Endorsements

"*Frank Urso, a native of Tampa's Ybor City, which was virtually a company town for the manufacture of cigars, grew up in a Sicilian family speaking little or no English until he entered school. His book is a masterful memoir—earthy and emotional—recreating a childhood mingling with a predominantly Hispanic culture in a community surrounded by an often antagonistic Anglo majority. There's never a dull word in this fascinating story.*"

—Leland Hawes, *The Tampa Tribune*

"*A raw and unvarnished recollection of growing up in Ybor City during the 1930s, '40s and '50s. Frank Urso's autobiography adds to our understanding of that remarkable place. The son of illiterate but resourceful Sicilian immigrants, Urso tells a story rich in detail of extended families, cold-water duplexes and the struggle for survival in Tampa. It is a tale of urban decline, racial and ethnic friction, and hope—always hope for a better future. For those who believe present-day Ybor City suffers from a malady of quaintness and cuteness,* **A Stranger in the Barrio** *is a must read.*"

—Gary R. Mormino,
—Professor of History, University of South Florida

A Stranger In The Barrio

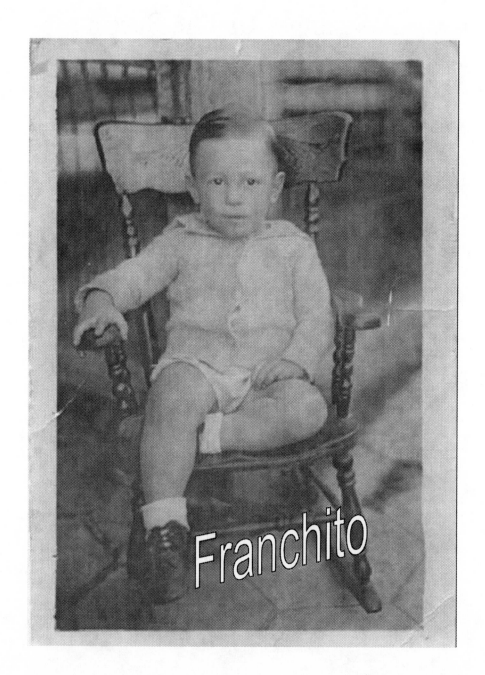

Franchito

A Stranger In The Barrio

◆

Memoir of a Tampa Sicilian

Frank Urso

iUniverse, Inc.
New York Lincoln Shanghai

A Stranger In The Barrio
Memoir of a Tampa Sicilian

iUniverse books may be ordered through booksellers or by contacting:

iUniverse
2021 Pine Lake Road, Suite 100
Lincoln, NE 68512
www.iuniverse.com
1-800-Authors (1-800-288-4677)

Some names have been changed to protect privacy.

ISBN-13: 978-0-595-33537-4 (pbk)
ISBN-13: 978-0-595-66964-6 (cloth)
ISBN-13: 978-0-595-78339-7 (ebk)
ISBN-10: 0-595-33537-3 (pbk)
ISBN-10: 0-595-66964-6 (cloth)
ISBN-10: 0-595-78339-2 (ebk)

Printed in the United States of America

To the despaldilladoras who stripped the leaf from the stem

    And to the mojadores who wet it.

To rolleras and rolleros with chaveta markings on their hands,

    And to those who slapped machinettas like guillotine machines.

To strong-arm boncheros that pressurized wooden molds,

    And to those that cowed to Hispanic foremen.

To gentle faces shaded by parasols from a noonday sun

    And to their garish dresses and widow black, too.

To men who walked out of factories at quitting time

    With hidden smokes bouncing like "love handles" inside their shirts,

And to those who wore straw hats.

    Oh yes, pagliettas, as they were called, were there, too.

To all the Sicilian cigarmakers now asleep—

    I dedicate this book.

Contents

Preface

I lived in Tampa's *barrio*, Ybor City, until I was twenty-three. I germinated Sicilian, frozen in time. Sicilians, perhaps unlike other immigrants, never sought to be Americans, never wanted to be what they were not. In me, Ybor City created a character whose tongue flips between Sicilian, Spanish and English, but I am never in doubt of who I am.

Any inaccuracies of dates, names and places in this memoir are due to the ignorance I grew up with, or simply because I cannot remember.

Today, tourists who visit Ybor City see a rejuvenated Seventh Avenue, the old business district. Much of it is the stuff tourist traps are made of, but national historic plaques tell us of a unique past. Restaurants, shops and boutiques line the streets like any "old town" in any old city. Vicente Martínez Ybor's original cigar factory is now Ybor Square, an office complex, and the old Bien Publico Clinica is a historic inn. A four-story Hilton Inn sits on Ninth Avenue. The Centro Español Club has become Centro Ybor—a dining and entertainment complex. A crumbling, boarded up V. M. Ybor Grammar School, away from the tourist area, has been restored for disadvantaged children.

Never did I dream where I bought Italian bread, Ferlita's Bakery, would become the Ybor City State Museum. Across from it is Centennial Park where life-size bronzes honor Nick Nuccio, the first Sicilian-American mayor, who performed my parents' marriage ceremony in 1933, and Tony Pizzo, the local historian—my mother's first cousin.

What has been razed or devoured by time and termites remains alive only in the minds of those of us who grew up there. City blocks have vanished, streets have been closed and one-ways created. Only tourists making a wrong turn see the blight of a black ghetto that looms behind the renaissance. The duplex I grew up in will never have a historic plaque out front, nor will any of the slum homes that made up the once proud *barrio*. They are the leftovers that don't make it to the menus of travel magazines.

Today, my parents' tobacco-cutting tools, *chavetas* and *machinettas*, sit on my bookshelves. Nonna's crocheted doilies fade in the sun. Papa's homemade cheese grater grates truth next to my nonno's cheese crock filled with memories. Yellowed naturalization papers peek out of a Perfecto Garcia cigar box, and black and white photographs stare from walls as if requesting Mascagni's opera, *Cavalleria Rusticana*, one more time. And I? Well, I sip a cup of Cuban coffee, turn on the music and puff on a Honduran cigar and say, *"Bravo Siciliani,"* but there will be no encore. I cherish the sacrifices and *la dolce vita* the immigrants bequeathed me. So, I pump more Sicilian words into English and tell their story, my story, with contradictions and conflicts—folly and frivolity. Each depressed key breaks the Sicilian code of silence.

Frank P. Urso, M.D.
Naples, Florida

Acknowledgements

Leland Hawes, History and Heritage writer, *The Tampa Tribune*, for believing I could write, his never-ending encouragement and endorsement of this work.

Gary R. Mormino, Professor of History at the University of South Florida, for his support, endorsement and for helping me fill in historical gaps with his book, *The Immigrant World of Ybor City*.

Meg Files, Professor and Chairperson Department of English and Journalism, Pima Community College, Tucson, AZ, for teaching me the ABCs of the craft.

Carol Hay, for her patience and assistance with the manuscript over the years.

Historic photographs are the courtesy of the Special Collection Department, University of South Florida Tampa Library.

1

Ybor City was my skin, and skin covering poor people wrinkles faster than the rest of the city. It was an immigrant world, a world of *tabaqueros*, cigarmakers, who clung to the middle part of the Florida peninsula as if the rest of America didn't exist, didn't care it existed. It was the *tabaqueros* world, and it promised to be mine. I entered the enclave unaccompanied, and America, well, she was there, too, standing at my side, at a distance, but it was Sicily who napped under my bed, and the bogeyman, well, he was never the devil, although he stood around at arm's length from poverty.

Many buildings were two-story in the business district, La Sèptima, and built from both wood frames and old red bricks. Jews lived above businesses on the busy street. They were an insignificant number, as I recall, and lived in flats with overhanging porches where clotheslines and ornate wrought iron railings watched over me. But I never met one. Each Saturday, Miranda, the Devil Crab Man, parked his bike curbside. A white box hanging from its handlebars was filled with fried croquettes of *habia* or crabs. The dark-skinned man gesticulated with Tabasco Sauce in front of S. H. Kress's five and dime store and saturated the air with the smell of crab croquettes deep-fried in lard. The five and dime store was known as "La Casa Barata," literally the cheap house.

Nationalistic attitudes prevailed inside the shotgun homes and *casitas* of Cubans, Spaniards and Sicilians. Sure, there was no little Italy or little Madrid or little Havana, but Ybor City was as Cuban as Cuban coffee and Cuban bread. Spaniards occupied second place in the three-tiered pyramid of immigrants. They had an ongoing feud with Cubans since the days Imperial Spain ruled Cuba, so there was no love lost between them. Sicilians, at the bottom of the stack, tried to survive as a minority among minorities. Only the southern Negro lived in relative tranquility, ostracized and segregated in abject poverty next to the *barrio*, making me believe I was not poor.

Negroes from Cuba lived inside the *barrio*, too, so full-strength segregation applied only to southern blacks whose language Latinos didn't understand. The use of the word Negro wasn't disrespectful then, only "nigger" was. Cuban Negroes were different, having previously lived in an integrated Cuba. They mixed with white Latinos, and some were neither this nor that, for their blood was mixed. Those we called *mulattos*, and, of course, they were considered black, for the slightest drop of black blood made them Negroes. Cuban Negroes and mulattoes rolled cigars alongside Caucasians in cigar factories and spoke Spanish like everyone else. They were not banned from socially mixing in public, but they never were welcomed in Sicilian homes. Tampa Anglos didn't understand that Spanish-speaking blacks never walked into my home. They thought we were all one potluck dinner of Cuban niggers, and that was what Tampa Anglos called us. As long as they believed integration was limited to Ybor City, it was all right with them, but Italians were a far cry from anything Cuban and anything black. It was just our fate we lived where we did.

A lifetime has elapsed. It's the new millennium, and not much time is left, yet whenever I visit Tampa, Ybor City beckons me. Today, my people's progeny live the American dream with green-laced lawns in the suburbs of Tampa where no one knows anyone else, and their houses, like the people who live there, look alike. But Ybor City memories are riveted in my mind, and the old people remain just a few handshakes away in old cemeteries, *tabaquero* cemeteries. Each time I visit, cigarmaker handshakes squeeze my hand hard, welcoming me back, promising never to let me go.

As I made plans to leave Ybor City in my early twenties, Spanish and Italian words ebbed in the narrow streets, eyes dimmed and Latin smiles straightened. Immigrants watched the southern Negro move in next door in the late 1950s and early '60s. I saw Ybor City die, and its vibrant cigarmakers metamorphose into granite and marble headstones in the Latin cemeteries. L'Unione Italiana Cemetery is where most of my family is buried, a few city blocks away from what was my cosmos, where cigar factories dominated our lives.

As I remember it, Sicilians never sought to be Americans, never wanted to be what they were not. They came to America for jobs and were content to live in America's alleys with their own, saying to me, "Franchito, take what is good in America and push away its bad." I tried to do both, but it was an impossible task.

On a Sunday morning, my cousin Vince and I visit old Ybor City. Neither of us are churchgoers, but we have a mission. Oh, there was a brief time, back in high school, in the1950s, we went to mass at Our Lady of Perpetual Help Church because we attended the Catholic school there, but it didn't last, didn't take hold. We decide to visit the neighborhood that holds much more meaning than we ever found inside a church.

"Think it's safe?" Vince says, as we drive up East Columbus Drive and park near the cross street of Nineteenth Street.

"Sure, why not?"

"Hope you know what you're doing. We're worse than sitting ducks out here. We don't belong anymore, you know."

"Hell, it still feels like home, Vince."

"Hasn't been for a long time," he says, stressing *a long time*, saying it as if he's trying to shake me into reality.

"Just take decent shots. Don't give me your grief," I say.

From different angles he points his camera at the old two-story house. He snaps photos of where we began life, where our grandfather Ciccio died when Vince and I were five. He pans and snaps the duplex I moved into at age six, only a half dozen houses away. The duplex sits due west on the same side of the street, on the north side of Columbus Drive, and it was there I lived until age twenty-three. Vince is wrapped up in his camera. It's obvious he's not much at taking pictures, so he keeps looking at the camera's parameters as if it were manual. He flips levers this way and that, so I wait and look around and watch him check and recheck the number of frames left. Adjusting his bifocals, he peers through the viewfinder. Maybe he thinks wire-rimmed glasses make him look younger or chic. He's fussy that way. Oh, yes, always that and undeniably fidgety.

"Take good ones," I say, trying hard not to pressure his already stressed high-tech skills.

"It's user friendly, Frank, see?" He holds the camera out in his palm. "A Canon Elph."

I nod. "Nice and compact."

"Did you ever think we'd want pictures?" he says.

"Did you?"

We sit in my Ford Bronco, parked in a neighborhood that no longer bears any resemblance to the Latin district Vince and I grew up in. It had been more Latin than the Latin Quarter in New Orleans.

I'd driven by the old neighborhood when I visited Tampa before, but I never told anyone. I didn't want any of my old buddies thinking me sentimental, a damn fool for risking my life, driving by what is now the East Black Ghetto of Tampa. It consists of dilapidated *tabaquero* huts with leaky roofs that leaked even then. I remember when *casitas*, wooden houses where cigar workers lived, stood erect and proud in the shade of factories. Now many are crack houses.

I still see their insides as if blight has not taken them over. I haven't forgotten how women swept them clean with straw brooms on Saturday mornings and washed windows down with newspapers dabbed in kerosene. I spent as little time as possible inside mine because freedom and becoming a man was an experience to be found in the streets. The houses were jammed next to each other since their conception on the city's grid map in 1886. That's how cigar factory owners built them for a pittance and rented and sold them to cigarmakers, assuring the factories their workforce was permanent, and that's how a cigar town was born.

Graffiti snakes along *casita* walls and tin garages. Winos lie in once quaint streets, and look up at me when I drive in as if I don't belong—not the right color. With each visit, I see houses consumed, boarded, condemned and razed. It's a war zone to those of us who once coexisted with blacks in a segregated South. Then came the war years. The late 1950s and early '60s became my Civil War years; the real Civil War; the only Civil War I identify with, for it was all about Negroes again—Civil Rights.

During the Civil War of the mid 1860s, my ancestors were in Sicily, so there is no catharsis to that war. Cubans, Spaniards and Italians didn't die in it. It was an Anglo war—Anglo against Anglo. No one ever occupied my turf, but in the late 1950s, I saw black invaders swarm, replace white Latinos rocking and swinging on front porches. I saw my people retreat as Ybor City fell to the vanquishers, and perhaps it was then I understood the meaning of the word *vanquishers*.

My first home, the two-story I shared with Vince, stands abandoned and uninhabitable. A white condemnation notice proclaims it to be so. The notice hangs tattered, weathered, nailed to the wall next to one of its front doors like white tags hang from great toes in county morgues, keeping identities straight, keeping the dead from running amuck. And so it is also with discarded homes.

We hear yells around the corner. We see teenage boys looking up at a steel rim protruding from the backside of a rotting wooden garage. Jumping, they glance and bounce the big ball at their feet, rim it and watch it teeter and fall inside the rim. They bounce it harder and harder on hard sidewalk cement. I watch their eyes flick back and forth, and bounce off my cousin and me.

Poverty is indigenous here, always has been, but its people now are different. There is no tradition or culture—no sense of honor inside the homes—not even the one said to be found among thieves.

Dark silhouettes peer out from behind torn screen windows and front doors as we sit inside the Ford, ignoring the black women who rock on porch rockers. Winos, like slugs, lift their heavy heads, contorting themselves as if there is perhaps a way to find comfort on curbstones and sidewalks along storefronts, clutching brown paper bags, overnight bags, outlining the necks of whiskey and wine bottles. Broken glass with labels of Calvert and Seagram litter gutters as if awaiting the runoff of a spring rain.

I'd driven into the ghetto slowly so as not to highlight our presence, as they say, keep a low profile, not awaken the damned, but only few sleep—most know we are there.

I hear a smart-ass teenager cry out, "Whitey, go home."

I turn to Vince and say, "But it's our home, too."

He says nothing.

"How can I tell them? Sure, I'm white, but it doesn't mean I don't understand the indignities of a ghetto life. Who better than me, than us? Who better understands a muzzled mind?"

"Don't bother," he says.

Some things in ghettos never change, stay the same, and it isn't the lack of materialism wasting minds. It's the not knowing there is something different, another way of living, another way of thinking. It happened to me before I could read, before I could write. Then one day, fate twisted my arm and led me away.

"Vince, those two by four studs weren't propping up the porch of the two-story the last time I came by." I flip down the car's visor to block out a bright morning sun.

"You really think it's safe?" His eyes meet mine, linger, and then move away.

"Sure, don't worry. I got a .357 magnum in my duffle bag," I say, glancing at the back seat.

"You gotta be nuts!"

"Well, you never know."

"Yeah, but still, it's illegal."

"Shit, don't worry about it. Just take good shots. I'll be in charge of keeping us alive, okay?"

He worries about weapons, fears them, always has. It seems strange to me, for there is something in my blood attracting me to guns, something innately Sicilian. I never dreamed I'd need a pistol to visit home, but here I am with the magnum in the back seat, and he and I are at odds again.

So what's new? I ask myself. Different traits, different strokes, sure, but we have the important parts in common. After all, our fathers were brothers, stereotype Sicilians who emigrated at the turn of the century.

Vince doesn't approve of my ways, never has and never will. So what if I have to pack a gun to visit the ghetto for old times sake? At least I visit—blacks or no blacks. You'd think he'd visit the place, pay his respects—pay his dues. It deserves better, deserves at least that, but he sits next to me with a quizzical expression at the mention of the .357. It's the same face that, as a youth, warned, "Better not.

Take it easy." He said it with a grimace, lifting one eyebrow like one lifts a cheek to squeeze out a fart. "Don't be so crazy, Frank."

I recall the inseparable cousins forging a single identity, laughing at our distorted reflections on storefront windows. The Urso boys, that's what teachers called us, and that was about right, for it was the name joining us at the hip.

"Look at those beauts." I point across the street at the duplex.

A heavy-ass black woman drapes a beat-up rocker on the front porch. Her ass molds itself outside the seat, and her arms are as big as pig thighs. A string bean teenage girl hovers over her, braiding cornrows.

"Never saw cornrows around here before," I say.

"Corn?"

"You know, the way blacks style their hair. Looks like rows of corn, doesn't it?"

Perhaps to the worldly who live and work among blacks in big cities, cornrows and dreadlock hairdos are a given, household words, but not to those of us who grew up isolated and sheltered from a diversified America. Those of us in Ybor City were always the last to know. I recently learned about cornrows, so it didn't surprise me Vince was unaware.

"Oh, didn't know it had a name," he says.

"Where the hell you been?"

"Don't be corny," he says.

"Everything happens here last."

"Always did."

"Except integration," I say. "Cause no Kennedys lived here."

He doesn't smile, telegraphing he's a Democrat.

"Just saying it like it is. You think you'd ever find a Kennedy living next to colored town?" I slap his back.

He gives me a limp smile.

So I say, "It wasn't until my folks rented out my half of the duplex that Papa plumbed in hot water. Damn blacks demanded it, said it was a civil right. Mama was so pissed after having done without all those years. She kept saying, 'He put it in for the blacks but wouldn't do it for me.'"

Papa kept saying, "We can't rent it, Mary, without hot water. Doesn't matter they're black."

"You've been gone too long, Frank."

"No shit."

"Looks like people live in both sides," he says.

"What do you think of taking a walk through? You know, like landlords do when one checks out of an apartment, a quickie, that's all, a quick look-see. Think they'd let me if I ask?"

"You crazy?"

"Hell, I'll pay them. Just a peek."

"Don't be a fool, Frank. Addicts and prostitutes live around here now. They might think you're an undercover cop, A.T.F. agent, or something like that. That's no place for a white man."

"That's probably what Anglos said about us when we lived here. 'Those Latins aren't fit for consumption—not a place for decent folks to visit.' That's what they said. You know it. Said it to their kids."

He shakes his head.

"But we didn't care. Hell, it was all we knew," I say.

"Didn't make it easier."

"I know."

"Look, if they know you're in the car waiting, they wouldn't start crap. I could offer that fat woman five bucks. See what she says. It'd only take a few minutes."

Recklessness plagues me still. As a child, Vince didn't take risks, played his half of growing up safe. Nothing changed—physically either. He rigidly does daily sit-ups, confessing last night he watches his fat intake, too, unheard of among Sicilians. I saw it happen, saw it evolve. It wasn't his fault his mother stuffed him with raw eggs, cod liver oil and Ovaltine to butterball him up. Mine didn't spare me either and left me equally scarred, scars rooted in rigidity and superhuman frugality. No, no one escapes Sicilian mothers, not even Sicilian fathers.

Until the day fate twisted my arm on the duplex porch and led me away, I only dreamed of how life might be outside the ghetto, living in a house instead of a duplex, a green lawn instead of cement, a chimney to welcome Saint Nick, central heat warming my clothes on winter mornings instead of a gaping gas oven barfing heat in my face, a daily newspaper I didn't deliver, parents attending P.T.A. meetings, a full-fledged Christmas tree instead of a Florida Pine branch and roller skates and a scooter I never got. I knew it was different some place. I just didn't know how different.

I never asked Vince if he had thought about things like that, but it happened so long ago, so irrelevant now. He's preserved his slim physique, kept his hair, sense of humor and amiable smile, but he grayed prematurely. As a child, he was the taller, light-haired one, actually blondish. He was the cuter one with hazel eyes. That was a rarity in the culture of low slung, swarthy Sicilians. Vince was probably a throwback to Vikings. I'd read somewhere Vikings, called Normans, rescued Sicily from Ottoman Turks. Short and stout was common, and that was me. I was his flipside, flipside in personality, too. Even today, I sport a bushy mustache, and he's clean-shaven. I enjoy pasta, fatty beef close to the bone and fat Honduran cigars—the fatter the better. After dinner and a bottle of Chianti Classico last night, he called me Zorba the Greek and cracked up. He pointed his finger at me. So what? I'd said to myself, aren't all Sicilians Greeks anyhow?

Vince was my alter ego when I'd blundered like a bull. Mama told me he was cautious as a cat learning to walk, walking down stairways, gauging each step, taking them one at a time preparing his path with feely hands. Then there was me who missed each one, ending up at the bottom of the stairwell screaming, "Mama." We were a pair all right, intricately woven but different.

Cugino, cousin, is a word *gringos* think Italians use indiscriminately, but it's not so. It only appears that way because we have large families. Perhaps some Anglos liken us to the English and to Shakespeare, whose characters call each other *cousins* in plays although the characters may not be blood related. Italians are a far cry from anything English and anything Shakespeare, who, by the way, loved Italians, setting many of his plays in Italy and naming many of his characters with Italian names: Othello, Antonio, Malvolio and Romeo to mention a few.

I grew up oblivious to Shakespeare, Ovid and Dante and the rest of that literary bunch, including Mark Twain. It wasn't until high school I rubbed shoulders with the greatest Italian of them all, Julius Caesar. Goose bumps trumpeted under my skin as I read Mark Antony's speach to the Romans. It was as if I was there at the funeral pyre listening to—*The good is oft interred with their bones.* So I understood, understood early on that line referred to me, for those were words Anglos translated to *the only good wop is a dead wop.*

Vince and I were tobacco seeds, knowing all about *vitolas, capotassos, picadura* and *claro tabaco* at an early age. Our parents and our uncles and aunts all worked in cigar factories.

We knew early on that master cigarmakers worked the better *vitolas* or better quality cigars, and that they commanded more pay. Cigarmakers took a year or two of apprenticeship before being allowed to roll anything worthwhile. A good paying *vitola* was a status symbol in the factories and the neighborhood, establishing a pecking order of sorts.

Breva was one of the lesser expensive *vitolas.* The cigar was short, made for brief smokes, and the word meant brief just like it sounds. *Cheroot* was a very low-end cigar—made from *picadura*. *Picadura* meant the guts of the cigars were not long filler or intact tobacco, but instead minced tobacco—cut and blended. Until this day, when I think of cheap cigars, I think of Hav-A-Tampa. It was a factory where machines rolled cigars, and redneck women operated the machines in the large wooden building on Twenty-Second Street. No self-respecting Latino cigarmakers would work there. "Pure shit," was what Papa said about Hav-A-Tampa cigars—"pure shit."

"A couple more should do it?" he says. His tone tells me he's ready to leave.

Vince fingers his collar button like our grandmother fingered rosary beads. He keeps his collar buttoned in all seasons to cover up a hairless, asthenic chest. He's so prissy with his long sleeves slightly rolled up and hair premeditatedly fluffed to hide a receding hairline. I bet he uses a blow drier. I'd almost forgotten how different we are.

"Ah, come on, them blacks aren't interested in us, keep shooting. There may be nothing left to photograph next time we visit."

"Frank, you're crazy. We're outnumbered and not young anymore. There isn't a white around for miles," he says. "We should get the hell out of here."

I'm silent.

"Frank, did you hear me? We're supposed to be having fun, strolling down memory lane, not looking for trouble."

He's right, but I'm wondering what might be recognizable inside the duplex. Would the old claw-footed bathtub still be there? Would its feet, like mine, be clutching the past, remembering me after hosing down blacks for forty years, remembering how I took baths with a beat-up aluminum pan diluting hot water I heated on a gas stove? Would BB holes from my air rifle still be in the window-panes of my bedroom? Would the closet Papa turned into a water closet by plumbing in a commode still flush in the dark? Papa never did put in a light. Would it now flush leftover feelings? When my parents moved out in the early '60s, they junked their worthless, termite infested 1930s furniture. No personal effects were left behind, just lives.

Since my last visit, the squat columns of the duplex porch have been painted black. The tasteless vulgarity whacks at my dignity, whacks low down at my crotch. Once the cement columns so typical of vintage homes were white, not lily white, but off white. Papa said the paint wouldn't fade, wouldn't yellow because he tinted the white with a few drops of black he called "color." The house was my identity growing up—1816 East Columbus Drive, the second house from the corner with twin palm trees, one on each side, providing stingy shade on the front porch.

Barrio homes were unique. Most were made of wood and were white with open front porches and steeply pitched roofs. They were not typical row houses of the Northeast but quasi row houses of southern ghettos.

Growing up I didn't distinguish between cigar workers and cigarmakers. The terms were synonymous to me, but now I make a distinction. Cigar workers are all those who worked in the cigar factories. It includes employees who wetted the tobacco; stripped the leaf; selected and graded it; put paper rings on the cigars, the banders; and those that placed cigars inside boxes, the packers. Those who actually rolled the cigar, the bunch-makers and wrappers, I call cigarmakers or *tabaqueros*. Except for the period just before the Christmas season, when factories orders often ran high, cigarmakers did not work on Saturdays. It was a five-day workweek and the weekend set them free.

On Saturday mornings, as a boy, I smell the aroma of frying garlic, onion, green pepper and olive oil suffusing the narrow streets. It is a distinctive scent I learn to identify early, and it's called *sofrito*, used to make a variety of Latin sauces. The fragrance drags me by the nose, pulling me from one redbrick paved street into another.

In summer, sidewalks bend to the sun at midday. With blistered feet, I seek shade. In winter, I find the sun and bathe in it, playing in a moth-eaten sweater. Old clothes are never thrown out, nothing ever is.

In the evenings, I watch men sit on front porches, hear them bemoan baseball scores, cringe at the extra inning run that lost the game. A perfectly executed bunt topples the champions of the Cuban League. They argue as if they'd been there, seen it, laid it down, the ball spinning like a top, going nowhere on yellow clay. They hear all base runners advance on short-wave radios.

From porches I hear feminine voices percolate Andalusian recipes of pigs feet and *mondongo*, tripe, called *tripa*, and the common *picadillo*, ground beef with white rice or yellow rice made with saffron. The price of saffron soars, costs more than gold by dry weight, so they settle for artificial coloring. *Arroz con pollo*, yellow rice and chicken, made with or without capers, is accompanied by black beans, with or without *platanos*. Everything is with or without, like coffee with or without milk—*con leche, sin leche* with or without *azúcar*, sugar.

I learn to distinguish Castilian and Asturiano Spanish when Spaniards say, "*peros, hombre.*" They say "but man" like haughty gentlemen say it in Spain. I compare it to base Cuban Spanish. Cuss words like *conyo* and *máricon* are staples in Cuban Spanish. Yes, that's what Cubans say all the time: *pussy* and *queer*. They say it second nature. It's not exaggeration, simply Cuban conversational Spanish.

I'm four or five, walking a narrow street, holding Mama's hand, listening to Spanish *novellas* floating from radios across wire-fenced yards. When Pepsi Cola makes its debut, Spanish stations play the musical ditty over and over, distort the word Pepsi, skim off the *p*, so it's Pesi Cola *es la cola para me*. I sing along in Spanish—"Pepsi Cola is the cola for me," like it's number one on the *Hit Parade*. Yes, Pesi Cola is the cola for me, *para me*, the hell with the *p*. In teen years, I flash by homes on my bicycle, speed by the vernacular, jumping street curbs, and Spanish and Sicilian merges, blurs, and the wind fills my ears.

Spaniards call porches verandas, sit there in the evenings clustered. Cubans call me *muchacho*, but most say Pancho or Franco as smoke swirls, mixes Havana with Cuban coffee as if blended in demitasses. Swings glide, move barely, and handheld fans swish back and forth. Heavyset women dig out handkerchiefs from sweaty bosoms and wipe sweat off tired faces. And Sicilians call sidewalks *marciapiede*—marching feet—but I never make the literal translation. It's that way with most things.

Staked out in the sun, the *casitas* bleach, sealing in relics of the day. Degrees multiply exponentially inside. *Tabaquero* huts have no air-conditioning, no shade trees, and tin roofs inhale the sun and exhale it into bedrooms at night.

Mosquitoes are a nuisance. Wings fan my ears, so cuss words fill the night. We do our best to keep the bloodsuckers at bay, sitting on porches trying to snag a breeze, stuffing galvanized buckets with rags, lighting them with stick-matches. Ragged clothes smolder, as the thirsty vampires ignore the smoke burning my eyes. Dim streetlights, cigars and cigarettes light up the night, and smoky swirls create *sfumato* scenes of people and shadows on swings, not unlike DaVinci paintings of the Italian Renaissance. But for my people, the Renaissance never comes.

Straits of air between homes separate *casitas* and circulate intimacy. Heavy rains in summer thunder on tin roofs. Overhangs dump rainwater in the narrow corridors. Late at night, I hear myself breathe. I listen to windowscreens take breaths. Privacy in the *barrio* doesn't exist. Life is out in the open, exposed, so occasionally I hear a neighbor woman say, "*Peros, hombre, no tienes verquenza. Nada.*" "Husband, have you no shame?" She places the emphasis on "shame" as if she knows I can hear.

The flatulent old man offers no defense, finds contentment in commitment to explosive relief. I hear him again and again, as if he's aiming at my window. Men of the era keep nothing in, absolutely nothing. The cacophony of cicada does not drown out intimacy in my part of an urban South. I hear moans and grunts. I conclude husbands and wives are orbiting the moon, making it hard on squeaky bedsprings, which seem to uncoil in deference to love. Nothing is sacred where I live, absolutely nothing.

"What do you think of those columns?" I say, expecting him to comment on the tackiness of it all.

"I'm telling you they're hostile. Just like those athletes at the Olympics, holding up a fist during the national anthem. Do you remember? I wouldn't want to go in there."

"But those Olympic games were years ago. Surely they've settled down by now," I say.

I recall my godfather sitting on the duplex's porch swing after dinner, and I hear him saying, "Le Negri." Saying, "*Tizzune.*"

I know blacks painting the columns black would not have surprised him. No, not him.

Shotgun "quadriplexes," duplexes and *casitas* struggle to survive the new millennium. Note the intimacy of front porches. The two-story house with a dormer was my first home. It was razed shortly after this photograph was taken.

Decaying and neglected, the duplex lives to see another garbage day. No one tells Sicilian stories inside anymore. A "No Trespassing" sign is nailed to a palm, and an American flag flies backwards over its front steps. Columns have been painted white once again.

2

Every Italian boy has a godfather, or he wouldn't be Italian. Mine lives in the other half of the duplex, and it's said he'd led a spirited life. Well, as lively as an immigrant cigarmaker could, yet an air of melancholy hovers over him like the odor of tobacco radiating from his plaid shirt.

The names godfather and godmother are pronounced *parrina* and *parrino* in Sicilian. The words are said different than in mainland Italy—*padrina* and *padrino*. Sicilian is not a written language, just a spoken dialect, driving Italy's mainlanders crazy. And it has no future tense. That should have told me something.

Conversations with my godfather start early. He tells me about cigarmakers and factories and *capotassos*—Spanish foremen hover over cigarmakers like vultures. He tells me great stories and practical things, too—how he makes *bonches*, the guts of cigars, putting out over four hundred a day. A bunch or *bonche* is the filler of a cigar, and it is what defines my godfather as a *bonchero*.

He strokes tobacco leaves into submission, rolling them into rough cigars. Tobacco leaf called a binder covers each *bonche*. The "bunches" fill the receptacles carved out in the insides of wooden molds. A steel press tightens the ten or so *bonches* in the mold. The mold is allowed to set for a while. A wrapper or what is known as a "roller" performs the final steps. The roller wraps *bonches* with a high-grade tobacco leaf—what cigar smokers see when they look in a cigar box. Most *boncheros* are men, so my godfather is my idol doing a masculine job.

After work my godfather stops and slugs down whiskey in cafés. It's my godfather's favorite time of day—happy hour of sorts. Cafés are located near cigar factories, and I have been told that before I was born there were nearly two hundred and fifty cigar factories in Ybor City and West Tampa. Finding a café is never difficult. Even after factories fold, bars seem to stay open. My father tells me there'd been a time my godfather embraced the trinity—three vises, *vicios*. In colloquial Sicilian the word translates to "habits," and the connotation is never good. In his prime my godfather was a drinker, a gambler and a womanizer. He also does not like blacks, but that is not a vice, for none of the Sicilians where I live do.

"Parrino, why do you call blacks *tizzune?*" I say in Sicilian, looking up at him from the porch floor.

Oh, I learn about blacks all right—learn it all early. Blacks live nearby and use our sidewalks, so, in those early years of porch confinement, I see them daily. "Colored town" abuts the *barrio*, just east of my home. That's where the gun and knife club comes alive every Friday and Saturday night. Sicilians call blacks *negri*, but my godfather calls them *TIZZUNE*. The word is catchy—starts with a high note, *ti*, and ends thunderously with *zzune*.

"Because that's what they are," he says in Sicilian. "Franchito, come sit by me."

"What does *tizzune* mean?" I jump on the swing, rattling the chain that links us to the porch ceiling. The ash from his cigarette falls on his undershirt and stops at the crest of his paunch. He looks at it as if he's not sure what to do, as if the ash might burn its way through. He stands, shaking it off, shaking and disrupting his thoughts and mine. He had been sitting there peacefully after supper, gazing at lumbering traffic, enjoying a rare breeze passed on from porch to porch of stringed *casitas*. He loves waving at cars, waves at people he knows, all cigarmakers from factories, inhaling with after pasta soporific ease as if he doesn't have a care in the world. He gives me a sense of security as I breathe in secondhand-nicotine tranquility.

"Be still," he says. "And don't do that again."

I smile at my impishness and say, "Parrino, *scusa*, I'm sorry."

He reconstitutes, taking a drag that sinks both of his cheeks. "Franchito, *tizzune* in Sicilian means troublemaker, *capisci*?"

"*Capisco, capisco*," I say. "I understand."

The word "*Capisci*?" simply asks, "Do you understand?" In Italian it is commonplace to reply with almost the identical word—as if responding in kind—but without a question mark, and the terminal *i* changed to an *o*—meaning I understand. It's another habit of his, his nature to keep asking *capisci*. Pretending to understand, I respond with—"*Capisco, capisco*, Parrino."

"So, anyone who's a troublemaker is a *tizzune*," he says. "*Capisci*?"

"Me, too?" I say.

"No, no, you're Italian."

I smile as if he's just initiated me into the family.

He exhales. "In Sicily *tizzune* was a stick we used to stoke fires. We didn't have tools like we do in America, so we picked out a straight stick and set it aside for stoking fires. Over time it charred and turned black."

"So, they're *tizzune* because they're black like the stick?"

"No, no, troublemakers, Franchito, troublemakers. They're always stoking trouble. Whenever you see one, watch out," he says.

He lights up and continues, "You know, Franchito, we live with them, so when you get older and get in a fight with one of those *figlio di puttani*, sons of bitches, don't hit them on their heads. Never bust heads. No, no, never that, unless you use a two by four."

"Why not, Godfather? I hit wherever I can." I swing my fist like a windmill, two left jabs and a right uppercut at the smoke. He floats smoke rings at me, and I nail each one. I giggle.

"Hasn't your father told you?"

"Told me what?"

"About black people's heads."

"*Tizzune* heads?"

"Who else?"

He knocks on the swing's armrest with his bony knuckles. "Heads of concrete—documented by science, you know. I saw their skulls in a famous museum in New York—The Metropolitan Museum. You can break your damn hand on those sons of bitches. Take it from me, I know." He flicks the ash from his cigarette towards the porch railing. He misses. It lands on the porch. "Franchito, kick that ash into the yard before your aunt sees it. She worries I'm going to burn this damn house down."

On my knees, pursing my lips, I blow and blow, blow the ash gently, keeping it intact, watch it roll on the floor, onto the yard as if it's diving off a cliff.

"So, I punch them in the stomach?" I say, running back and jumping on the swing.

"No, no. The *figli di puttani* have a weak spot. Every man has a weak spot, Franchito. So, that's where you hit them."

"Godfather, when Papa says son of a bitch in American, he says *somma ama bitcha*, but you always say it in Italian. I never hear you say it the Americano way."

"There's no reason—a son of a bitch is a son of a bitch in any language, *capisci?*"

"Yes, but it's so funny how Papa says *somma ama bitcha*. I wish I was allowed to say it. Please say it, Godfather, please."

He stiff-arms me with a penetrating glare. "You got to know where to hit blacks, Franchito."

"On their nose?" I say. "A one two punch, right?" I assume the attitude of Rocky Marciano.

"Aww…come on, that's too easy." He swats my hands down. "Their nose is already flat, so why pick that, that's no fun, eh?"

"Right."

"Franchito, it's their lips. They stick out like portabella mushrooms—*le funghi*—that's the weak spot—*la funga*. That's the target, can't miss it." He takes a drag and exhales.

Funghi or mushrooms are what Sicilians call lips, anybody's lips, so he teaches me a Negro's Achilles' heel is plastered on his face, and *tizzune* is a word synonymous with nigger, yet Sicilians seldom used the word nigger. Even after they learn to speak broken English, the word is *tizzune*, as if they understand prejudice.

I choke on the smoke he sends my way. He laughs. "To be forewarned is to be forearmed," he says.

My godfather smokes Lucky Strike, Camel and Chesterfield and tells me smoking is taught in school in the boy's room. Although it's said to stunt one's growth, it is native to America, so I inhale smoke when he isn't looking, placing my nose near his face, behind his ears when I hug him. He doesn't know I'm inhaling and dreaming of the day I'll smoke my own or maybe roll my own.

Immigrants contribute to my education without euphemisms, and Negroes, oh, well, they dot the landscape like splattered ink in a Rorschach test. Twenty-Second Street is the dividing line, my Mason Dixon line. Some infiltrate and live a few houses east in the next block, creeping closer each year. Immigrants don't make a big deal about them, but their proximity is everyone's concern. Even I know it's rougher in "colored town."

From my front porch I watch trolleys hobble, clinging to an electrified steel cable running high off the street. Trolleys have double rows of reversible seats, and open windows in summer permit muggy air to circulate. Their clanging bells excite me. When steel wheels slide on steel tracks, titanic goose bumps punctuate my skin and, overhead, the hum of the cable sparks, making it visible at night.

The trolley operator depletes his belt changer with a push of his thumb, punching coins out one at a time. I watch my grandmother drop them, watch coins tumble on a steel slide inside a glass box. On rainy days huge windshield wipers hug expansive glass and, sitting inside the trolley, I listen to an irksome rub, a rub, no doubt, Negroes who sit in the back can also hear. White men offer seats to standing white women, but never to blacks, even if pregnant.

A cleaning woman steps in and walks to the back. Speaking Italian allows me to ask questions without black people understanding what I'm saying.

"Nonna, why do *l'negri* sit in the back?"

"Don't stare," she says.

She doesn't hate blacks and doesn't understand the intricacies of the Deep South, doesn't realize what slavery was about, doesn't know about the Civil War and Lincoln. And, although she's not prejudice, she fears blacks as perhaps I fear the dark.

"Is that why the cleaning lady eats her lunch on Aunt Felicia's back porch?" I say.

"*Sì.*"

"So, if that black lady visits our house, she'll sit in the back porch?"

"Franchito, you don't understand. She's not going to visit our home."

"Parrino calls black people *tizzune,* Nonna. He says they have concrete heads," I say.

"Maybe that's because some of the cleaning women drink his whiskey and dilute it with water, so he won't know. Felicia says it makes him furious."

When my grandmother isn't looking, the black woman winks at me.

"Why do they sit in the back?"

"People in charge of America make them sit there."

"But why?"

"It's a form of ignorance."

"What's ignorance?"

"Ignorance is the devil."

"Is he black or white?"

She shakes her head.

"The devil can't sneak inside our house, right?"

"Right," she says.

"Is he afraid our family will gang up on him?"

"*Sì,* Franchito, the devil knows Italians would break his legs."

I nod. "Nonna, did you have Negroes in Sicily?"

"No, but the first Negro I saw was paraded through the streets of Alessandria della Rocca in a cage when I was a little girl. Never saw anything like it again. *Grazie* Dio."

"A big cage?"

"He looked so sad, Franchito, and my papa said he was a savage from Africa on his way to America. He was big and strong, and I was afraid to go near."

"That's how I feel, Nonna—sad."

"I know," she says. "It's just where we live. It was different in Sicily."

Nonna's best stories are told at night in the solitude of our bedroom. After my grandfather Ciccio dies I enter her world. Each night is a flashback to a world she never relinquished. It is from the fountainhead I glean all that happened before I was born, and there is not one American word or thought in her stories. From her I learn racism is an American tradition, does not exist in Sicily. It is just the way things are in the South. Sicily becomes my Utopia, my lost horizon, and it is as if sometimes I'm there in her small village, and I see the people living among cacti and see the cacti tower over stone huts in Alessandria della Rocca.

Like giant deer antlers, forked pallets of prickly pears soar into the sky, and, like Sicilian vespers, they invoke God from dawn to dusk. They grow tangled, escaping the craggy Sicilian soil. Between crevices, seeds incubate until one day they peek over clay roofs. They grow tall toward the sun reflecting itself in the wavy mirror of the Mediterranean Sea. Without regard for winter rains or summer droughts, the fleshy skeletons cast crooked shadows upon hovels and the people inside.

Up, they grow, up, through the centuries, while marauding conquerors claim the island: Greeks, Romans, Islamic Turks and French. The island people remain aloof and stand mute. The Sicilian code of silence, *omertà*, is born. The disdain for authority, disdain for the *carabinieri*, roots deep and Sicilian anarchy is born. Never tell on a *paesano*, never spill your guts, I'm told.

The cacti's white flowers, in surrender, greet the conquerors each spring. The conquerors gloat. The delicate pear-shaped fruit flourishes in summer, and oval pallets like rustic parasols shade the people from the sun. The fruit's peel is punctated with warts and, if left unpicked, wrinkles with time. Foreigners and *paesani* alike pick the fruit. It is not overtly hostile until grabbed. Then the fruit's anarchical demeanor stings the hand.

The cacti ignore pestilence, ignore famines, ignore the ammonical stench of livestock stirring the senses and mixing man with beast. Life exists on the island in the raw without vanity or frivolity. Inside huts kerosene lamps illuminate the glare of the unprinted page, illuminate each step of stoic, illiterate existence.

The cactus portrays the austerity woven into dusty Sicily. It produces a fruit not understood by America, a fruit whose sweetness camouflages its innumerable seeds. Seeds the uninitiated mouth spits out without thought, with disdain, while the Sicilian accepts them without hesitation and swallows them whole. The people of the island eat the fruit until the day thousands flee. From rooftops they point to America and shout with eyes too dry to cry. Corralled near the rudder, thousands are herded into steerage, below deck. They leave their bucolic homeland behind and take seeds with them.

Speaking Sicilian on a hot afternoon in Tampa, Nonna pulls a basket from the refrigerator. "No, no, don't touch. Put them on newspapers."

The lopsided fruit rolls onto the printed pages covering the kitchen table—four, five, six, no, eight in all.

"Look very cold, Nonna," I say, sitting, sweating at the table.

"That's how you eat them, Franchito, cold. Don't touch the skin. Chew easy," she says. "*Sèmpre adagio.*"

Olive skin hands peel the fruit held with newspaper. One escapes. She hesitates and reluctantly sticks it with a fork. She amputates both ends of the prickly pear with the kitchen knife, slices longitudinally and splits its peel twice. She forces the fruit to puff its seedy chest out. I pluck it, do not touch the peel and chew the fruit easy like, never gnashing the pulp. I dislodge its seeds, scatter them inside my mouth and savor the flavor. Flipping the flesh from side to side with my tongue, I give deference to the seeds, love each one and swallow them whole.

She is old, toothless and her mouth sinks like a withered blossom.

"Tell me a story of Sicily, Nonna," I say.

"I'll tell you one tonight. I have work to do now."

"No, no, Nonna, now, *per favore.*"

"Don't you want to go outside and play?"

"Please, please."

"Tonight, Franchito, tonight."

Though I live in America, I know Sicily is my home, my second home, or maybe it's my first? It's like living in one place but having allegiance to another. I feel like a child from a broken home feels having two fathers or two mothers, some they call ex's and some they call step's. Those children never talk about feelings and neither do I.

Nonna reminisces. "It was a different world, Franchito, a different world."

I listen and keep slurping the succulent fruit.

"Well, you know, prickly pears grew wild there."

"Wild?"

'The air was dry, never humid like Tampa, and we had little to eat. Your grandfather worked in the fields and I made pasta and sold it to the villagers, so we could get by."

"Is dry air good?"

"Good for prickly pears, but I never saw my father and mother again, Franchito, never did. I knew I never would."

"Tell me more, Nonna. Did they have cigar factories there?"

I close my eyes as she wipes the sweat off my face with a wet dishtowel. Nonna doesn't ask why I shut my eyes. She knows I see better in the dark. I sit and try not to squirm, don't say a word and let her words fill the room.

"So, you see, Franchito, Sicily is a country with olives, almonds, music and *ficodindia*." My grandmother calls prickly pears *ficodindia*, figs from India, literally translated, and, if the word is said slowly, it is—*fico-di-india*. But I never see the printed word, never dissect vowels, so I have no concept where the fruit originated and don't care. I slur over its name like I slurp its sweetness, for, you see, illiteracy has no beginning and no end. I only know its teachers who brought it over on the big boat and parked next to "colored town" where it thrives.

3

The storyteller's words are vivid, always are. Grandmothers are a premium in a working *barrio* where most couples work in factories. I lie next to her on the sofa. She cradles my head on her lap, and I gaze at a ceiling I cannot see, as headlights flash on the walls.

"Nonna, do you remember when I was born?" I ask.

She doesn't respond.

"I know I was born, but I don't know where, Nonna."

"It was not a happy occasion, Franchito."

"Why not? Did Mama want a girl?"

"No, although mothers do pray for girls."

"Are girls easier to take care of?"

"No, it's just when mothers widow, they feel more comfortable living with a daughter than a daughter-in-law. It's the Italian way."

"Oh."

My head acclimates to her lap. I shut my eyes. She clears her throat, but the words I hear are not hers.

"*Migliore morto che deforme,*" I hear a man say.

"Better dead than deformed," are the words in Sicilian spewing from under a fedora shading a face where patient rooms line corridors like cigarmaker cottages back up to alleys.

The man, in his early thirties, has grown comfortable being uncomfortable. He no longer stares at scuffmarks janitors failed to erase, marks he placed there the night before. He no longer hears tinny distortions in the operator's voice weaving static into names of doctors, nurses and visiting hours. He doesn't hear the chatter coming from a nurses' station near his wife's room where nurses grab medical charts, slide them across counters and stack them. The nurses hang on to coffee mugs, slap on lipstick, confide illicit affairs, record vital signs, medications and progress notes. In between drags of smoke, they scribble as if their lives depend on it. They do it at the end of each shift, night after night, and then hang charts alphabetically in racks, as if to allow the wet ink to dry.

The man ignores bedpans slammed like cymbals as aids sashay in and out of treatment rooms. Frozen faces tell him they have just flushed shit into Hillsborough Bay. No longer does a urinal or a gurney turn his head, nor do red lights blinking above patient doors elicit distress. No, not anymore, and nothing but nothing prevents him from engaging in conversations with himself. It doesn't seem wrong to implore death, to wish it on his own flesh. Where the man sleeps, myths dominate medical facts, and all things are traced back to God or His antithesis. One or the other doesn't matter, doesn't matter if the mirror images of good and evil function as one. Birth deformities are accepted with a traditional "O *mio* Dio."

It was his world before it is mine. A world fettered with punishments and rewards, so-called instrumental ethics—rewards for the good done and rebuked for any bad—something Christians understand, abide by and brag about. It is how they secure their salvation, nudging of believers by priest to the right side of God and shoving the unrepentant into Hades. The man believes there is nothing to be ashamed of if his baby dies, nothing at all, but if it—and that is what he refers to me as—*it*—if *it* lives, then what? He'd seen others take the bait, seen them take on the cross. There was always someone in the neighborhood carrying it, embracing it. Martyrs they are called. He believes death is infinitely better than his own crucifixion—stuck for life with an imbecile child.

A dead baby would be as if it never happened. It wouldn't know he'd been born, wouldn't feel pain, not a thing—wouldn't know it lived, or died. The man is convinced infancy is a state of nothingness because no one remembers infancy, the womb, being aborted or miscarried. It is no different than before making love, before conception—so-called creation. Sure, that's what it is, just a black hole, a big bang in a world without sound, but living deformed is another story. It might mean a watermelon head, a hydrocephalic rolling on his front porch like a Florida watermelon. Friends would watch his baby drift from society—roll like a tumbleweed pushed by the wind. And each time the child takes a spastic step someone might cheer, "Bravo." Perhaps they'd even say, "Encore." The man will have to swallow his pride and smile at those who cheer for a cerebral palsy child.

The man is good at keeping things to himself and listens to babies cry and watches dirty diapers changed as he stands in the hall outside the nursery.

When he goes home, his mother comforts him. But, beneath her reassurances, she shares his presentiment.

"No life at all is infinitely better than being deformed, Mama," the man says.

"How is Maria, Filippo?" Her eyes do not meet his.

"The doctor says both are getting better."

"Filippo, *praga*, pray."

He shrugs his shoulders and sits at the kitchen table.

"There is leftover pasta in the colander," she says. "Eat, *mangia*."

She fries pasta in a cast iron skillet, adding meatball sauce as she stirs.

"Filippo, God has reasons."

"Mama, he's like a baby in a tiny casket."

"Can you tell who he looks like?"

"Impossible, looks like he's been in a fight."

"I'd like to see him, Filippo."

"No, Ma, no."

That's how my father welcomed me to the world.

The man and his wife live in half of a coldwater flat. Adjoining doors never close. His older brother and sister with their families live upstairs. All are cigar-makers except for the man's father and mother who were too old to be hired—too old to learn when they emigrated in 1904. It is a time of informality. His mother knocks on the ceiling with a broom handle to get her eldest son to come down and visit.

The neighbor next door, trying to sleep on his son's wedding night, wallops the floor next to his bed with the heel of his shoe, telegraphing to the newlyweds downstairs they're making too much noise. It is a togetherness of the times—cramped quarters all around.

My mother's labor was prolonged after I splashed water on the linoleum. Rhythmic contractions picked up the beat. At the end of the day, I'm stuck in never-never land—somewhere between this world, and the one I left behind. Mama languishes in a hospital bed urging me on with unladylike grunts, but I do not budge. On the fifth day extraction forceps tear at my head, and a pair of scissors divide my cord.

My head is swollen and discolored, blood stained. Hematomas and lacerations are pronounced and extend down the right side of my face. When nurses take me to Mama to nurse, they make sure my head is propped good side up.

Visitors peer at me through the nursery's window as if paying their last respects. It's how visiting the sick, wakes and funerals is done, doing one's duty in kind—something akin to the golden rule.

"What a shame. A little boy, too," I hear them say. "Dio, help Maria and Filippo."

They give me ominous stares. Sicilians understand stares, and I understand them, too. It takes one to know one, and well, I'm one of them. Life is personal, real personal, and Sicilians don't wait for obituaries to spread bad news. When death happens, it's read myopically, close up, from sidewalks and slow-moving cars. Heads peer out windows at funeral wreaths nailed to front doors with a four-penny nail. Immigrants don't read newspapers. They don't read a thing or brag about what they'd done in life or whom they'd created making love. It's all left behind, and it is certainly nothing *The Tampa Morning Tribune* cares to write about.

When Mama with a baby in hand doesn't return, news of the debacle spreads, and my father keeps saying, "Better dead than deformed." And I don't know how to respond. The downward pitch of Papa's fedora hides his face. It's a cocky style of wearing a hat in an era when celebrities and presidents wear them cocksure. Bogart, Roosevelt, Dillinger and both Hoovers, Depression Hoover and J. Edgar, the queer, wear them. Pretty Boy Floyd and Baby Face Nelson wear them, too, and so do immigrants. They'll be worn until President Kennedy bares his mane on a cold January presidential inaugural, but until then every man owns one. Immigrants wear them inside cigar factories, inside homes. Hats bob down the Latino business district, and Papa wears his to the hospital each night. Papa's fedora is *machismo,* from what I can see. It isn't bad looking except for frayed edges.

His suit is threadbare, but I understand it gives him a sense of dignity, yet the suit's rough fit speaks a language of its own. Clothes speak for immigrants without permission, and Americanos read immigrants at a glance, at a distance, without getting close. Immigrant sleeves fit noticeably too long or short—nothing is ever right. Trousers are short, too, like pay-envelopes and evanescent childhoods that walk into factories. Cuffs hang high-water, high off cigar factory floors, and immigrant necks, oh well; they're pinched off or swimming freely, deceiving them into believing there is no sliding knot in America's noose.

He crosses himself and looks both ways in the hospital hallway as if hovering over an invisible cross. He's bent over like a street person lighting a cigarette under a lamplight, protecting it from the wind, touching each member of the Catholic triangle. Papa's right hand touches his forehead, the pit of his stomach, two shoulders, left and right and kisses the tip of his fingers. At first, I think he's throwing me a kiss, but I realize the Sicilian is kissing me off. Destiny is playing with his toy, and there is nothing he can do. Toying with me, it rolls me over like gamblers roll dice, cut decks, flip cards, face down, some up, some down. Hit after hit destiny holds me close to its vest, never letting me know if I'll live or die.

"Mr. Russo?"

"*Sì,* but it's no is Russo—is Urso—Filippo Urso," my father says.

"I'm Doctor Cook. We need to talk."

The man walks behind Papa. He guides him like a gentleman escorts a lady on a first date with an outstretched hand—sort of prodding airspace, walking behind.

The doctor opens a frosted glass door stenciled PRIVATE. A motorized gaze motions Papa inside. The physician makes his way around a desk. Hesitating in front of a swivel chair, he waits for my father to sit.

Papa backs up and says nothing, perhaps hears nothing. Certificates hang on a wall. State of Florida is arched over James A. Cook, M.D., and another with a gold seal next to—VANDERBILT SCHOOL OF MEDICINE—CLASS of 1915.

Papa takes off his hat and holds it over his crotch.

"Sit down, Mr. Russo."

Whatever it is the doctor wants, Papa knows it won't take long. It will be one-sided as it usually is with Americanos. Papa seldom leaves the *barrio*, but when he does and conversations ensue, they're always short. Like the time he ran out of gasoline and purchased a couple of gallons of gas pointing at his two fingers.

"Sit down, Mr. Caruso, please. We need to talk."

"Sì, dottóre."

The physician opens the desk drawer and pulls out a Colt .45, a semiautomatic, model 1911. He places it on the desktop as if afraid it'll go off.

Papa, sitting in a cane-back chair, fingers the brim of the fedora, turns it between thumbs and forefingers. The leather sweatband feels like the smooth rim of a tire.

"Relax. No need to be scared, but, if you repeat what I'm about to say, I'll blow your brains out." The doctor picks up the gun and rips the slide back, slamming the hammer into the cocked position.

Papa puts the brakes on the fedora. He squeezes it hard like automobile brake pads slam on steel drums.

The doctor called him Russo, Caruso, common Italian names that sound like his. It was a not uncommon mistake, but so what, aren't all *wops* the same to Anglos?

Papa shrugs and says, *"Dottóre,* I no understand."

Doctor Cook lights a long corona cigar.

Papa knows tobacco, knows it well. He despises rolling the *maduro* leaf the doctor drags on. It's dark and heavy in aroma, and it makes him sick whenever he works the *maduro* at Perfecto Garcia Cigar Factory—also known as El Paradiso, Paradise.

"I no understand *la pistola, dottóre. No e necessario."* Papa points to the pistol.

"Oh, but it is *necessario*, Caruso. It's not a pretty picture I'm going to paint. If you repeat what I tell you, I'll deny it and come after you, understand?"

"But it is Urso, Filippo Urso, you know, right?"

"I have the right man." The man, in his mid fifties, rakes the hair off his forehead.

"I no know."

"Your wife, Maria…"

A gray ash breaks up on the floor.

"She is critical, *cri-ti-ca-le*, *muy ma-la*, understand? Bad. You need a specialist, *uno especialista*, to-mor-row. *Comprende?*"

"Whatta ever you say," Papa says.

The phrase gives Papa time to figure out what's been said.

"The nursing supervisor, Andersen, was present in the labor room. She saw the delivery. She's a good nurse and keeps me posted." Cook, tilting back, pivots on the swivel. Papa leans forward, but it isn't necessary. The doctor's voice is stentorian.

"*No es bueno.*" Stretching out the not good, the doctor rolls the cigar as if tonguing it into submission.

He goes on. "Andersen insisted I look in, so I reviewed your wife's chart. It's not my place to monitor physicians. I can get into problems with the medical community, *sabbe?* So, I'm going to say it straight-out. Maria is dying and the baby may be brain damaged."

Papa slumps into the chair.

"Your wife had dystocia, a tired uterus. It stopped contracting. Gonzalez used forceps, tugged hard at the head."

Papa focuses on each movement of the physician's lips, blink of eyes and rolls of the tongue. The doctor's eyebrows wrap themselves around words he doesn't understand. Words seesaw from English to Spanish, touch Italian and back off again. He intercepts frowns, and watches them recede. The doctor's words are formidable, constructed in stiff English. He understands the situation is worse than he suspected. It isn't just me at death's door but Mama, and she means a hell of a lot more to him than I do.

Papa hangs on to what he understands. Key words are only key because they're locked in grimaces, and each time a word is repeated, he better understands the gravity of the situation.

"Here's the name of an Italian doctor. Call Frank Adamo."

"Frank Adamo?" Papa stands as if the name propelled him out of the chair. "He grow up in Eighth Avenue before he go be a doctor."

"Here's his number. Call tonight."

"*Grazie, dottóre, grazie.*"

"Remember, breathe one word of what I've just said, and I'll come after your ass."

With his thumb, the doctor lets the hammer down, un-cocking and returning the pistol to the desk drawer.

Papa sticks out his hand.

The doctor nods."Good luck, *paesano.*"

Papa walks back to the nursery. The worse case scenario has declared itself—Mama dead and me a handicapped child.

I see Papa from my bassinet. He looks like a child who's lost his kite.

"Mr. Caruso?" A voice startles him. He seems preoccupied, never heard her walk up. He'd seen her before. I know, for she checks on us newborns all the time.

"*Sì,* Filippo Urso."

"I'm Nurse Andersen. Would like to hold your *bambino*?"

"*Infirmiera* Andersen?"

"Yes," she says. "Yes, a nurse."

"Come on, I'll fetch him for you."

"*Grazie,* but no."

She opens the door and motions him in.

"No, no."

"Oh, come on."

"No, Ma'am. Is okay. I look from here."

"Come in and say hello?"

"No, Ma'am, no."

Andersen picks me up and holds me close and places my face on her bosom. I take a deep breath and smell toilet water emanating from silky skin. She carries me to the window, tickles my chin and, in midair, shakes me, startling me. Failing to elicit a Moro reflex, a primitive neurological response normally found in newborns, she releases me to my bassinet. I know Papa cares. I saw him wince as though he felt my pain.

Surgical steel has torn me apart, banging me up, laying waste my head. I'm also what's called a "banana-head"—banana-shaped that is. And if that were all, it'd be fine, for a banana-head is no big deal. It's created by the molding of a baby's malleable head hitting a bony pelvis for hours, like hitting one's head against the proverbial brick wall.

Noting the absent Moro reflex in my chart, Ms. Andersen stands, straightens and tosses her head back—unraveling her blonde hair. She rearranges a striped cap. The cap reimplanted, she steps outside the nursery into the corridor. She's long-legged and voluptuous with striking Scandinavian features. She looks at Papa over half glasses.

"Mr. Caruso, ended up doing a double shift today," she says. "Looks like you could use a break yourself. Join me for a smoke?"

He doesn't understand but doesn't resist. She leads him to a room away from the patient care area where nurses' aids carry urinals with stiff arms, away from starched uniforms and orderlies with noses turned up to avoid the stench of bed-pans.

She gestures for him to sit and plops herself in the conch concavity of an upholstered sofa. She pulls out a pack of Old Gold and tapping it on her wrist, coaxes a few cigarettes out.

"Here," she says with an outstretched arm.

"*No, grazie,*" he says. "I no smoke."

"No smoke? Heard you're a cigarmaker, and you no smoke?" She smiles.

She taps a cigarette on the armrest, packs it, flips open the lid of a metal lighter, thumbs its wheel and lights up. Inhaling deeply, she lets smoke flare out her nostrils. She's sensually molded in the comfort zone of the sofa. Papa skims legs, thighs, and hips and moves out of the range of her eyes. Sicilian women don't smoke, and those who do are viewed askance, for there're three things Sicilian women don't do: smoke, drink and drive cars—Americanas do all three—do them unabashedly.

"Got *bambinos* at home, Sir?"

"No, Ma'am."

No one had said sir to him before, sounded foreign. It's not at all what he expected. It was more like a hello when she said it. Intimidation no longer seemed married to the word, and he'd ma'amed her like he ma'amed his third grade teacher the day he told her he would not return. At eight he began an apprenticeship at Perfecto Garcia Cigar Factory, a year without pay. He began his career rolling cigars, carrying pots of Cuban coffee to cigarmakers for change. In the evenings he swept the factory floor. That's how it happened to all of them. No one cared, and no one was the wiser. It was how children were birthed into the tobacco industry.

"I was the nurse at the delivery," she says. "Just want you to know I'm doing all I can for your baby."

Andersen snuffs out her cigarette and walks to the door, holds it open. "Philip," she says, straightening her uniform. "Baby is going to be a good-looking man—take after you."

He understands she noticed more than his name. She peeked beneath his reticence—saw the man.

"Got to get back," she says. "Call me any time, hear? Any time. Tell the operator you're inquiring about a patient on the critical list. Ask for Carol Andersen. My father emigrated from Oslo, so it's spelled with an *e*." Catching herself, she adds, "Never mind. I'm just trying to say I understand."

"*Porco* Juda." Papa invokes Judas the pig and watches buttocks sashay out of sight.

The operator announces the end of visiting hours.

He paces off. "*Uno, duo, tre, quattro.*" Thirty-three steps, thirty-three short Sicilian steps from the nursery to the elevator, perhaps ominous. That was the age of Christ when he was pinned to the cross. Papa is thirty-three.

He smiles at a Negro woman who slides the elevator door open.

"Going down. Watch yo' step."

He moves to the rear.

"Down, going down."

She rattles the door shut, turns a spear-shaped handle on a numbered brass dial. Passengers in the suspended cage avoid eye contact, peer at open spaces created by a harlequin-grated door and watch black numbers on concrete floors flash by. Papa's eyes lock on the floor. He thinks of me, thinks if I survive, I'll never go to school, never let go of his hand.

The Negress opens the door. "Watch yo' step."

He had watched his step. Papa didn't marry until he was twenty-nine—disillusioned with the strife he saw in his brothers' marriages. Through the years, Mama told me the story of how their paths crossed, walking to and from the cigar factories during lunch breaks. Papa walked to El Paradiso. Mama, with her mother at her side, walked to El Reloj. The factories were a block apart. It was a time few immigrants owned cars, and since most lived a few blocks from factories, they walked home for lunch. Frugal immigrants did not eat at restaurants. Mama noticed Papa's smile. He paced himself to meet the two women head on. No matter which side of the street my grandmother took, he was there.

Mama began to smile back with her eyes. Of course, her mother noticed. Their courtship was traditional. Relatives interceded and brought the couple together. Dating was prohibited. All activities were chaperoned. Papa received visitation rights after a background check by my mother's father, and within a month, Papa's parents presented themselves at my mother's home. Glasses of wine and traditional sugarcoated almonds came out, and my paternal grandfather, Ciccio, fulfilled his duty to his last unmarried son. He said, "Signore Domenico, my son Filippo wants to court your daughter with the intention of marriage."

Mama's father limited Papa's visits to weekends, but soon Papa broke the rule, and showed up nightly.

When I was growing up, Mama bragged how she rejected four previous marriage proposals. Two Cuban and two Sicilian cigarmakers wanted her, and *want* was the operative word—*Te quero*. It meant I love you as well as I want you in Spanish—indistinguishable. The number of proposals a woman received reflected desirability, so Mama clung to her proposals like blue ribbons. Their engagement lasted a year, and Papa squeezed in kisses when chaperones relieved themselves in bathrooms, and it was then, no doubt, Mama was squeezed, too.

4

The old man visited my mother earlier that evening and gave Papa a pessimistic stare in the hospital room and walked out. Now he sits outside on a cement bench smoking a cigar.

"Do you think Maria is going to die?" Mama's father says to my father when he walks out of the hospital.

"Dottóre Cook said Doctor Gonzalez botched it," my father replies.

"That bastard. I don't think there's a good one in the bunch. They import Cuban and Spanish physicians because American doctors won't work for the pittance Latin clubs pay."

"Adamo is coming in the morning," my father says.

"Did Gonzalez come by today?"

"He saw her briefly, said nothing to worry about. Maria said he seemed rushed."

"Still the fever?"

"Rattling the bed at night."

"Maybe you should've taken her to a midwife."

Papa's generation was shifting to physicians, realizing midwives were unprepared for obstetrical complications, unable to use forceps or perform Caesarian sections. Spanish and Cuban physicians came cheap, as a package deal with an Italian club membership—about a dollar a week. It covered hospitalization, outpatient visits, pharmacy costs and house calls. Sharing physicians by mutual aide societies was a cost effective method of delivering healthcare—a form of early HMOs. Fernandez, Gonzalez, Dominguez, Paniello and Trelles were familiar names in the *barrio*. *Barrio* doctors drove Cadillacs like chariots of fire with big M.D. logos lighting up their auto tags, and some lived in palatial homes.

"It's *lo brutto destino*, Filippo. You and Maria have the baby in an Americano hospital, and there are problems."

Papa agrees with my mother's father. Destiny is brutal, but the couple had feared cerebral palsy. A few children delivered by midwives in the *barrio* recently had been afflicted.

"The baby might be brain damaged," Papa says to the middle-aged man.

Glaring into the passing traffic, his father-in-law sticks his hand in his mouth and chomping on it, exposes his teeth. He doesn't bite hard, but the grimace highlights his anger. His hand flings straightaway from his face like a karate chop aimed at an opponent's neck. An audible grunt terminates the maneuver.

Sicilians of my grandfather's generation used the Sicilian gesture, and old ladies used it, too, kept it hidden in black purses and under black shawls ready to let fly, but that's as far as it went. I never saw it used by my parents' generation. The karate chop, signifying *vendétta*, implying I'll get even, disappeared with those who grew up in Sicily. The middle finger replaced it in America, so my father's generation flung the analog with the rest of Ybor City Cubans.

"We should put a gun to that bastard's head. Let that son of a bitch know he can't play around with Italians."

"Let's see what Adamo says," my father says.

"Filippo, want to wait for my son, Tony? He can drive us home. He's visiting a mechanic with a bad appendix."

"That's all right, Papa. I'll walk."

Papa glances inside well-lit homes as he walks the sidewalks and sees how Greater Tampa lives. He sees cars in driveways newer than those parked in the *barrio*—on average ten years old when purchased. Florida live oaks and broad-leafed magnolias amplify the South. The outskirts of the *barrio* are not yet called suburbs. Well lit homes tell him Anglos don't care about electric bills. Saint Augustine grass in well-watered lawns is lush.

He turns onto Columbus Drive. He crosses Nebraska Avenue, the western boundary of the *barrio*. Walking east he comes to Sixteenth Street. He looks up at El Reloj Cigar Factory's clock tower where my mother is employed. It is dark, ominous as the clock strikes ten o'clock. Directly in front of the factory stands La Económica Drugstore. On the opposite side and catercorner from the drugstore is a café. The café is where *tabaqueros* stop before going home from El Reloj and El Paradiso cigar factories. El Paradiso is a block north and where Papa is employed.

"*Joven*, come, come here," a man yells when Papa walks through the café doors. "Never see you anymore, Felipe."

Heads at the bar turn, then go back to cloistered existence. The dark-skinned older man paddles the seat of a four-legged stool, inviting Papa to sit next to him.

The man is disheveled, mid-sixties. Most cigarmakers are younger than José. José has been a *bonchero* for fifty years. Papa knows him from his early apprenticeship days.

José doesn't remember names, for alcohol has shorted out his brain. He's like a politician, knows many, slaps people on their backs and flips them off with his broad smile—everyone knows José. The glib man calls people *joven*. Cubans often call their friends *cabron* and *hijo putta*. Testy goat or son of a bitch is not necessarily a put down, but it can be. It's all in the tone the words are said. In a culture that is mired in cuss words, and Goddamn is not heard, *cabron* is often used as a term of endearment, and so is son of a bitch, but "young man" is always non-inflammatory and complimentary in every sense of the word.

José works at El Paradiso Factory where Papa works, but both were once employed at the Clock Factory or El Reloj, where Mama is currently employed.

José speaks only Spanish. Italians working in cigar factories speak Sicilian and Spanish. That's the norm. Spaniards and Cubans never learn Italian. They don't have to. It's simply a numbers game. Italians are outnumbered about four to one.

"Armando." José waves at the bartender. "*Dos* whiskeys, *por favor.*"

"*Bueno*, all right, I'll have one," Papa says to the older man.

"*Sí, sí*, one to start, Felipe, but you look like *mierda*, shit. He slaps my father's thigh, clasps down as if to steady the young man's response.

"No damn good, José. I think Maria is dying. I'm not going to work tomorrow. Will you tell Panchito?"

"Die? No, no, don't say that, Felipe. Panchito will understand. Besides, he knows Italians rather work than play hooky, eh? Not like us Cubans, *bon vivons*."

José slugs a shot and looks at the empty jigger as if it just short-changed him.

Panchito is the *capotasso*, foreman, at Perfecto Garcia, nicknamed El Paradiso, where Papa is a roller. *Capotassos* hire and fire arbitrarily. There is no appeal process in cigar factories, so *capotassos*, mostly Spaniards, receive the utmost respect. Panchito knows Mama from the days when he was the foreman at Regensburg & Sons Cigar Factory.

The factory is called "El Reloj" by Spanish speaking cigarmakers and "Lo Rogio" by Italians. The clock gives identity to the city block long factory. Its tower looms above *casitas* and shotgun homes. One of them will be mine. The four faces of the clock face the compass winds, and after hurricanes from the Gulf of Mexico batter Tampa, its black hands sweep clean turbulent skies.

The Clock's tower is the highest structure in the *barrio*, but cigarmakers can't pronounce the Jewish name Regensburg, so they also call it "Rey-hing-boy."

"Felipe, *tiene que tener corazon*—you got to have heart."

"Ah, José, first I worried about the baby, now Maria."

José spits between his legs on sawdust covering the floor. "Bad things happen fast, but good things slowly, *amigo,* but all will be well. You'll see, Felipe. We drink, eh?"

"*Quién sabes,* José, *quién sabes?*"

"You will see—it will be *bien, joven.* That's *la differenza* between Cubanos and Italianos. Italianos worry about this and that, worry about shit, you know. That's what it is, nothing but *pura mierda.* Cubans don't give a damn as long as we have a bottle, and a woman with a tight dress squeezing a big ass. We're happy, *en cielo,* heaven, *hombre.* Don't worry. We're all waiting to die."

"José, do you have to talk about death?"

"Felipe, drink, drink. It helps a man sleep, sleep like *un muerto.*" José winks then snaps his fingers and yells, "*Otro* whiskey, *dos mas,* Armando, *por favor.*"

"O right." The bartender lifts a fifth of Seagram off the shelf. "Want water?"

"*Sí, con neive, sí, sí,* with ice *y agua.*" José bottoms up and slams the jigger next to the water glass, lifts his buttocks, scratches his crotch and breaks wind. "*Perdona,* Felipe, *peros* better out than in, no?"

They drink bourbon straight, putting out fire with ice water. No one drinks mixed drinks in the *barrio.* Straight bourbon reflects the *machismo* of the three cultures. It's how they down life, perhaps drown life, straight, one jigger at a time.

When his wife goes to Mass on Sundays, José hits the café early. On Saturday afternoons, he awaits *bolita* results. Winning numbers come over the radio, beamed from Havana. *Bolita,* Cuban lottery, translates to little ball. It is little balls with numbers they pull out of a bag, supposedly at random. It is illegal, but no one cares, "gives a shit," as they say. Men and women play numbers, but, in actuality, play dreams, for each dream has a designated number.

Dreaming of a rat is number 29, death is number 9, and other dreams have numbers, so dreams are tagged—numbered commodities. If a black cat crosses their path, it's a number, too. There are numbers for all living and dead things, and *bolita* runners or bookies are everywhere. They are seen in factories, cafés, and social clubs and out in the streets, and if one is a prodigious gambler, they'll come to the high roller's home to jot numbers. *Boliteros,* as they are called, give out slips of paper called receipts.

José insists whiskey is infinitely more redeeming than the white Eucharist. He tells my father he doesn't have to pour out his guts to a hypocrite hiding behind a black screen to receive unmerited grace. He pours it eighty-six to a hundred proof. Each swallow, in his mind, translates to a Hail Mary, and gulping in succession constitutes a fine Act of Contrition. At least, that's what he says.

He views the Catholic Church with disdain, yet his wife, a cigarmaker, is a devout Catholic. Men despise the clergy, yet wives frequent Mass and *novenas* and make *promesas* (promises), bribing saints with acts of public humility. It's common to see a pious woman crawling on her hands and knees on church steps or walking barefooted on blistering sidewalks near church. It's payback for a requited prayer, a quid pro quo, one publicly acknowledged.

"*Bueno*, José, I have to go. I need to be at the hospital early *mañana*. Another doctor is coming to see Maria." Papa slides off the stool.

"Who is the doctor on the case now?"

"Gonzalez."

"Ah, *sí*."

"You know something about him?"

"Well, I hear good and bad."

"Tell me, José, tell me."

"Sometimes it is best to say nothing, *amigo*."

"Please, José, tell me what you hear."

"You come ask a Cuban about a Cuban?" José pauses, lights a cigarette and blows smoke in Papa's face. "Well, I say he is nothing horrendous like Doctor Garcia. Gonzalez is okay, but he's a pussy monger."

José's audacity nudges Papa's buttock back onto the barstool.

"The bastard got caught with the wife of a friend of mine at Palmetto Beach. The two of them so tired of *cingando* they fell asleep. Water coming in the floorboard told them they were worse than stuck in the sand. The wrecker found them watching the incoming tide trying to float away the Cadillac. The mother of three, can you believe, Felipe, such a whore? No shame left in this world, liked to fuck in the doctor's Cadillac."

Papa sips and lets out, "Ahh," as if to smother José's words.

"Felipe, Cubans are not like Italians. We love whores, oh, yes, love the whole fucking mess. Don't forget we got some of that Africano *sangre*, hot Negro blood from the Caribbean, and it makes more than our skin dark—our desires, too. It makes us crazy for *papaya*."

Papa understands *papaya* to a Cuban is not just a fruit; it's a metaphor for female genitalia. It seems the anatomical structure is intricately woven into Cuban existence—something around which all things revolve like the Copernicus theory.

"Don't make me laugh, José. You're married to a good woman."

"My wife, Esperanza, is Catolica, faithful to me and Jesus, but if she had her druthers, it would be with him she'd cuckold me."

"You're a crazy old man."

"*Sí, sí,* I know." José spills bourbon on his shirt.

Papa eyes him. "But about Doctor Gonzalez, tell me."

"Ah, Gonzalez, *sí, sí,* a nice man, okay for pimples and shit like that, but heavy-duty stuff—no good. Sounds like your woman has *problemas.*"

"Doctor Adamo is coming to see her in the morning."

"Ahh, *sí,* Adamo sees Cubans and Spaniards, too. Says pay later when he knows he's not going to get paid, but at least he says, 'Later.' Has a good heart, *corazon,* understand?"

"*Sí.*"

"I hear he's cocky. Nobody has died under his knife lately that I know of, but, if he says Maria is going to die, you better go to Lord and Fernandez Funeral Home and pick out a casket her father will like. If he says he can save her, come tomorrow and buy me *un* whiskey."

Wiping tabletops and flipping chairs, Armando, the bartender, hangs chairs on tables, tucking them in for the night, sprinkling fresh sawdust from a bucket.

"Felipe?"

"What?"

"You know Adamo was my roller. He was not bad for someone who became a doctor. He was fast with his hands. Loves to cut, so be careful if he wants to open up Maria. All those bastards like to make money—cut first, sorry later."

My father nods.

"Adamo is opinionated but smart. Cuba and Spain don't have medical schools like America. I think it's good you bring Adamo in on the case. If I had to go under the knife, it would be him. I know Cubans and Spaniards go to Doctor Trelles."

"Italianos go, too," my father says.

"*Sí, sí,* but the man runs a meat market in his *clinica.* He thinks he's a surgeon, but he's the butcher of the *barrio.* His mistress Conchita gives the anesthesia, and El Bien Publico or the Gonzalez Clinic on Fourteenth Street is not any better. That Trelles is nothing but a society doctor for haughty Latinos. He's a good friend of the pharmacist across the street, J. B. Those Spaniards stick together. You know Pacheco, no?"

Papa nods.

"Like they say one Spaniard greases the hand of another. So, Felipe, it is best to go to Centro Asturiano Hospital with Adamo, or to Centro Español Hospital on the Bayshore where Doctor Winton operates—nice man that Winton. But, Felipe, never go to Trelles, never, unless you want to die, *hombre, comprende?*"

5

And "Adamo" was what Italians called him.

Dr. Frank S. Adamo, the patron saint of Sicilian medicine, exemplified to me that a poor boy born in the ghetto in 1893 could be a *somebody*. During World War II, the Japanese imprisoned him, and he distinguished himself administering to soldiers in the Bataan Death March, returning emaciated with vitamin deficiencies, a shell of his former self. "Skin and bones," I heard Italians say. "An authentic war hero from Ybor City."

The colonel was paraded downtown in a convertible, and Mayor Hixon proclaimed Frank S. Adamo Day. I didn't attend. It was just another workday for my parents. I was about ten years old, so I didn't see the hoop-la, didn't see the parade, didn't have to—I knew the legend.

Growing up, I admired him, saw him making rounds at Centro Asturiano Hospital, cutting a wide swath in its dingy corridors. He was an old man by my standards, older than Papa, but I felt proud when he said, "Hello, Fili," to my father. We didn't know doctors, lawyers, or Indian chiefs, only cigarmakers, cigarmakers and more cigarmakers.

A highway was named Adamo Drive, so Americanos were finally made to say an Italian name, and it was as if I heard them say, "Uncle."

But in 1935 I'm still casketed in the hospital's bassinet, and the morning brings a drizzle to the gulf coast. The sun is hiding behind clouds east of Tampa, beyond the town of Gary where Italian farmers and rednecks live. It can't seem to decide if to shine.

"*Che dice*, Filippo, how've you been?" Adamo says.

The bespectacled man in his forties bear hugs Papa Italian style.

"Nice to see you, *dottóre*," Papa says.

"Where you work, Filippo?"

"El Paradiso."

"Remember lo Coralli? If it had not been for the ten-month strike I'd still be rolling cigars there. Went to Chicago looking for work and ended up in medical school."

Lo Corrali was what Italians called the cigar factory Corral y Wodsika.

"I know. I heard the story," Papa says. "You remember José Rodriguez, *dot-tóre*?"

"He was my bunch-maker when I was young, nice man."

"Said to say hello. Saw him last night."

"Oh that José was some crazy Cuban. Got to be getting on in years."

"Hasn't changed. He works at El Paradiso now."

"A good *bonchero* but drinks like a fish." Adamo shakes his head. "Not a bad Cuban," he says.

"Maria is sick, *dottóre*—chills, fever, cold one minute, hot the next."

"I'll go to the nurses' station and look at her chart." He starts to walk off.

"Nurse Andersen knows the case, *dottóre*, the head nurse. I saw her a while ago."

"All right, Filippo, all right, I'll talk with her."

Adamo returns. "*Minga* everything is running late in this place. Can't get a case started on time."

The physician's gaze fixes on the floor as he talks to my father, "Mary ruptured her bag five days before delivery…went into labor, contractions continued a day. Patients need to deliver within twenty-four hours after the bag breaks, Filippo, a cardinal rule or infection sets in. Chills, legs swelled up, right?"

Papa nods to the physician rattling off facts like a rattling gun.

"The sun must never set twice on a woman in labor. *Minga*, can't let a woman labor indefinitely. I give them twenty-four hours, give them a chance to do their thing, but if it doesn't happen, I go get the baby." Adamo pounds his open palm with his fist. "No, no, never wait."

Minga is a word like *capisci*, one I learn early, and it is ubiquitous. It's said by men, means "dick" or "prick," encompasses both without preference. *Minga* adds no substance—only punctuates with passion. It's not a womanly word uttered in the presence of women. Chauvinism respects women where I live. At times the word substitutes for Goddamn since there is no Goddamn in Sicilian, still isn't, not in the land of the Pope, only Porco Juda, Judas, the pig whose name my people take in vain.

"If I can't take the baby with forceps, I section…cut, cut, cut, understand? It's not a matter if you want to go to the dance, baby, you're there, in the middle of the dance floor, and the band is playing, and you will dance, whether you like to dance the Tarantella or not. I would have sectioned her with a pocketknife if I had to. There's your problem, Filippo, in labor too long, so infection set in. The nurses tell me she didn't put out much urine the last twenty-four hours. We'll hydrate her, Filippo. You got to get rid of Doctor Gonzalez."

"*Dottóre*, I'll pay in installments."

"Don't worry."

"Just want you to understand we don't expect anything free."

The physician walks into Mama's room, observes her pallor while palpating her abdomen. His approach is gentle first, then vigorous, palpating liver, spleen and pelvis deeply in that order. He moves quickly to the chest.

"Will these stretch marks go away?" Mama says.

"Don't worry, Mary, need to get you out of here."

Mama slumps back. "Ahh, I'm so weak."

Propping her up, he slaps a stethoscope on her back. "Take a deep one, Mary. Go on breathe one more. I hear you got a nice baby."

She exhales. "That's what Dottóre Gonzalez says, '*Un macho hombre.*' But he's sick, too. Nurses bring him and put him on my breast. They won't let me see the right side of his face, and he won't suck."

"Shush, breathe. Deeper, all right, let it out. Fine, fine."

"Dottóre Gonzalez used forceps."

"I know."

"I'm so weak, *dottóre.*"

He lets her down easy.

Adamo doesn't count respirations or pulse, for counting isn't his style, believing in the overall scheme of life and death, it's the big picture that counts. To him, counting stuff is pedantic—a leftover brouhaha from medical school days.

He feels what he needs to feel, feels it instinctively. After all, Mama's history told him what it was, and the physical examination confirmed it. He feels no trepidation in a snap diagnosis. It comes with the persona, fast, like rolling cigars.

He struts out of the room, hands in back pockets, cocky-like. "Well, I can't promise, but it's clear what she's got."

His eyes meet Papa's head-on.

"What, *dottóre?*"

He shoves the stethoscope in his pocket, puts his arm around my father and leads him away from Mama's room.

Adamo chooses his words. "Filippo, I saw lots of carnage in Chicago, lots of bad cases. Pathetic people came to the hospital to die. They believed that's what hospitals were for, like our old people in Ybor City do. Cook County Hospital was full of Negroes and immigrants, unbelievable ignorance, yet we cured many against terrible odds."

Papa says, "*E vero, dottóre.* That's how my parents think of hospitals. A place to die."

"Oh, by the way, tell the hospital staff your wife's name. They got her down as Russo in admitting and Caruso on her chart. Don't want Mary to volunteer for someone else's surgery."

"Doctor, does she have a chance?"

"It's an abscess and blood clots in her legs, Fili. Serious? Yes, very—if the abscess is not drained, she'll die. Infection will eat her alive, or if the bag of puss ruptures inside, peritonitis will set in. Either way it would be fatal. First, I need to know where it is—hate to go in blindly. I'll wait to see if it will make itself accessible to the knife. It's best if it's in the pelvis, outside the peritoneum, but, wherever it is, it's going to have to be drained. Understand?"

José's comments of the night before prey on my father's thoughts. Adamo is reluctant to cut. The situation is formidable.

"An abscess is a collection of pus," Adamo says. "Has to be drained surgically—no other choice."

A week later the abscess is drained, and foul smelling pus saturates the operating room.

Doctor Gonzalez practiced a lifetime in Tampa, and Papa never failed to point him out as the man who delivered Mama and me to death's door. The man lived in a posh house made of yellow bricks. It was a time when brick homes were luxurious and yellow was chic. It was a time a yellow brick house had no other meaning to me. I knew nothing of The Wizard of Oz, Toto, the Tin Man or the Wicked Witch of the West.

When my parents encountered Doctor Gonzalez in Ybor City streets, he patted me on the head and said to my mother, "See what a *macho hombre* I delivered, Maria."

Mama smiled and acted as if nothing had happened. After he left, Papa would say, "That *somma ama bitcha*."

He wasn't a bad man, just a bad doctor, and maybe it wasn't even that but just the times when we all lived with a different mindset.

Mama said, "You be nice to doctors, Franchito. One never knows which one might be called in an accident or an emergency. Whoever it is will hold your life in his hands—don't want bad feelings influencing him at a time like that."

I heeded her admonition—woe unto me if the doctor held a *vendétta*.

I envisioned Doctor Gonzalez would retire and bask in the Caribbean sun somewhere, sitting on a veranda of a big house, wearing the same embroidered Cuban shirt he wore on house calls. It was one of the things that impressed me the most—the way the flowing white shirt hung over his black belt next to his medical bag as he went up and down wooden steps of *tabaquero* homes. But Doctor Gonzalez never left Tampa. He passed on like the rest of my immigrants, for things in the *barrio* were not always what they seemed. Some visions existed only in my dreams.

The legend of Dr. Cook and his Colt .45 was told and retold until Papa died in his eighties. It happened during a time physicians did not testify against each other, and to talk to a patient or a patient's family about another physician amounted to treason. If the word had gotten out Dr. Cook was monitoring patients in his hospital, doctors would have stopped admitting their patients there. Perhaps pulling a gun on a patient is unheard of today, and in an age of litigation it is incomprehensible something like that could happen, but it did. Papa saw it as Doctor Cook's way of helping out an unwary immigrant. Papa described easing out of Dr. Cook's office like one backs away from a Catholic altar, never letting the supplicant's ass get between him and the Host.

Dr. Cook endeared himself to my father by pointing the loaded forty-five. It was a language all immigrants understood. A Colt .45 was a hell of an adjective and a bullet a hell of a period. I never met Dr. Cook, but his legend served as a reminder to me during my fledgling years in Ybor City that good Americanos existed, even if they didn't speak Italian, didn't live in the *barrio* and threatened my father with a Colt .45 loaded with compassion.

6

I remain hospitalized for two months. Spring arrives early in Ybor City in 1935. Dill, fennel, mint, collard greens, tomatoes and basil leaf flourish in backyards next to alleys. Saint Joseph flowers arch high above vegetable gardens and remnants of dilapidated outhouses. The flowers bloom and tower over short Sicilians hoeing rows in gardens. The flowering stalks fold over near flowering tips as if bowing in prayer. The flower and stalk take on the configuration of a shepherd's staff, so Italians aptly call the flowers St. Joseph's staffs. It is the first flower I call by name.

A bitter winter ravishes the middle part of the state with freezes in January and February. Smudge pots burn between rows of orange and grapefruit trees in the outlying citrus belt. In the ghetto, water pipes attached to outside wood sidings of homes pop like kernels of corn.

To Sicilians March is festive, the resurrection, the renaissance of Jesus and spring, and mothers and grandmothers buy shoes for children and sew clothes in anticipation of Easter. But on Saint Joseph's Day, the nineteenth of March, the old ladies of the neighborhood focus on the old man with a shepherd's staff and a beard.

They prepare offerings in the form of food and drink and place them on planked tables covered with an assortment of mismatched oilcloths. The feast day of Saint Joseph, patron saint of the poor, is a glorious affair. The feast consists of roasted goat, *capretto arrosta*, hot Sicilian sausage, pasta and sauce, chicken soup, homemade bread, *manicotti* and *cannoli* and *sfinge* (doughnut-like cakes deep fried in lard). Flower arrangements placed next to a ceramic statue of Saint Joseph or a painting of the man on the face of a calendar embellish the room with colors. Twelve men down on their luck are invited to play the roles of modern-day apostles, and the Last Supper is resurrected.

"Oh, it's so good of you to come on this holy day. Saint Joseph takes care of us all," my widowed great-aunt says—stooping, searching, reaching for the hem of a black apron to wipe a toothless smile, as she readies herself to plant a kiss on her guests.

"*Grazie, signora.*" The men thank her and congregate in the parlor before she leads them to an enclosed back porch where the Last Supper will take place.

"We wait for the others. Go on, drink wine, just pressed this year. You know what delicious *vino* Don Pietro makes, eh?"

One of the so-called apostles pours red wine from a gallon jug. "*Puro* like Cristo and full of faith, Signora Grazia."

She crosses herself as if she's the priestess at the altar.

He sips and smiles. "*Bello* dago red."

Bringing his sleeve to his mouth, he wipes. "Don Pietro makes *bellissimo vino.* I swear it on my mother's tomb, and Santo Giuseppe, too."

"Pepe, apostles don't swear. Their word is like the Lord's." She cackles as she does all the years I know her. "But what is this dago thing—*che cosa* you say?"

"That's what Americani call us, *signora*—dagos." Pepe laughs. "Don't worry about what it means. Hell, I don't know what it means, but it's nothing good. Nothing those bastards call us is good."

The old lady glares. "*Va dare lo culo le* Americani *figli di puttani* (Go give their asses those American sons of bitches)."

"Now, now, *signora*, no need for anybody to give up their asses." Pepe smiles at the vulgar admonition. "Is Don Pietro still having trouble with the police?"

"*Sì*, they say he needs a license to sell alcohol." She places her hands on her hips. "A poor old man can't make a little money from the vine—what a shame."

Pepe picks grapes from a bowl. He tosses them singularly in the air, catching each one with an open mouth.

Aunt Grazia scurries and sets plates.

"Let those police go give their asses," she says.

"Watch your language, *signora*. You're in the company of apostles."

She laughs. "How can I forget you're an apostle today, Pepe? It's the rest of the year I worry about."

The men savor a collage of aromas emanating from the kitchen.

"During prohibition we kept his winemaking hush-hush in the neighborhood—never a problem. We had all the wine we needed." She sighs. "Ah, but now things are different."

"A sin, a damn sin, *signora*."

She pulls out a chair hugging the table. "*Setati*, everyone, sit."

She folds her arms on her chest. "The mayor drinks the old man's wine, you know. The old man is intelligent, takes a gallon to him at Christmas and on New Year's. That's how the word got out. Now lawyers from City Hall come looking to Jew him down."

Pepe nods. "Lawyers let anybody put a stitch in their assholes for a penny, *signora*."

The old lady waves Pepe off. "Come on—you go too far."

It's an expression Sicilians use. It is a metaphor implying extreme frugality at the expense of honor, at the expense of one's ass and, as a boy, I visualize painful stitching of an asshole with needle and thread.

Jiggling rolls of fat under a black silhouette, she laughs. "We'll eat soon. Pick on sausage. Have more *vino*?"

"For a penny, those..." another apostle revs. "Those assholes should be cinched, cinched tight, so they can't breathe." He mimics sewing with needle and thread, grimacing as if he's smelling an asshole. "Suffocate the bastards." His speech is slurred.

"Gustavo, *per favore*, leave your anger at the door," she says. "Apostles didn't keep grudges." She scurries into the kitchen. "Ah, *lo pane*, the bread's burning, Madonna!"

"It's true, *signora*," Gustavo yells into the kitchen.

"But lawyers are worse than the devil. At least the devil makes no pretense of being a friend. For a penny, the bastards would turn Christ in—one damn penny," he says to the men.

Turning to Pepe, Gustavo says. "I never paid that asshole lawyer. What the hell, I was innocent. I did six months in the county jail. No work—no pay, I said to him." He eyes the kitchen door.

"But, Gustavo, they found the *bolita* tickets on you. What the hell you expect? Got you dead to rights. Should have flushed the receipts down the toilet."

"Yeah, yeah, but how about if one of my customers claimed a winning number, then what? Without proof where would I be? I don't need that kind of shit with Charlie Wall. Better to do time than end up in an alley. That lawyer could have made up a story; said I picked up the wrong shirt at the whorehouse instead of admitting it was mine."

Pepe grins. "Yeah, yeah, *stupido*, but you got no one to blame but yourself. Should work for Trafficante not Wall. Santo is the *capo-boss* of the future. He takes care of his boys. What do you expect from Charlie Wall? He's Americano. He don't give no crap about wops. Next time get a lawyer like D'Arpa or Grimaldi to defend you. Can't trust Americanos."

"But the judge was Americano, Pepe, Americano, *capisci*? The jury was Americano. Not one Latino." Gustavo stands with hands on his hips.

Pepe pulls him down by the arm. "Come on. Let go, man, does no good to fester. Give you an ulcer, Gustavo. Why ruin a beautiful Santo Giuseppe lunch?

Just don't take numbers from strangers. Never know who's working for the cops."

"Damn right, but it pisses me off."

The old lady wipes her hands on her apron returning from the kitchen. "There will be plenty for you men to take home to your families. There's lots of goat and sausage in the oven."

The men smile and in unison say, "*Grazie, grazie, signora.*"

"It's nothing, *niente, niente.*" She relishes compliments, saying it's her pleasure, "*Mio piacere.*"

She looks over the seating arrangement. "You look like St. Peter, Pepe, so you sit here. Move over, Gustavo, and, you, Ignazio—my God—you are the spitting image of Santo Stefano. Sit at the head of the table, *per favore.* Stefano was the first martyr, you know—stoned because he stood up for Cristo, and Saint Paul looked on. Did you men know Santo Paolo was a Jew called Saul?"

"No kidding," Gustavo says. "An Italian saint—a Jew?"

"One with a snarling upper lip. He persecuted Christians until Jesus twisted his ear—blinded him on the way to Damascus."

"Damascus? Where's that?" Pepe says.

"*Demonio*, how would I know, but that's what the priests in Sicily said," she says.

Demonio is a word I learned early, means hell, derived from demon.

The men laugh, never realizing Jesus and Saint Joseph were Jews. Everybody in the Old and New Testaments were Jews, but I didn't know. It's never presented that way.

"It's time we eat," she says.

The faces of Ybor City and the apostles change. It is the time cigarette smoking takes hold. Young men prefer smoking cigarettes to cigars. It's the modern thing. The tobacco industry falls prey to booming cigarette sales. Slowdowns in cigar factories become the norm, and encores of Saint Joseph's Day continue to play year after year. Apostles find embracing work more difficult than the cross.

I see apostles making their rounds on the nineteenth of March, feasting at one neighbor's home one year and at another's the following year. Year after year they pass themselves off as saints, drinking dago red, not saying much and checking in vices at front doors. Aunt Grazia knows most are a far cry from canonization, knows they hide run-ins with the law, sell *bolita* to supplement their meager salaries doing piecework. Apostles are often laid off, so some embrace *bolita* fulltime, flourish, and drive black Buicks, flicking cigarette butts out car windows. Many languish in cafés and the Italian Club—gambling, womanizing and importing American whores into Ybor City. They find it difficult to resist the path of blond, blue eyed, freckled American women. It's the first installment of the American dream.

Saint Joseph's Feast is a grand affair, all right, in those years following my birth. But on March of 1935 I do not taste Don Pietro's dago red, feast on roasted goat or feel the bite of hot sausage. Life goes on without me as if I don't exist.

7

I survive the malpractice debacle except for a minimally shortened right leg with no limp. Mama is left with a messed up birth canal and the fear of pregnancy. Mama's bad delivery is legendary. Relatives refer to it all the time, but I thrive sucking on Florida Dairy milk while everyone waits to see if I'm retarded. I hear them talking about how Doctor Gonzalez tore up Mama's birth canal and my head with the steel forceps. There is talk she might not be able to have any more children, and that suits me fine. I learn to walk, say Mama and Papa, and reach for a *piruli* on time, so my mother says, "*Grazie,* Dio."

Piruli is hard candy sold by a Cuban vender called the "*piruli* man." He walks Ybor City streets yelling in Spanish, "Cry, little babies, cry, so your mama will buy you a *piruli.*" The hard candies are stiletto-shaped and brightly colored: red, blue, green. With pointed popsicle-stick handles at one end, each is stuck on a discarded banana stalk, as if the candies are resurrected multicolored bananas. The short, wiry man in a *paglietta*, straw hat, blows a whistle as he goes by my house, carrying the stalk jammed with *pirulis*, selling each for a penny.

My grandmother Anna is more discriminating, perhaps less forgiving of my mother's not so perfect baby. When she gives me a bath, she stares at my legs, compares one leg to the other and shakes her head. I go through baby shoes like a crippled racehorse.

I'm introduced as a miraculous birth, something like the Jesus resurrection. Sicilian women pick me up and embrace me, squeeze my face into their big breasts. Most women work in cigar factories, but, whether they do or not, it seems to me they all shop at La Sèttima on Saturdays and all smell like tobacco.

La Sèttima in Italian, or La Séptima, in Spanish, translates to Seventh Avenue, and that is the way it will be with most things in Ybor City. Italians have an Italian word for every Spanish word, but when they don't, they make one up. In a culture where few are literate, it's easy to bastardize a language, and they do it with Spanish.

"Maria, the boy looks like you," a *tabaquera,* a woman cigarmaker, says on a Saturday afternoon, but any woman might have said it, and they did without regards for my feelings.

I'm four and I'm made to go shopping with Mama and, although she buys me a dime-toy at five and dime stores, shopping is something no little boy concedes to willingly. Mama continues her conversation on the sidewalk. I stand next to her and hear the woman say, "*Hoy,* Maria, is Felipe working?"

"No, not yet," Mama says.

"They say they're going to be hiring at La Pila."

"*Buenos,*" Mama says. "Do you think you can talk to your foreman about a job for Felipe? We would be indebted."

It's a time of layoffs. It's the Great Depression, and labor strikes occur frequently. Some last months, but no one in my family crosses a picket line. Being a strikebreaker is a lifetime stigma among anarchist Sicilians. It's as bad as the big letter *A* Hester Prynne wore in Nathaniel Hawthorne's *The Scarlet Letter.*

There is an "us against them" feeling among cigar workers directed at factory owners. Italians, Cubans and Spaniards stick together. When it comes to labor issues, there is no distinction. It is as if the three cultures scream in unison, "One for all and all for one." They are *The Three Musketeers.*

Mama earns about seven dollars a week, and Papa is laid off a lot. On Saturdays, when she visits the business district, I hear her say repetitively in Spanish, "Just looking." Clerks are Latinos. Mama dresses me in a miniature suit, wobbly fedora and a spring-loaded necktie. I hate the miniature suit, particularly the fedora. Encased in the outfit, I strut like a Maas Brothers Department-store mannequin, as if Seventh Avenue is first class, something like downtown's Franklin Street where the haughty of Tampa shop.

Mama clings to me, and she isn't bad to look at if one likes women short, five feet. I can't wait to go home, change-out, jump into tattered clothes befitting my style, but I'll have to wait, make rounds on W. T. Grant and Kress before climbing the gradual Nineteenth Street slope home.

We enter Kress's five and dime store, and I say, "Mama, I don't want to look like you. The lady said I look like you. 'Just like you.' That's what she said, Mama."

"She was just being nice. You look like Papa."

A fat Cuban buttock swerves in the aisle and delivers a bolo punch to my fedora as if she is the Cuban prizefighter Kid Gavalan. I reach for the hat, expecting a kid's right-of-way, but the fat lady just misses spiking my hand with high heels.

"I hate this hat. Why do I have to wear it?"

"You want to look like Papa, don't you?"

I can't resist. I smile.

Mama humors me, but I know it's true, for when I go out with Papa my mood lightens, and most people I meet say I look like him. To resemble one's mother is the ultimate insult, for she's synonymous with woman. There is no worse fate for a boy in a patriarchal society.

Papa has recanted his "better dead than deformed" mantra, and I've forgiven him and joined his world. Papa tells me he is the before, and now I am his after, and that's exactly how he puts it, making me feel like the one and only hereafter.

Women are necessary to birth babies. I understand that, but the world I've joined is chauvinistic. Chauvinism is monogrammed in my diaper, dyed in every fiber before the loom wove my name into Franchito. There is never confusion, never an illusion, never an identity crisis, never any thought of changing me to an alternate anything. I'm never circumcised to make me doubt I'm Christian. After all, Italians have no covenant with Moses' God, and unlike Muslims, Italians drink wine, so we're what God intended us to be, his favorite sons—Sons of Italy. Papa says no matter where we live, there is a Sons of Italy Society. Italians are everywhere in America. Being a member of the club means men play their roles to the hilt, and women pantomime theirs. I didn't know it then, but it was male bonding, and it happened without fanfare or pretense—peewee football or Little League games.

No doubt the Florida sun bleached my images, but I remember the four pigeonholes that make up my first home. Like four barrels aimed south from a two-story frame building on the north side of East Columbus Drive between Nineteenth and Twentieth Streets. Across the street stands a Negro Catholic School whose name I never learn—St. Benedict the Moor School.

It is common to see an occasional broken street sign. There aren't many, a rare one here and there, but they let me know there's been a name change on the street where I live. Broken off posts read—gan Ave. The neighborhood has become predominantly Italian my relatives say, hence the name change to Columbus Drive. But my grandmother continues to call the street La Michica. I have no inkling La Michica refers to a state. It isn't merely Nonna pronouncing it La Michica throwing me off, but the fact I am never told America consists of a slew of states, forty-eight of them then. Michigan is one of my many unknowns.

Instead of "apartments," cigarmakers call homes *canons*, meaning cannons, a word almost identical in Italian to *cannone*. The word apartment is unheard of. It connotes upscale, and we are anything but upscale. Rooms are laid out in sequence. Instead of a string of pearls it is a string of rooms: parlor, bedrooms, followed by a kitchen and bathroom. A tiny bathroom occupies the backs of homes, abutting alleys used to drive jalopies into paint-starved garages that shelter a plethora of rats. Because of the bathroom's terminal location, Sicilians call it *backaouso*, Italianized version of "back of the house," said as one word.

I smell garlic, onions and green peppers frying in olive oil when peering into doors, and sweet basil and mint flourish in recycled one-gallon olive oil cans sitting out front on porches. My eyes perceive the insides of these homes as tubes. Each is a dark abyss, an illusion, if you will, like looking into a giant telescope. The front door is the ocular piece and the back door the lens. Light pours in at both ends.

Use of bathrooms from the *sala* requires walking a shotgun or cannon home's length. Visitors wishing to relieve themselves inspect these homes twice—once rushing to the bathroom way in the back—and again on the return trip. Homes are built from a no frill point of view. The architectural design reflects uncomplicated lifestyles, sort of like Byzantine art—two-dimensional—like immigrant existence—to work and home. It is a one-two punch that would have floored Frank Lloyd Wright, no twists, no turns, no angles and no curves. There are absolutely no diversions—in the front and out the back. So, a *canon* is where I roost, am shot out of, and a granite curbstone underscores my address.

Summer afternoon rains flood gutters, and I float paper boats into sewers. On sunny days, curbstones transform themselves into playpens, fencing me in. Mica particles embedded in the granite flame in the sun, glittering like diamonds. Oh, it is a hell of a landscape with sidewalks and curbstones defining my existence. Sidewalks are my boundaries where I play hopscotch, stick ball and hide and seek. When playing hide and seek, I enunciate the "base" and the "it," but I never find the English words hiding from me between parked cars. I scream "hang-go-see, hang-go-see." It will be years before I realize what the words are.

From curbstones I wave to cigarmakers walking to and from factories. I wave at Italians in funeral processions and wave at black hearses heading east to L'Unione Italiana Cemetery. I cover my ears to sirening ambulances crossing Twenty-second Street, picking up the knifed, the dead and not so quick from a string of colored bars.

Swinging on my porch, I feel imprisoned. I am no different than a yellow canary my Aunt Felicia keeps in a domed cage in her parlor.

The bird swings on a bar, and I swing on a swing. He and I are comfortable—him and me—him swinging on his and me on mine. On weekends, my aunt sets the cage on the front porch. She calls it the bird's "rec-time." She says it's a place for him to sun himself, stretch his wings and air out his head. I see it as a chance for him to make a break for it, so I open his cage and say, "Fly, birdie, fly. Get out of here!"

Each time I stick my hand inside the cage, I prompt freedom. He goes stir-crazy. First he rattles his cage then clings afraid. I understand. I see his cage, see his dilemma, but he doesn't see mine. Mine is a bigger world, and my cage is not physical. My aunt says he's a lifer. He's too domesticated to make it on his own, so, in our own way, the bird and I commiserate.

"Franchito, don't dare let him out, hear me. He'll die," she says.

The bird stretches his throat and sings. I watch mockingbirds dive-bomb his cage. A splattered *Tampa Tribune* looks up from the bottom of the cage. The bird dots the *i*'s on the page. He remains serene, unaffected, as if he doesn't give a shit. But he does. He just did. He dotted the printer's ink, so perhaps he understands it is not always a matter of choice.

On damp evenings, after hard summer rains, termites fly erratically. They swarm the street lamps and the inside of homes. They drop their wings in Mama's kitchen. All homes have termites in the *barrio*. A light bulb dangles from an electrical cord above a kitchen table. Termites, attracted to the light, pound their heads on the bulb and fall. Picking themselves up, they fly back for more. Papa fills a basin at a sink hung from a tongue and groove wall, and Mama takes charge next to the drain board.

"Mama, what are they?"

"Termites, termites." She pushes me away. "Stand here. Some people think they're flying ants, Franchito, but, no, they're termites—believe me."

Papa says, "*Sì, sì, comehayne, comehayne.*"—the Spanish word for termites.

She waits for him with hands flailing in the air as if she could bust each one.

"*Filippo, premura, premura,* hurry, hurry," she says.

"Franchito, watch. See how they go for the light. Filippo, the sons of bitches are going to get inside the furniture."

Papa is rushing and splashing water on the linoleum. He places the basin in the center of the table. The incandescent glow of the bulb bathes itself in the water below. Termites dive-bomb and some plunge. I see them dip their wings at Mama and, like Kamikazes, they circle the bulb to make their approach. She fires back a sardonic smile, moves the basin a little to the right and then left and watches them play follow the leader into what I imagine is a vast Pacific Ocean. The battle over, Mama peers into the basin and takes no prisoners.

"Franchito, need to check your bed tonight. Termites bite," she says. "If they chew wood, imagine what they'll do to you."

Something bites, all right, bites all night, bites like bedbugs, and sometimes they are bedbugs or *cìmici* as we call them in Sicilian. Mama keeps turning my mattress each week, spraying it with everything she hears is lethal—even kerosene.

As I grow older, I realize there're other Franks in my family. I'm the fifth grandson christened Francesco after my paternal grandfather. It's a name that is miniaturized to Franco, Ciccino, Ciccio and translates to Frank. It is made diminutive by Americans with Frankie. Italians flip it back to Italian with Franche and, again, reduce me to the diminutive Franchito. It makes full circle. There is no *k* in the Italian alphabet, so *ch* is pronounced *k*. The number of Franks creates confusion when I listen to, "Frank? Which Frank? Frank, who? Whose Frank? Not you. Yes, you."

So it's imperative appositives are tagged to the Franks. Initially, relatives use our fathers' first names for appositives, and it goes like this: Franche di Vincenzo, Franche di Stefano, Franche di Pedo, Franche di Nino and Franche di Filippo, me. Later our occupation singles us out—Franche, the fireman; Franche, the bartender; Franche, the doctor; and so on. If a Frank changes his job it throws relatives off. It happens when Frank the bartender becomes Frank the shoemaker.

Names are not chosen because parents like them or because they're in vogue. We are not like blacks that run around with names like Washington and Roosevelt or like Cubans who go as far as to name children after Jesus. It's all a matter of historical facts, Sicilian facts, for the naming schema is derived from an ancient Sicilian custom. It simulates what breeders of thoroughbred racehorses do—pass on names like Man o' War and War Admiral to their offspring, clarifying and emphasizing the genetic pool with names of champions.

Firstborn males are named after paternal grandfathers, and second sons after maternal grandfathers. That's how first names are chosen. The same patriarchal process chains girls to their grandmothers, and there, too, paternal grandmothers pull rank. The only unknown prior to birth is the gender of the child.

8

"Blew out his brains," Papa says.

"Sure it wasn't in the car?"

"No, no, Mary, in the house." He breaks up day-old Italian bread into hunks.

"So that's the one that's for sale?"

He nods. "Buried him Thursday. Felicia and Peppino went to the funeral. Nice man she says."

"I heard about it at my factory, too—bunch-maker."

"A good one. Worked a good paying *vitola*."

Mama brings her cup of Cuban coffee to the table. "Goes to show you."

"Shows you what?"

"A good *vitola* is not everything."

"It's like new, Felicia says. She saw it a few times." Papa dumps the bread into the bowl of Cuban coffee and scalded milk. When he finishes he stands and says, "Franchito, want to go?"

I nod.

"Maybe, you shouldn't take Franchito. People are still paying their respects."

"It'll be all right. It's too early in the day for that."

There are no telephones—no advance notices. Most cigarmakers don't have telephones, and Papa knows the car is sure to go, as soon as the grieving stops—maybe before. Who knows? Maybe it's already gone, for a good deal doesn't wait for a widow's eyes to dry where I live.

Papa takes my hand, and we walk a far distance. We go past El Reloj, past Fifteenth Street, past V.M. Ybor School and Cuscaden Park.

"How far are we going?"

"Not much more, a few more blocks—other side of the park."

We walk up creaky wooden steps onto a sun-bathed porch. A wreath droops from a nail in the wood siding between the duplex's doors. Ceramic pots sit on both sides of the steps on top of slabbed brick pedestals. Bright green asparagus ferns spill over their sides. Papa hesitates. He eyes the wreath and knocks, rattling the screen door. He stares at the flowers reflecting the morning sun, knocks again a bit louder, and I look up. "Are we in the right place?"

"Should be," he says. "The flowers are closer to this door."

A woman dressed in black with dark circles hugging deeply set eyes opens the front door. She plasters down her dark hair. The woman has no makeup on, and her eyes squint as if she's shunning the glare. She doesn't seem older than Papa and smiles a lukewarm smile as if smiling is sinful. It's a smile teetering between life and death.

She says, "*Buon giorne,*" and lets us in. A solemn conversation, initially strained, ensues. It's a conversation a five-year-old perceives from low down, below eye level, near linoleum where I'm often left to play while adults talk. They stand in the parlor, talking and gesticulating. She points to the back of the house, then to a parlor table where I see white carnations in a vase in front of a man's photograph. An unlit candle stands next to the black and white portrait. The man in the photograph doesn't seem older than Papa, and it's the same man who stares down from another black and white photograph on the wall. There he's thinner and younger, but it's the same man dressed in a black tuxedo. The widow is also in the photograph dressed in a white gown with a train arranged in a swirl hiding her feet. She holds a bouquet of white lilies. Both smile. The picture is similar to a picture that hangs over the sofa in my living room.

A child's close-up view of feet is unique. It is an asset in judging grownups in a totalitarian world of adults. I'm able to judge from low down, judge all their feet. I've come to believe feet speak to character. After all, feet are the foundations of those who trounce my world. Some feet of Sicilian women are built to bear weight, klutzy and stout, hinged to swine-like legs stuffed in shear stockings like grocery store hams hang on hooks, and some feet wiggle, crimped with deformed toes. Others peek out from cutouts. Some feet are peripherally rimmed by leather, so-called pumps, but all threaten those of us who spend time on floors. All can seek, crush and destroy toys. Other feet dent railroad tracks and crush dump trucks, but some are delicate, cautious and aware of my world. Hers are graceful—fitting into pink slippers, perhaps like Cinderella's.

She speaks to Papa in a soft voice and reaches for a paper bag on the parlor table. She stoops over and holds it out. "Would you like some?"

I know it's candy from the rattling sound. The white bag is a tip-off in a world of brown paper bags. I thank her and grab one wrapped in silver paper. I know it's chocolate. I've had them before, expensive from Kress's five and dime. My parents call them Kress's.

"Oh, go ahead take more Kisses. It's just me, now."

I feel sorry for her and hope Papa won't get a good deal.

I say, "*Grazie.*" I take two more and say thank you again.

The man with the wavy hair smiles from behind the carnations, as if he is eye-ing my chocolates, but he doesn't seem to mind. I know he's dead. Papa says he'd like to see the car if it's all right with her. So, after the usual *mi dispiace,* or the I'm sorry formalities of shaking of hands, nodding and shaking of heads and shrugging of shoulders, she leads us into a bedroom. It's the next room, for that's how shotgun homes are laid out. Bedrooms follow living rooms and stop before kitchens. She pauses, explaining to Papa how she found the man dead on the floor and shows Papa where a bullet lodged in the wall. I'd like to put my finger in the hole, but it's high up. Papa stares at it like he stared at the wreath, shaking his head.

"I didn't know he was hurting so badly," she says in Sicilian.

Papa puts his arm around her shoulder and whispers, "*Mi dispiace.*"

She wipes her eyes with a handkerchief. "I know."

"Did he leave a note?" Papa drops his eyes.

"Couldn't write, so I didn't get a goodbye."

"Too bad. You had no idea?"

"No, but he left a red rose on the bed." She whimpers.

"*Mi dispiace,*" Papa says again.

Mi dispiace is a term which is ingrained in me early, so when things are sad, and I don't know what to say, I say it. It makes me proud as if I'm of some help, makes me feel like a man.

"Put it to his head. Couldn't have a viewing."

"Too bad, very sad."

"I should have known."

"Don't be so hard on yourself," Papa says.

"You know, Filippo, his father killed himself, too. About the same age, blew his head off with a shotgun."

"I know," Papa says. "I know."

Papa keeps shaking his head and looking at the floor, and, out the corner of his eye, he eyes me. Nothing is a secret in the *barrio,* particularly suicides. We go through the kitchen and emerge in a back porch. Cats run off under the house when she rattles the screen door.

We walk over to a detached wooden garage. Papa rolls open the garage door hanging from a rusted steel track. A 1936 Chevrolet two-door sedan stands parked inside on paired strips of cement lifting four black tires off the sand. It stands in the dark as one might imagine a dealer's showroom at night. The sun spotlights the rear of the car and license plate. The car is black, mint and has no dents. Papa's eyes light up as he opens the driver door and peers inside. He walks around the front and looks under the hood. Hoods are bi-valve like tin oysters, so, from each side, he peeks at the engine as if he knows what he's doing. He walks around kicking tires, soothing fenders with the palm of his hand and looks at the spare inside a hump the lady calls a trunk.

Papa sits behind the steering wheel, looking into a rearview mirror. He turns it one way and another. He turns a key, and pressing on the clutch with his left foot, he moves the gear stick rising from the floor. Flipping it into neutral, his right foot slams a knobby starter, and a grinding sound erupts. He swings his right foot onto the accelerator as if his leg is disjointed. The engine backfires and throttles. I can see he loves the sound, feels power in his foot, but he doesn't know how much the widow will take.

Papa says, "Nice. Low mileage."

"Fili, if you buy it, I'll be happy. I'll never learn to drive," she says.

"You won't try?"

"No, no, not a woman alone. No chance. You know that."

She's an attractive widow, but widows seem not to remarry no matter how attractive they are. There is always younger, fresher meat for men to chase. Sicilian men marry virgins. Most will have it no other way. There's something about not being a virgin that turns Italian men off. Old men are more likely to contemplate widows. When wives die in my culture, men go back to the starting gate and give it another try. Papa justifies it by saying women age faster than men, and besides, taking on a widow is different than buying a secondhand car. Used cars bear no stigma. Cars, unlike wives, are never a matter of honor.

"I brought cash. I can pay now, if I can afford it."

"It's hard doing business at a time like this, but I'm sure you'll be fair," she says.

The purchase is somber with Papa first offering condolences then mixing in his best price. There's no haggling as they throw out numbers foreign to me. Papa smiles, as is his nature when he turns on his charm, does it automatically when he's nervous. He seems more like a kid than a papa. She smiles coyly when he pulls out a roll of bills wadded with a rubber band. He counts them into her pale hand. She doesn't do a recount like I know Mama would do. She trusts Papa and tells him to keep the keys and go inside and have coffee.

The lady places official looking papers on the kitchen table while water boils in a small pot. Neither can read, so they pass papers back and forth. She explains where she is to sign. A line is marked with an X.

"There will be no mistake. Once I sign it's yours," she says.

She writes her name cursively, slowly and deliberately, pressing hard, one letter at a time as those who can write in my neighborhood typically do. She purses her lips as if her lips are wrapped around the pen. She gets up from the table and dumps heaping tablespoons of Caracolillo Cuban Coffee into the boil, causing a momentary stall in the roar. Resurgence in the boil tumbles the grounds and they rise and climb over, staining the sides darkly. She shuts off the gas and strains coffee into a *culatore* hanging from a nail above the sink's drain board. *Culatores* are flannel strainers like wind catchers in airports except they point down, vertically down. The strainer bulges, steams and turns darker brown, dripping dark coffee into the coffeepot. After placing demitasses on the table, she pours three cups, and I look at Papa and smile.

I normally drink coffee with milk, but, today, I drink it like a man, black and strong and undiluted. I can't remember when I started drinking coffee, but I know it was after I was weaned. It's not a big deal for me since most children in my neighborhood drink it. It is a time before decaf and preoccupation with frivolous details.

But today I stir lots of sugar in my coffee, and that means slurping and mixing it with air to avoid burning my tongue. Oh, it's good coffee, the best there is, so I savor each slurp and lick my lips. Papa thanks her, and I do, too, with a mimicking *grazie*.

Papa has not bartered, for there seems to be more to the deal than just price. She's a nice lady, so I'm sure the car isn't overpriced. Papa seems a little unsure as though he thinks he paid too much. I sense his discomfort as he drives his treasure home, and a treasure it is.

"She was a nice lady, Papa. I'm glad you bought it."

"Yes, nice," he says.

"Do you know her from the factory?"

"I know lots of people from the factory."

"I loved the candy and real black coffee." I grin looking out the passenger window, watching the neighborhood flash by. It's one of the few times I've been inside a car.

He looks at me and says nothing.

"I like coffee without milk, Papa. Mama puts in so much. I hate milk."

"It's just the way Lilly is."

I'd heard him call the woman Lilly. She never introduced herself, but there was lots of stuff I couldn't hear from my low-down position near the linoleum. I'm glad Mama isn't with us. It's my first man-to-man ride with my father. I feel like a man. Without Mama, I command the passenger seat, but the rest of my years growing up I'm relegated to the back seat, giving me a sense of how Negroes feel in trolleys, and I don't like it.

I never tell Mama how much I liked the woman, never mention her name or the black coffee without milk. *Omertà*, the Sicilian code of silence, is a sign of a man.

I've never seen Papa drive a car before, and I am sure he's learning as we go. I know he's unlicensed, and he drives awfully slowly, always will.

"Papa, why did the man kill himself?"

"Don't know, Franchito."

I play with a knob on the dashboard and wake up windshield wipers. I open the glove box to see if the dead man left anything inside like maybe his gun or extra bullets. I look at Papa, but he's looking straight ahead.

Papa sticks his hand out the window each time he turns—sometimes points up and other times straight out. When he comes to a stop sign his arm and hand disappear. Doing the machinations he smiles, as if the wind in his face is lifting his smile.

The car has no radio, and Papa never turns on the heater. He doesn't realize a heater doesn't cost extra to run. He never buys a car with a radio or air-conditioning in his lifetime. He is steeped in frugality—the fear of ending up broke. It's a glorious winter day, and the sun is warm, reflecting off the back seat of the black car. I see the car's image whizzing by storefront windows, so I wave as, at thirty-eight, Papa drives home his first car.

9

Partitioning doors between my paternal grandparents' home and my side of the cold-water flat never close. Life is shared as I ride from one side to the other on a broomstick horse.

"No privacy in this house," is what Papa hears Mama say.

My side of the shotgun home is flush with furniture compared to my grandparents' Spartan side. Our parlor accommodates a brown sofa and a matching chair the color of *maduro* tobacco, and as the years go by, I realized the furniture will reside with me all the days of my life. It outlives all my grandparents, and in time, I learn it has human qualities: legs, arms, feet, backs and even bald spots like my father's side of the family. A worn wool carpet in the corridor resembles a heavily traveled Sicilian donkey path.

Mama's venerated dining room table stands in the center of a tiny room. Next to it is a china cabinet. Single light bulbs hang in each room, occasionally swinging like I hear lynched Negroes swing. I worry because I overhear *Latinos* might be next in line with the Ku Klux Klan. We're different than rednecks, not as different as Negroes, but different enough. All we have in common with them is our skin.

Short Sicilians have no problems negotiating low hanging light bulbs or short doorways with overhead transoms that circulate flies. Tan roller shades shield us from neighbors living barely five feet away. Parlors boast wedding photographs of incumbents, hanging from moldings encircling *salas* high above low wainscots. Wallpapered rooms display brown rings in their ceilings—products of water leaks. China cabinets are filled with delicate figurines, which I'm instructed never to touch, or the crochet doilies lying flat on parlor tables and under radios.

But the most interesting homes are those of old widows that I visit. *Salas* are loaded with photographs of dead relatives. Chivalrous women pose standing in long dresses next to sitting mustachioed men. The furniture I sit on is Victorian, too. A strange odor hovers inside the homes, making me think of musty mausoleums. Bizarre faces of ancients hang out in photo groups as if they're the original Darwinian species that gave birth to my grandparents' generation. Oh, it is a hell of a voyage with toothless docents telling me stories of Sicily and of bandits hiding in snowcapped mountains. The old women offer me sugarcoated almonds as they give me personalized photo tours. But I'm too young to appreciate the sub-text, so I stand bored, staring at stern faces that have passed on. Though dead, they gather on parlor tables as if the tables are miniature pantheons.

My grandparents Anna and Ciccio live a monastic existence on their side of the flat, a lifestyle reflecting Sicilian simplicity. Their kitchen is heated with a charcoal heater, and Nonna cooks on a kerosene stove. The coal heater gave off headaches, and Papa keeps objecting to its use, saying somebody might die if windows aren't cracked.

My cousin and I take naps in an iron bed next to where Nonno Ciccio stores explosives. Some are stored under the bed. None of those old houses have closets, and Papa keeps explosives in our side of the flat, too. They arrive by Railway Express in wooden boxes.

Papa walks out on the front porch one evening. Nonno is sitting on the swing, and I'm playing on the floor.

"*Buona sera,*" my father says.

Nonno agrees, and my father and grandfather talk in Sicilian as all of my family does.

"How'd things go at the factory today?" Nonno Ciccio says.

"We need to talk," my father says.

Nonno is smoking a cigar. My father hands him a couple more he brought home from the factory.

"*Grazie,* Filippo, *grazie.*"

Porches are an integral part of the South. In summer, men sit on swings after dinner and listen to mockingbirds sing their last song. After dishes are washed in hot pasta-water and dried with wet dishtowels, the women join them on the porch. Porches are shared, a gathering place, in multiple-dwelling homes con-structed in the late nineteenth and early twentieth century. Homemade swings hang by chains from steel hooks screwed into tongue and groove ceilings.

The short men sit suspended in midair with feet off the ground. I hear the crunching sound of chain links, alerting me someone is readjusting a buttock, seeking relief from hard slats. When my cousin and I are alone, we pretend the swing is a two-men clipper ship floating in a vast ocean. We ride it and imagine ourselves Gasparilla pirates, and now and then our ship capsizes. But this evening the sea is peaceful and calm. Nonno puffs on a cigar as if he doesn't have a care in the world, and the two men drift on an outgoing tide.

"What do you want to talk about, Filippo?"

"*Gioco di fuoco,* Papa."

"What about the fireworks?"

I know about fireworks. I love them. My mother makes my father swear he won't allow me to make or shoot them when I grow up. I'm only five. My grandfather and father shoot them on feast days at the Italian church grounds on Seventh Avenue. Papa burned his eyes last year and visited an eye doctor for months. The family prayed to Santa Lucia a lot during the time his eyes were bandaged, and he couldn't work. That is how I learn Santa Lucia is the patron saint of eyes.

Occasionally, Papa and I run into one of his cousins in Ybor City stores. The man is missing fingers on his right hand. Papa tells me he blew them off making fireworks. I guess there are no patron saints for fingers and hands. Papa says making fireworks is more dangerous than setting them off. The family has a tradition of playing with fireworks in Sicily, and that's exactly how Sicilians refer to fireworks, *gioco di fuoco*, game of fire. Haughty mainlander Italians call them *pirotecnico*, pyrotechnics—a hell of a complicated word for my vocabulary.

"But now that I have a child, maybe it's too dangerous to keep them inside," Papa says and bunches up his lips. "You know how children are."

Nonno drags on his stogie, pauses, and lets smoke out of his nose—short bursts like bulls do in movie cartoons. "Too dangerous? We've been keeping them in houses all our lives. In Sicily my father kept some near the stove. It's never a problem as long as you don't flick a match on them. They're safe, won't explode on their own. It'd take an act of God."

"It makes Maria nervous, sitting on the sofa with explosives behind her. Maybe we could move the crates to the garage. Get rid of those under your bed, too."

"Get off it, Fili. What kind of woman did you marry? What does she know about fireworks? You're letting her put a dress on you. Tell her she married into our family, not the other way around."

Papa doesn't respond.

A month later, my grandmother leads me out of the house. "*O Mio* Dio. Hurry up, Franchito. The house is on fire. Let's go outside quick." She screams for my grandfather, "Ciccio, Ciccio."

Neighbors run out into the street, and screams crisscross, and nuns run out of the colored Catholic school across the street. Nuns yell back to Negro children to stay inside, and I watch the children stick their heads out of windows. Some make faces as the school bell rings and rings louder each time.

Hermina, a fat woman, administers ammonia salts to my grandmother whose body is now limp and slumped. Two nuns run up and help her get across the street. I sit next to my grandmother at curbside near the school. Black children yell, "Fire! Fire!"

Others point, make funny faces and cheer. A fire engine arrives and blocks the trolley tracks. The motorman and passengers get down. Suddenly there are more people watching the fire engulfing my home. Firefighters unroll flat hoses from the fire engine and run back and forth, and others hang on to huge axes and point upstairs. A red sedan with the words Fire Chief on its side panels arrives. A portly middle-aged man steps out and struts as if he's a maestro entering the stage. Squad cars and policemen join the commotion, and the colored children, well, they're still yelling, delighted, cheering the flames. Another white oppressor home is being torched like the Klu Klux Klan burns theirs.

Nuns are charitable, bring glasses of water to my grandmother, and a young nun asks me, "Would you like to come with me inside the school?" I don't understand English, so I shake my head.

My grandmother yells, "Ciccio, Ciccio."

He's running out of the house. It's the first time I see the old man run, and he's running like hell, never looking back.

"Can anyone speak English?" the fire chief says.

His red helmet shines in the noonday sun against the drab black of firemen, nuns and Negro children. After checking in with a firefighter who's shouting orders, the chief walks up to the young black-hooded nun. He points to the house, and she points to my grandmother whose head is wrapped in a black shawl.

It is my first exposure with ammonia salts, and pungent fumes swirl around my grandmother's head. She crosses herself again and again, so it's as though I smell an invisible halo trying to engulf her. In time ammonia defines itself as the harbinger of womanly distress. I smell the salts whenever there's death, family feuds, a gashed hand in the kitchen or an auto accident. Any crisis will do. Ammonia salts hover over all debacles, and the tiny bottle, gripped tightly, is waved under noses. It penetrates with an invisible sting, making eyes tear, and I watch groggy heads roll, retract, rotate and shake loose at the neck. Sicilian women are good at fainting all right, relishing undeserved attention, something like unmerited grace received in the sacrament. Times aren't too remote from the Victorian era when fainting was feminine and fashionable, so I witness resurrections often.

"What the hell do these people keep in their homes, Sister?" The fire chief adjusts his helmet, tightens the strap under his chin.

"I have no idea." The young nun shrugs her shoulders.

"Damn, there's got to be explosives inside. Did you hear that blast, Sister? That ain't no damn timber exploding in there."

"Watch your language, Chief. There're children around."

And there are. Many are leaning halfway out windows by now, and some dart out, cutting out of school through the back door.

The chief hangs his head. "Sister, can you speak their language?"

"I speak some Spanish, but they're Italians."

"Give it a try, Sister, please, can't be that different."

"*Señora, que tiene entra su casa?*" The nun asks in Spanish what's in the house. With hands defaulting to sign language, she tries to create an explosion, sort of like Mama mixes spaghetti with sauce in a pasta bowl.

"*No capisco, no capisco,*" my grandmother says. She's never worked in a cigar factory, so she doesn't understand.

The nun shakes her head.

The fire chief points to the house and screams, "Joe, grab the old man, he's trying to go back in."

"O Dio *mio*, O Dio," Nonna waves as if to say, Ciccio, forget it. "Ciccio, *sta bene*. Don't go in."

A blast blows out a front window, and firemen retreat. They drop a hose on the street and it snakes wildly, resembling a giant serpent like the one I see in pasta boxes labeled Saint Giorgio, ones with a man on a horse slaying a dragon with a spear. The hose is hissing and splattering spectators like a coiled giant serpent, knocking some down. The crowd screams louder, disperses, loses cohesiveness, but never dissolves. Several firefighters regain control like they did with my grandfather and hug the hose. It's unprecedented excitement with the liberated hose making old folks jump like I jump rope. I giggle.

I hear a neighbor say my grandfather wanted to retrieve a cigar box. I know he puts lots of things in cigar boxes, but all immigrants in the Cigar City do. Cigar boxes are full of dreams, most unrealized, tucked in boxes year after year. Cigar boxes are safety deposit boxes, full of everything from immigration papers, wills and a little cash. When I crawled under Nonno's bed, I'd seen his cigar box squeezed between the mattress and spring next to a double barrel shotgun like a stagecoach's strongbox.

"Get the hell back. These damn I-talians probably have ammunition stored inside, Mafia, you know." The chief shakes his head. "They're all connected, a string of cousins."

A policeman walks up and interjects. "Could be arson, Chief. Don't put bombs past them bastards. There's one little wop called Pastashutta…"

I focus on his gun and gun holster. It's a very big gun, a beauty.

"Who?" The chief says.

"Yeah, don't know for sure, but the name means dried pasta, may be a nick-name. Don't know for sure, but that's what Cubans tell me he's called. If you see that fucker in the crowd, watch out. No doubt, he started it. All wops know he's the one to talk to if they need a building torched. He's always around when times get tough. That *dago* leaves no evidence, one slick bastard."

"Just keep the crowd back. We'll worry about who started it later."

"We never can pin it on that son of a bitch, Chief. Sure could use your help." The policeman walks away mumbling what sounds like Patashutta and son of a bitch.

"I don't think they're like that," the nun says to the chief. "They're poor peo-ple, honest from what I've seen. Young ones work in cigar factories, see them file in and out like clock work at noon. The old people stay home and take care of grandchildren, seems a family all right."

Another explosion and red and blue smoke pours out of my grandfather's bed-room. The crowd is in awe and swings back as if a giant sigh overwhelms them, pushes them back into the schoolyard. The heat intensifies, and we're forced to move back, too. The nuns bring out chairs, so we abandon the street curb and sit in the schoolyard. The vantage point is still good. It is as ringside as it can be con-sidering the size of the blaze. The wind blows the acrid smoke towards us, and I cough.

The chief walks up to the head firefighter. "Joe, tell the boys not to take chances. Can be disastrous. Get some bulletproof vests from the cops."

Joe waves to firefighters to get back.

"Exploding ammo can be a hell of a trap. Better get the crowd farther back. Bombs—just never know, Joe."

The chief turns to the pale-faced nun. "Are you sure the old lady can't speak Spanish, Sister? Sure would like to know what's in there."

The nun runs back to Nonna.

"*No capisco, no capisco,* help us Dio." My grandmother makes the sign of the cross.

"Sorry, doesn't seem to understand a word. The neighbors don't seem to know much either, Chief."

"Damn it, nobody knows a f—ing thing. Shit, didn't mean it, Sister."

"In your work, you should stay on His good side." She turns away.

"Ciccio, Ciccio." My grandmother waves my grandfather to stay back. He's covering his face from the heat, trying to go back into the house.

"Stop that old bastard," Joe yells.

Two firefighters restrain my grandfather again.

"Have the cops handcuff the bastard," Joe screams.

They place him in the back seat of a squad car, and I watch him sit dolefully looking at us. He waves in slow motion with lips barely moving, body slumping, and there are tears in his eyes as he looks at the fire and then fixes his gaze on the floorboard.

Mama arrives and swoops me up off the sidewalk, hugs and kisses me, ravishes my face, and I wipe saliva off with my sleeve. I see better perched on her arm like a hawk. I see my cousin sitting even higher, straddling his papa's neck as if he's riding a horse. Uncle Vincenzo was having lunch when the fire broke out. He carried my cousin Junio down from upstairs. That is what my cousin Vince is called as a child. Junio is the Italianized version of junior. The terminal *r* is dropped by those who neither read nor write. It is a name that sticks to him well into adulthood.

We look at each other serious like, for we know it is, and he waves at me, so I smile and wave back. He whips his father on the head as if, indeed, my uncle is a horse. The crowd keeps pushing the two of us apart, but we know it's temporary.

The chief walks up to Mama after a neighbor points her out of the crowd.

"Mrs., Mrs., you live in that house?"

Mama nods.

"What the hell's in there?"

"In the house?"

"Yes, inside. Anything we should know about?"

"Nothing, I know nothing," Mama says.

"Nothing? You hear that? See those green flames. Is your family in the Mafia or something, Ma'am? Is there live ammo in there? Bombs, anything dangerous?"

"Ammo? No understand."

"I got men to be concerned with, Ma'am, need to know. If you know you have an obligation to tell me."

Mama shakes her head. "I no understand."

But she does, understands, understands every word and knows all the answers. She recognizes explosions from sound patterns and colors, heard them before, witnessed them in the night skies at the church, but she's Italian. She isn't about to rattle off a list of: devil wheels, crazy wheels, Roman candles, multi-break aerial shells with electrifying colors and thundering salutes.

Flames flick in and out of windows. Shattering glass, the flames retreat back inside the house as if they forgot to ignite something. In and out flames leap, setting off explosions. Mama knows my grandfather is the cause of the fire just as sure as if he lit the torch.

"Ma'am, do you know a man called Pastaschutta?" the fire chief says.

She shakes her head and purses her lips as if they are sealed for eternity.

"Would you rather talk to the police? They're here you know." The fire chief points his finger at her.

Mama glares and remains mute. A cloud covers her eyes, and she puts me down on the sidewalk. I sense what's coming, so I give her berth. She wraps her skirt around her thighs. She knows Anglo questions are harbingers of the state's opening remarks directed to an all Anglo jury, prosecutorial pleadings to an Anglo judge in the state's case of arson against anarchist Italians. This time it will not be Sacco and Vanzetti they'll lynch but her husband, so she crumples into the gutter.

"Ah, shit," the fire chief says. "Fucking emotional I-talians." He looks for the nun, but she's not nearby, so he sighs. "One fucking mess." He takes off his helmet and wipes his brow.

He waves Hermina over. "Are you a relative of this woman?"

"*No hablo* Americano." Hermina blurts out the Fifth Amendment, "No speaka English." She resumes the administration of ammonia salts, kneeling next to Mama.

Smelling salts respond to *aqui, aqui.* That's what Spanish-speaking bystanders say as they look at the two women, directing Hermina to this and that resurrection. Hermina runs back and forth between my mother and grandmother. My Aunt Giovanina arrives and joins the duet. She's a big woman, so I don't stand near. Flames reach the second story, and smoke pours out from her front window.

Giovanina cries out, "Help me, Dio."

Hermina gives her the treatment after two men ease my aunt to the ground.

Mama wakes up when the fire chief fades into the crowd. Giant hoses pour more water than I've ever seen in my short life, and water rolls out from inside my home, out the front door, flowing over the porch. Like a waterfall, water tumbles down three wooden steps. Soon, the blaze simmers and the crackling of lumber abates, and the murmur of the crowd softens, dissipates, but the odor of burnt wood permeates the neighborhood and indelibly stains my brain.

Papa comes running home from the factory where he's been misinformed as to which block harbored the fire. He blanches and prepares for Mama's wrath, but she hugs him and sobs.

The next day, I walk through the house with Papa. It's awfully dark. The walls and ceilings are charred resembling barbecued alligator skin. Glass and debris litter my home. Mama's precious possessions are ruined by fire, smoke and water—all uninsured.

The intense heat of summer with paint buckets lying around on the back porch, and with no insurance to constitute motive, the fire chief concludes there's a chance of something called spontaneous combustion. It's explained as something mysterious like the Immaculate Conception, something unbelievable that actually happens. My family clings to the nebulous theory and calls it an act of God. We believe in the Immaculate Conception so why not spontaneous combustion?

There're a few more interrogations requested by the fire chief, and Papa and Uncle Vincenzo meet with him. The three walk through the rubble, and I wait for my father at Hermina's, next door. Neither man is helpful in clarifying the origin, nor are neighbors who are questioned extensively. All of them say, "No speakea the English."

It's one hell of a fire, a hell of a day and another example of *omertà*. It is deemed an act of God and Italians always give deference to God.

I see the fire chief's car parked in front of the Catholic school a few times after the fire, see the young nun leaning into the car window around lunchtime, but I never see her get in.

Subsequent to the fire, explosives are stored in a shed in rural Palmetto, farming and dairy country. I enjoy visiting the shed built by Papa out of scrap wood and discarded tin. It stands tranquil underneath a Florida live oak. It's a beautiful tree standing solitary in a sloping pasture reminding me of a place Fernando the bull might live. He is a bull I will learn about in second grade. The Spanish bull is said to be addicted to the fragrance of flowers, so goes the story, and won't hurt a soul. He sports a smile on his bullish face and loves beautiful cows. Papa keeps the shed locked with a padlock, and we continue to visit for years, long after Nonno dies. It's my outing with Papa; one Mama never joins. It is my trip to what I think is country, and it was then.

Papa says, "Well, if the shed blows it can only hurt cows."

But that means Fernando and he's such a loving and gentle bull who sustains himself on dandelions. I don't want harm to come to Fernando, and I know if cows are around, he's sure to be there. I never see him, never do. I step in lots of cow-cakes the ensuing years and relish each one, knowing some belong to him.

Mama never mentions fireworks again to my grandfather after the fire, but she never lets Papa forget wedding gifts and furniture sacrificed as burnt offerings to Ciccio. She never lets him forget the comment Ciccio made about Mama dressing up Papa in a dress. She is sensitive that way, a less forgiving person than Papa.

Papa simply accepts it for what it is—a clash of the times between his generation and his father's. Papa should have never tattle-taled; after all, Mama is just a woman. What does she know about fireworks?

10

After the fire my grandfather swings slower and slower on the swing. I see his smokeless cigar dangle between fingers. He delegates more and more feast day fireworks to my father, and it isn't long before he takes to bed.

L'Unione Italiana Cemetery or the Campo Santo means holy or sacred field, and to Sicilians it's as sacred as the Holy Grail. It's located on the other side of Twenty-Second Street, in colored town. The name cemetery frightens me because of its onerous sound. Campo Santo is always said so somberly it hangs heavy on my mind, as if the name alone can weigh corpses down—pin them underground.

After Nonno's burial my aunts and uncles discuss options. I peek at headstone brochures and listen to them argue for about a year. Is it to be marble or granite, tall or short? And the facts to be carved on it are as important as if it were the Rosetta stone. The name on the slab reads in Italian—Francesco—*nato* 1863—*morto* 1939.

Unbeknownst to me, the stone will orient me, decipher mysteries, and at times, entertain me, as I look at my distorted reflection on its shiny surface. I realize the finality of death, *morte*, as Sicilians call it, is written in stone.

"We're all made of shit," my godfather says after hearing a relative is sick with cancer.

Another day I hear my father say that one of the old men he knows from the Italian Club is urinating blood.

"Poor man," Papa says. "The bad has come to him."

I begin to understand death is a common denominator. One day we'll all end up at the Italian Club Cemetery. It's a question of when—never where. We'll all be buried in colored town.

Oh, I was aware of death's existence peripherally before, but I hadn't experienced it first hand, with feelings, that is, with tears and loneliness. Two days before the funeral, the dining room table, China cabinet and buffet are moved into the bedroom in anticipation of the coffin. It is there on the day after the funeral that I position myself supine, on the floor, rigid and still in the exact spot Ciccio took a load off his feet. As if casketed, I await my invitation to his world. I imagine myself in a box, inhaling the fragrance of the previous day's gladioli.

"Oh, Dio, what are you doing, Franchito?"

"Nothing, Mama, just resting."

"With your hands across your chest and your eyes closed?"

"Why not? They're resting, too."

"Get up, Franchito. That's no place for you to rest."

"Are they bringing Nonno back?" I ask.

"Grandfather is never coming back."

Days earlier I had witnessed Ciccio's death, even though my aunts and uncles had said I was too young to witness dying. They said I'd have nightmares if I stayed in his bedroom. They told my parents a new bogeyman would enter my world. I was too young for death to do me any good. My father protested, insisted and said that was my grandfather they were talking about, my namesake who carried me in his arms, took me for walks and tossed me around for good times' sake when he was well and strong. Nonno had climbed roofs and repaired them into his seventies like he once climbed olive trees in Sicily, and now he couldn't climb out of bed.

Playing on the floor, next to a space heater, I feel the heat try to warm up the scantily furnished bedroom. From low down, I peer into the eerie glow of burning coal as it waxes and wanes like the hot furnace of hell.

It is a day all my aunts and uncles on Papa's side of the family play hooky from cigar factories. They arrive early that cold November morning and file into my grandfather's room. Some smile, some nod and, those who don't, hang their heads as if they don't see me playing with empty pasta boxes and sewing thread spools on the floor. Only a few brush me aside.

"What you doing in here, Franchito?" Aunt Felicia says.

"Nothing, playing."

"Better if you go play in the other room."

"But everybody is in here."

I hear about the death rattle, but the only rattle I know is the one babies shake and stick in their mouths.

Continuously and mechanically the death rattle had attached itself to my grandfather overnight. Loud, heaving respirations fill the room that morning. Nonno's eyes no longer look at me. Clouded over, they stare at the ceiling, reflecting the *Sacred Heart of Jesus* hanging above the head of the bed. Death, the alien, sits on my grandfather's bed, demanding his prize. Like the Black Hand of Palermo I hear Death's raspy voice say to the old man, "*Signore*, please, today, you come with me."

The women finger their wedding bands, turning them on dimpled fingers, seemingly knowing they can't get them off. Some relight candles to the Virgin on the dresser, and the men grasp the foot of the bed, pushing it back and forth as if trying to push death away. Sicilian hands are agitated, and Sicilian faces peer into the bed as if it's taxiing for takeoff. All know the flight into eternity is about to commence.

"Filippo, how long has he been like this?" says the youngest of my father's brothers.

"Happened during the night, Nino," Papa says.

"Maybe we should call Dottóre Winton?" Stefano says.

"I called earlier from next door, 'It's a matter of time. He's got pneumonia,' the dottóre said."

Mack Winton, M.D. is an Americano who administers to poor whites and blacks free of charge.

"Ah, Filippo," Stefano says.

The three of them search for inspiration on the floor. The shortest and most roly-poly of the brothers is Pedo, short for Giuseppe. He sits in a chair next to the bed, sits as if sitting at ringside watching his hero get clobbered. Women bang pots in the kitchen, making Cuban coffee while Nonna Anna sits in an oak rocker fingering a rosary.

Then comes the moment Catholics call "the Assumption." It's the instant stillness holds hands with silence, and my grandfather leaves the room. All hear Ciccio take his last breath, and each one of my aunts and uncles sighs as if letting it out for him. It's as if each one feels guilt, some for what they have done or said to the old man, and others for what they haven't done or haven't said, but all seem guilty. I sense that's how adults feel when parents die.

Pedo reaches for the ceiling as if to try to influence heaven. "O *mio* Dio, e *morto.*"

The little man's big voice rounds out the angles of the room and it frightens me. I jump on Nonno's bed.

"No, no, Franchito, get down from there," my mother says.

"I want to go with Nonno," I cry.

My father picks me up.

Nonno's hand slides out of mine.

I don't know it, but it's the beginning of pomp and circumstance that will play for a week.

I feel emptiness wipe hair off my brow like Nonno used to do when I ran up to him sweaty from play. My grandmother's black rosary falls to the floor. It's an old rosary, one she carried on the big boat, primitive and held together by string. Its beads are twisted and can't be strewn.

I respect the rosary. My grandmother taught me it made all things right. Each bead is sacred and blessed by a priest, each an Our Father and an Ave Maria; she insists—nothing more, nothing less—priests gave it the power. The rosary represents Catholicism at its complex best to me, yet it lays paralyzed, unable to move, uncoil itself from death's sting, unable to speak out and say, "Get thee behind me, Satan." Despite its black magic, it's unable to gain traction on the slick linoleum. It is worse than sacrilegious to allow it to lie there entwined, so I pick it up.

"Here, Nonna," I say.

I hand it to her, and she smiles like a handicapped person does when one opens a door. "*Grazie,* Franchito."

"It's her crutch, a collapsible crutch," my aunts say whenever she rolls it into a ball and hides it in her pocket, her pocketbook, under her pillow, or sets it on her makeshift altar on an old oak dresser.

My grandmother never questions the rosary's sweetness, or the bitterness death shoved in her face. Sweetness to her is found in reflection, not in a flash flood of tears. She rolls beads like rednecks roll "roll-your-own" cigarettes. It is in beads she finds solace, each a memory of life with Ciccio.

"Ah, Papa, don't leave," screams Aunt Giovanina.

In my culture death is legendary, and there're things to be said, things to be done according to tradition, but for my grandmother there is only *il lutto*, a lifetime of wearing black.

Death is the one thing Sicilians can't undo, so they immerse themselves in the process. The voices soar, trying to thwart death, shoo it away or kick it in the ass like Nonna kicked a kitten's ass off our back porch. They try to steal one more second from eternity, one that won't be missed. The room, full of sighs, bulges and begins to float like a balloon. I look for a place to hide, hunker down as the chaos intensifies.

"The ammonia," someone screams.

The cork comes off and I smell the odor.

"Felicia, Felicia," another says.

Aunt Felicia swoons. Holding her breath, she ignores the pungent ammonia.

Limp body parts of voluptuous women drape themselves over cane back chairs. Felicia is the first to succumb, the first to slump. She outdoes Aunt Giovanina, who seems to take a late cue, but, nonetheless, she, too, does her *ra-cha-cha-tive.*

Adults shoo me away. "Franchito go in the other room. This is no place for you."

"But where can I go?" I say. "I want to stay. He's my *nonno*."

There is no place to go, no radio to listen to on either side of the flat. After deaths, radios are muted for a year. Death puts a damper on all things musical and recreational like movies and Italian Club picnics. I don't go to a neighbor that morning. No one takes me away. None take me on. Once the screaming takes hold, neighbors trudge in. I stay and watch, making myself as unobtrusive as I can, but stay in the room I do, stay and watch, watch it unfold.

An overhead light bulb casts bizarre shadows in the room. Its effect mixes shadows that swing from ceiling to walls, then pick themselves up and block the door. The hanging bulb, unprotected from flailing arms, swings to and fro as adults fuss over the bed. I hide low down and mix with the soft shadows.

By afternoon funeral plans emerge.

"Mama, I think it's better to put Papa in our dining room. Combined living room and dining room will give mourners more room, and it's still on the first floor," my father says.

"You're right, Filippo, *e vero.*" My grandmother nods.

Funeral homes are not in vogue, just coming into their own, aren't routine. Most funerals originate from homes. People in the *barrio* die at home. There are no nursing homes to catch the old and sick, at least, not for the poor. Besides it's a violation of ethics to dump parents in "Old People's Homes." Those waiting to die don't last long. Morphine is doled out generously to the terminally ill. There are no antibiotics, tubes or respirators to prolong misery. Family vigils take their cues when death rattles set in.

Funeral attendants pick up Ciccio, drain him and pump him up with pink formaldehyde. I watch the coffin squeeze into my side of the flat as perhaps attendants squeezed the blood out of my grandfather at the funeral parlor. They position the casket against the wall for the wake, rosary and funeral. My grandfather seems asleep. Oh, yes, asleep that's what Mama says, but I know he's dead, stone cold dead. That's how he feels each time I grab his hand, despite euphemisms proclaiming him so natural. Each time I go near the coffin, I'm admonished. "Franchito, no, no."

I walk away. "I just wanted to see, that's all."

"You can look but don't touch, understand?"

"I promise not to wake him, Mama," I say, but I try.

Ciccio's interlaced fingers form a bridge across his chest, bridging his world to mine. There are flowers, food, relatives and friends everywhere. Women sit in the room with the coffin and men sit and talk on the front porch. Tall candles flicker next to the coffin and flowers lay helter-skelter spilling onto the floor. The fragrance of gladioli is outrageously good.

It's an eerie feeling sleeping with a corpse near my bed that night, him asleep in an open casket allowing him to breathe. The corpse is my grandfather, so I love him and know he'll do me no harm.

"Filippo, you think this dress is good enough?" Mama says the morning of the funeral, holding it up against her short frame.

"Of course, it's black, isn't it?"

"How about Franchito? He's got no black clothes."

"Hell, something dark will do."

"You think it will be all right, Fili? You think so? It's his grandfather, you know."

"Mary, he's just a boy."

"How about the navy-blue sailor suit? It has only a few white stripes."

"Fine, fine. I don't think anyone will care if he's a sailor today."

That's how Mama perceives life, always worrying what people think. It's her curse as if it always is her unblemished reputation at stake. Banking on rigid protocols, she never lets her guard down, but this time I am her reputation, me at her stake. Oh, she tries to socially condition me, all right, but thanks to Papa, she only partially succeeds.

Two days after Death marched in, Death's puppets file out. Out the front door goes the black suited priest dripping holy water on the linoleum. Out go stage directors who with honor guard precision snap hearse and limousine doors. Out goes the short stature crowd, and gladioli wreaths wrapped in glittering gold ribbons reading Rest in Peace. Like beauty contestants with sashes, the wreaths had stood tall and proud on skinny tripod legs next to Ciccio's coffin for two days. Out come pallbearers wearing black ties they'd tugged on inside. Their hands hold on to the deadweight of the box. Half tripping, they go down three wobbly steps with uprooted six-penny nails. Papa fixed the steps months earlier but didn't replace rotten wood. He's a master at trying to make do.

"It's temporary," he'd said at the time, always does, but he never expected three small steps to be asked to take on the brunt of so many heavyweight Italians.

Papa's carpentry work is never fancy, but it's stout, sturdy and stalwart. But today his nails don't hold—nothing holds. Everything and everybody is coming loose—letting go. Ciccio is leaving the house for the last time, and we're letting him go. It's what old people who visited my grandmother during the wake said,

said it plainly to a face viewing life through a prism of tears—"*Mi dispiace*—Sorry, but you must let go."

Last, comes the stampede of unsteady high heels. Women who were sitting
near the coffin stand and walk out, clattering like a herd of cattle. Balancing
themselves and hanging on to spouses, they broach Papa's precarious steps. Black
veils cling to pale faces like fishnets trying to catch tears.

Ciccio introduced me to the traditional Sicilian funeral, introduced it with
zest, flair and with the roar of a hearse's eight-cylinder engine. I follow my grandfather sitting in the back seat of a plush limousine, never slowing or stopping at
intersections where a motorcycle policeman intervenes. My neighborhood fades
as I enter the world of colored town—the land of the dead. We drive under a
wrought iron arch reading L' Unione Italiana Cemetery, and I look up at Papa
and Mama, but no one says a word.

11

I readjust my schedule not to include Ciccio. He's tucked away in colored town. Shortly after his death, we move down the street to a duplex, a few houses west on East Columbus Drive, on the same side of the street, and my widowed grandmother comes with us.

"Don't forget *l'fiore*, the flowers, the flowers," Anna says to Papa, opening the screen door, running out on the porch.

Papa's black Chevy looks on. It is parked out front a few feet from our front porch—a sitting target for drunken blacks driving "niggered up" cars on weekends.

"Papa, I want to come," I say, running up.

"Just going to pick up flowers, that's all," he says.

The dead are respected, for overnight they've become defenseless underdogs, indiscriminately seduced by an insatiable underworld. I am told it is wise and prudent to revere them, for death is the ultimate example of what goes around comes around.

Anna goes back inside seemingly satisfied.

For years after my grandfather's death, Papa cruises Seventh Avenue on Saturday afternoons.

"Going to pick up flowers," he'd said in Sicilian, but it's more than just flowers. It is the cemetery he and my grandmother prepare themselves for. Visits to the cemetery are a routine of life.

We arrive in the business district, and Papa parks on a side street off Seventh Avenue. The street is bustling with shoppers. People are talking and gesticulating. There's a makeshift flower stand ahead right on Seventh Avenue. Papa stops and pulls up his trousers. He pulls on one side then the other and, when nothing happens, he loosens his belt and cinches it tighter. His trousers hang low, slide off stocky hips. Cuffs are frayed, and at home, I hear Mama say, "Filippo, you got no ass, no ass at all to hold up your pants." And he doesn't, and he doesn't care, replying every time, "But, Mary, I'm a man. Only women need a big ass."

Galvanized buckets with flowers sit in the shade of Kress's. Protruding like swords, the gladioli stand next to a beat up pickup truck.

"How much a bunch?" Papa says to a tall slim man.

77

The redneck towers over Papa, and looking at him, the man stretches his neck and spits out tobacco juice. It seeps out of the corner of his mouth, too. Each time he swallows, a large Adam's apple jiggles and the bulge filling his cheek mixes with words. Despite the man's constant spitting, the bulge never dissolves, and each time he spits, he blinks, and each time he blinks he swallows. A denim bib and buckled straps of his coveralls drape over the man's bony chest.

He looks down at Papa and says, "Fifty cents."

Papa shakes his head.

"Fresh as they gets. Won't find them cheaper." The man moves away from the truck, digs his hands into his oversized pockets and says, "Yes sir, them's a hell of a deal." He spits and splatters the redbrick street.

"Too high," Papa says.

"But they is fresh. I cuts 'em this morning."

"No matter, they going to cemetery," Papa says.

"Cemetery?"

Papa nods and says again, "How much a bunch?"

"Depends how many you take," the redneck says.

"How about if I take two?" Papa rummages the buckets with his eyes. "They no look so fresh. Is late you know. They gonna die and be worth nothing. Is time for people to go home."

"Well, it don't matter if they die, right? You say you gonna take them to the cemetery, right?" The man laughs and slaps Papa on the back.

Papa says nothing.

"Didn't get my joke, did ya?" The redneck straightens his cap. "Well, how many bunches will you take?"

Papa puts up two fingers.

"Thas all?"

Papa looks across the street, "Well, it depends on the price."

"Was you here last Saturday?" the man says.

Papa nods. "But most times I buy gladiola cheap across street."

"Can't just give them away, you know. Gotta make a living." The man removes his International Harvester cap, spits and runs his hand through red hair. "How about if I do you seventy-five cents for two bunches. That's a hell of a deal."

"How about if I take three?" Papa says.

"Four for a dollar. Deal?"

They seal it with a handshake.

I know Papa's making an effort, speaking the best English he knows how.

"Ain't you guys ever gonna learn to speak?" The redneck wipes his forehead with a red bandana and spits out a juicy one. I feel the spray hit my face.

"I gonna learn," Papa says, laughing and digging into buckets. "But, my boy learn first."

The redneck wraps the gladioli with newspapers around cut ends. I watch *The Tampa Morning Tribune* ink bleed print neither Papa or I can read. "Got a damn good price, Mister."

"*Grazie*," Papa says.

The gladioli fill my half of the floorboard.

"Franchito, go to school. Life is a race where a runner passes a stick to the next man and the next and the next. And sometimes one man makes up for the others. My father handed it to me, and I'm handing it to you, so don't drop it. Understand?" he says in Sicilian.

"But, I want to be like you, Papa."

"Promise you won't drop the stick."

He looks straight ahead.

I look out the window.

He sticks his arm out the window each time he takes a turn.

I know what I have to say.

"I won't drop it, Papa. I promise."

He reaches over and messes my hair. "Be like me, but don't talk like me. They'll teach you in school. You're going to talk nice, Franchito, real nice."

"Why did you quit school, Papa?"

"Too many mouths to feed in my family—nine mouths."

"Did they teach you Americano in school?"

"If I'd been given a chance, I would have been somebody, Franchito—a doctor, a dentist, a pharmacist, something—not sweat in the shipyard like a dog."

"But you say it's better than rolling cigars, right?"

"Much better. I'm out in the fresh air."

After Papa bought his car he quit the cigar factory and went to work for defense as a laborer at Hooker's Point Shipyard. World War II catapulted Papa out of cigar factories. He'd been afraid the American war-machine would draft him. Although he was forty, America was drafting forty year olds and said it didn't care if they were American born. All men were created equal when it came to dying, didn't have to speak English. As a defense worker he would be exempt from the draft. I worried those days in the back seat of the 1936 Chevy, listening to Mama and Papa's conversations about Mussolini, and the anti-Italian sentiment the Italian dictator had brought down on us.

"Lots of Crackos work at the shipyard," he says. Crackos is the Italianized word for rednecks. At the time I don't realize I am a Cracker, for I was born in Florida. All people born in the state are referred to as Florida Crackers, but the term never refers to Latinos.

"They give me the tough jobs, Franchito, the ones Americanos don't want, but I laugh, and they keep me on."

"When I grow up, I want big muscles like you, Papa."

"I joke with the Americanos, Franchito. They laugh at the way I talk. The foreman calls me Whapo."

"What does *whapo* mean?"

"Means tough, handsome."

I don't know the word wop, but there's a Spanish slang word that sounds like wop. Papa pronounces it w*hapo*.

"But it's going to be different for you. There are laws now that make children stay in school. You can be a somebody, Franchito—a somebody."

"Don't say that, Papa."

I'd seen his face blanch when the redneck belittled him. He doesn't know, but he's a somebody to me.

We walk into the kitchen, and my grandmother fingers the gladioli and smiles.

"Mama, like them?" Papa says.

"*Belle fiore,*" she says. "How much a bunch, Filippo?"

"Not much."

There is never a price placed on gladioli.

"I'll put them in water," she says.

A large vase is placed on a checkered oilcloth that drapes a small kitchen table.

Papa never brings flowers to Mama on birthdays, anniversaries or Saint Valentine's Day, but on Saturdays gladioli spruce up her kitchen.

Sundays evolve into D-Day, day of the dead. Oh, I celebrate the traditional Day of the Dead each year, all right, on the first of November. It substitutes for Halloween, and the dead are kind, bringing me candy, but this is different, quite different, a new experience happening weekly.

My grandmother, Papa and I leave early on Sundays. I sit bored in the back seat with gladioli bunched at my side, and the sun beats on a black 1936 Chevy each summer, and we drive under a wrought iron arch reading L'Unione Italiana Cemetery.

"All to the glory of God and Paradise," Anna says, after walking a sandy path, says it in Sicilian crossing herself, eyeing a photograph embedded in granite. Photographs similar to those found in Sicily's cemeteries depict the dead on headstones and mausoleums. In time I recognize the brief mantra is her preamble to fidelity. I watch her kneel and see wizened lips press against a granite headstone.

Piercing eyes stare back, and a single granite slab lays flat on a gravesite accommodating two, so it is as if I'm looking at a half-made-up double bed, for on the right side of the headstone, her side of the headboard, if you will, a scored, oval template like his awaits a photograph. That side of the plot is unslabbed, so for twenty years, her half, her side of eternity remains unoccupied, undated, unpictured and unscripted.

I'm designated clean up and water boy, dumping dead flowers in a putrid pile propped up against a chain-link fence and refilling vases with fresh water on command. I watch relatives bring flowers, no wax, silk or plastic, nothing fake. All is alive, so much alive, and fresh gladioli bring to dead immigrants a sense of redemption, better than Catholic Mass, yes, better than Communion, for there are more icons in the cemetery than Our Lady of Perpetual Help Church. I linger and stare at recently unearthed mounds, marvel at wilted flowers and wreaths dying in the sun, and it seems tombstones go up like subdivisions. Urban sprawl seems endless.

I stick to main thoroughfares, for to me, in the land of the dead, they are safer like heavily traveled interstates. I record a St. Joseph here, a lonely Jesus there, a cross, a hovering angel. Familiar names mark my route, but the stony landscape repeats itself, so occasionally, disoriented, my heart pounds, and I swallow hard. Tombstones are road signs held up by the dead, and some try to trick me, but each time I zigzag, rethink my way back.

I hold up a jar to my grandmother.

"Grasshoppers?" she says.

"*Sì*, Nonna."

"No wonder you took so long."

"No, got lost."

"Well, if you didn't go looking for grasshoppers, you wouldn't have."

"They were next to the spigot," I say.

"Well, better not run with a glass jar in your hand."

I'd found the jar among the pile of discarded flowers.

"See, Japs!" I hold the jar up to Papa.

"Set them free, Franchito. How'd you like to be imprisoned?"

"They look like Japs, Papa."

"Japanese are people, too."

"But they torture American GIs in the jungle."

"That's war, has nothing to do with people."

"I hate Japs."

Grasshopper uniforms are segmented yellow, orange and black like armor plates, camouflaging themselves like enemy tanks, and they cling to cypress trees like snipers. Grasshoppers are insects of choice, preferable to booby-trap laden honeybees, and grasshoppers smile fiendishly from behind yellow faces, faces I'd seen in war movies, yet their eyes are convex—too wide to be Asian. Their teeth protrude like Tojo caricatures I'd seen in *The Tampa Tribune*. I cajole them to swear loyalty to the land of the rising sun and incarcerate them in a larger jar at home, call it the brig. I smother them with grass, sandspurs and sprinkle water, sort of a last happy meal.

My cousin and I strap them inside paper airplanes and torch them. Standing atop his garage, we toss flaming "Zeros" boasting red dots of the rising sun, and we watch them tailspin to their deaths in a sea of weeds in the alley below. We shout *bonsai* and rush to crash sites and watch the bastards burn and take no prisoners.

On Sundays, widows in black descend on the cemetery, weeding plots. Bent over they rake them clean.

"Franchito, *viene qua*, come here," some say. "How is your Nonna?"

I address them *vocia,* an archaic word, means ma'am or sir in the Sicilian dialect. The word is loaded with respect and deference to older people. It's a word devoid of gender, a unisex word before unisex is invented or undressed, so I say it like a Sicilian gentleman of class.

When I return, my father looks at his father's headstone and says, "*Buono reposo*, Papa."

"But, Papa, Nonno can't hear."

I'd heard him say rest in peace many times. He makes me unsure if Ciccio is really dead.

When older I question the deeply rooted custom of gladioli every Sunday. I think it wasteful, inconsistent with our family's frugality, so I say, "Why, Papa? Why leave flowers to rot in the sun?"

Papa shakes his head.

"Nonno is dead, can't hear a thing," I say.

"Doesn't matter."

"Papa, he can't see us."

"No, but you can, Franchito."

"I don't understand."

"That's because you're thinking with your head."

He allows me to delve into what I think ponderous; doesn't say a word, looks at me, then at the headstone.

"He's dead, Papa, dead, yet you talk to him as if he's alive."

"There is much to be learned from the dead, Franchito."

"From the dead?"

"Someday you'll visit me, Franchito. Sometimes it's not only the dead who are lonely."

"Don't say that, Papa. You're never going to die."

We walk away. He jerks my arm. "Watch it, don't walk there. You are walking on a *morto*."

"Didn't know they stuck out that far."

"Be careful, don't need bad luck."

"Papa, I gotta pee."

"Can't you wait until we go home?"

"Don't think so."

"All right, go behind that stone. Aim at the aisle, not at somebody's face."

I didn't understand tradition is a form of catechism in my culture, didn't understand what Papa meant by—learn from the dead. It happened before I spoke English, before I could read. I never suspected Papa was carving me like a stonecutter carves a headstone. He did it Sunday after Sunday, and Saturday evenings he brought home gladioli.

The main entrance to the Italian Club Cemetery.

Ciccio and Anna share eternity's double bed. Not many visit anymore.

The Italian Club Cemetery is a duplicate of those in Sicily. My great grandfather's obelisk stands tall. Pietro Pizzolato immigrated in 1892 and died in the 1918 influenza pandemic. Empty urns are a sign of the times.

Mausoleums line up like row houses in the Alessandria della Rocca ceme-tery. Note the abundance of flowers, crosses, angels and Italian cypress trees, like those in the Tampa cemetery, standing sentinel in the back-ground.

12

"When does Franchito start school?" A woman says to my mother at a rosary at Lord and Fernandez Funeral Home.

"In September," Mama whispers.

"Where?" the woman says.

"Free School."

I stare straight ahead as if what they're talking about does not concern me. I focus on a satin pillow propping up a gray head.

"That's okay, Mary, but Franchito won't get the discipline he needs at public school. Nuns teach respect, you know."

The woman blows her nose in an embroidered handkerchief, and then shoves it inside the sleeve of her black dress.

"I know, Peppina," Mama says. "But in Free School they learn to deal with all kinds of people. You never know who they will run into in America."

Going to funerals and wakes are like rites of passage, for one must reach what my parents call the age of reason. A child must understand that no matter what—the corpse will not rise. That is the first step. I watch adults file in, take perfunctory looks at the old woman. A few wipe their eyes and cross themselves, peering into the coffin.

I walked up with Mama, when we came in, and I saw an ant crawl out of the dead woman's nose. I didn't think Mama saw it, so I nudged her, but she gave me a look that said, "Act as if you don't see it."

"Americans are not Catholics you know," Mama says to Peppina.

"That's the point, Mary." Peppina leans towards Mama. "You want Franchito to learn about God."

The priest moves in on the casket. Peppina smiles at him as if letting him know she's on his team—shares the same mascot.

Peppina leans and whispers again, "Mary, how else is he going to learn about God? Not from those who don't believe."

"Franchito learns as much as he needs to know at home," Mama says.

"In the name of the Father, the Son…" The priest makes the sign of the cross and sprinkles holy water on the corpse. Drops land on my face each time his container flips back to the starting position, and I am in the third row. He's vigorous with holy water, but all I think of is nuns are tough, and ants inside noses don't wake up the dead.

Well, I learn about God. There is someone my parents call Dio. Mama tells me Dio is a person they pray to, yet I never see my mother or father kneel, lace fingers, roll rosary beads or hang a crucifix or a picture of Jesus in my home.

"We pray in private," Mama says. "Praying is a personal thing, like something between a man and his wife. You don't have to go to church. Besides, it's nobody's business whether a person goes to church or not."

I ask Papa, "How come we don't say grace at the table?"

"Having pasta on the table is grace," he says.

Papa doesn't Hail Mary either, doesn't know how, but occasionally, when things go wrong, he exclaims Bada Madre, beautiful mother, and it makes do. None of us know the Lord's Prayer, but, after Nonno Ciccio died, my grandmother Anna moved in with us. Prayers are embedded in her existence, and churchwomen, Ladies of the Altar Society, visit her. My parents never realize my grandmother is filling me with something she calls the spirit. She shares my bedroom, and that means I'm stuck with the Patre Nostro and the Ave Maria every night. I never make the inter-lingual connection that the Patre Nostro and the Lord's Prayer are one and the same.

I didn't realize it at the time, but there was a history to religion. Ybor City was founded in the 1880s, and priests and nuns established themselves in the predominantly Spanish speaking community. They endeared themselves to factory owners, who welcomed clerics into their elite society. Babies, in fine lace, filled baptisteries on Sundays; however, attempts by clerics to rein in the laboring cigarmakers were met with resistance. Priests expected Christianity to be a cinch, a slam-dunk with Latins, but the cozy relationship between church and factory owners was viewed as a conspiracy of sorts by cigar workers.

"Mama, will I be made to pray in school?" I say, rolling marbles on a worn carpet one late afternoon.

"Don't worry about prayers," Mama says with her head half cocked, laying it on the sofa's armrest. She often lies down that way after a day in the factory.

Papa comes home and sits in an upholstered chair. "Mama's right, Franchito. All priests want is money. Those *somma ama bitcha* live off the sweat of the poor." Papa unties his shoes, and leaves the room to take a shower. I know how he feels about priests, but I also know he's never met one.

"That's okay, Franchito, don't worry. I was made to say prayers when I went to Free School. There's nothing wrong with prayer unless it commandeers your mind," Mama says.

My parents despise ministers and evangelists. Papa says they're worse than priests because they don't belong to the Roman Catholic Church, which, by the fact it's Italian, is the best of the scams. Mama claims we're Catholics—her own brand.

I walk into the kitchen, and Papa grabs me by the shoulder. His eyebrows angle and reel me in like a fish, a Christian fish. "We baptized you right away, Franchito, just in case you died. The most disgraceful thing for parents to do is not to baptize a baby, for if he dies, he dies a Turk. Then it's too late, and if he lives, he goes through life being a Turk."

My father never met a Turk either—didn't realize Islam existed, but he knew Turks were not baptized. If he had understood the Koran, Papa might have agreed with Islam's chauvinism, austerity and moral beliefs. I didn't realize there was bad blood between Turks and Sicilians. Centuries ago Ottoman Turks occupied Sicily, so anti-Turk sentiment was passed down via oral tradition.

I lie in my bed that night, and I listen to my grandmother's flipside. Before Ciccio died I was exposed to her days, but now it's a night and day phenomenon with me sleeping in her room.

She says, "Listen to the *Rosario,* Franchito."

"*Sì,* Nonna."

"Ave Maria, Madre di Dio, Patre Nostro."

A portrait of her father and mother, Stefano and Felicia, hangs above the head of her bed. Above mine hangs her dead mustachioed brother, Pepe. None ever wink.

Nonna created an altar on her dresser. Santa Rosalia and Santa Lucia are favorites hiding in grottos next to Mary, Joseph and Jesus. Votive candles dimly illuminate the room. She warns me not to play with fire, but when she's not in the room, I swirl melted wax and create merry-go-rounds, coating insides of the glass. Sometimes I snuff out the wick and tell her there's a breeze coming through the room. She smiles.

I cross myself and say the Ave Maria in Latin in the dark, whisper it in order not to wake my parents in the next room. I don't know what the words mean, but it doesn't matter as long as I say them like her.

"Franchito, repeat after me—Ave Maria, *gratia plena.*" She breaks into song and tells how she sang lead in the choir in Sicily. "Sing with me," she says.

I do, and sing the Ave Maria and Panis Angelelicus, and it too is beautiful.

I know I share the bedroom with an angel, one whose voice quivers reaching for high notes.

"My voice breaks now," she says. "But it didn't when I was young."

"It's still beautiful, Nonna, beautiful." And it is.

Under her bed there's a chamber pot, and I have one under mine. I learn to pee in the enameled pot in the dark. If I'm on target, I, too, make musical sounds, but when she pees, it's different, not a tinkle, more a lady's swish. Our privacy is the darkness of night, and she knows each time I'm awake, for angels, like God, know everything.

At night, our bedroom is the target of an invisible sun. The heat trapped in our neighbor's tin roof transfixes itself through torn window screens. She stuffs the holes with newspaper to keep mosquitoes out, but that doesn't keep the heat out. Dante's *Inferno* keeps breathing a good part of the night. She's the closest person I know to God. I hear her speak to him, and, if he isn't listening, she repeats herself. She's got what Italians call pull, inside pull.

"Franchito, are you still awake?"

"Why sleep?" I say. "It's a waste of time."

She clears her throat with a sound reminding me of a carpenter's rasp. I know she's smiling, exposing her gums to visionless night while her fingers pill-roll rosary beads. She never forgets where she left off. Beads are a substitute for counting sheep. I never hear of Sicilian old ladies counting sheep; typically it's beads.

I recall the day her teeth were pulled, and she couldn't eat. Her face becomes angelic like a baby's. Her children talk of getting plates, but false teeth are expensive, so they never materialize. She does well, develops calluses on naked gums that struggle to hold up her sunken smile.

She was seventy-one when I was born, yet age has not wiped away the memories of village life. She pauses before each story, as if thumbing through pages caught in her throat. I can't see her face, but I know she's about to start.

"I was forty years old when I came to America, Franchito." She sighs. "I never saw my parents again—never saw them in their coffins or saw their graves, but I remember the good."

Anna speaks one American word—"okay," not an American yes, not an American no or maybe, only "okay," the obliging American word. She tells me to be grateful I am baptized and have a Christian name. I think that one over since all members of the Mafia have Christian names, but she's right, even Mafiosi are better than Turks. The last thing I wish to be is a Turk.

"I can't sleep, Nonna, too sticky." I flip off my sheet like a matador twirls a cape.

"Here, take this. Fan yourself. It'll give you something to do."

She's folded a newspaper into a fan. I run to her bed and take it, another miracle performed in the dark. Electricity is at a premium where I live, so I maneuver in the dark, learn the room in Braille and watch the bedroom come alive in the dark.

"What will you use, Nonna?" I say, fanning hard.

"Oh, I have a fan from the church. They're stiff, don't flip and flop like newspapers do."

She slipped one out from beneath her pillow, and though I didn't see her, I know it's what she'd done. There are many things I learn in the dark. Each sound has meaning, and each movement makes sound, all interconnected, all tied to the dark.

When the candles on her dresser are lit, I see moving shadows. An overcoat hangs on a nail behind the door, and it takes on human form. It's a wool coat that Mama throws on me on bitter cold nights.

"Nonna, there's someone in here."

"You're dreaming. Go back to sleep."

"No, there is. I see him."

"Go to sleep."

I stare at the coat and it moves, moves closer, disappearing only when she gets up and turns on the light.

"Franchito the only person you need to fear is the devil," she says, crawling back into bed. I saw him in the old church in Alessandria della Rocca."

"You saw the devil in church?"

"Oh, yes."

"Tell me, what is he like?"

"You really want to know?"

"So I can watch out for him."

"*The Last Judgment* hung near the altar," she says, flipping her sheet and fanning herself as if the thought of the devil turned up the heat in the room.

"Yes, but give me details, Nonna, the devil, please, the devil."

"It was a copy of a famous fresco at the Vatican, a painting alive with death. It was judgment day, the day we will all be judged by God, Franchito, and I saw all those *povere peccatores,* poor sinners."

"Did a fat priest paint it?"

"Oh no, Michelangelo did, painted it on wet plaster. The original is in the home of the Pope. Those pathetic souls made me want to cry. Sinners were being dragged out of a boat onto the shores of a river floating dead souls to hell. The priest told us the story when we were children, tried to explain what we didn't know. One of the devils with pointed teeth gnawed on a sinner's calf like a fresh goat roast while another devil, called Charon, swung an oar, forcing them out of the boat. I never forget those faces."

"What's an oar?"

"You know, one of those sticks used to row a boat."

"I know, Nonna, I know."

"*Sì, sì*, it was Charon, or maybe it was one of his helpers. It's been such a long time ago."

"Devils have names?"

"In the painting they did."

"Charon doesn't sound Italian, maybe Cuban?"

"I don't know, maybe he was, for the devil has lots of faces, takes on different forms and names they say."

"So how do you know when you see one?"

"Well, Charon's eyes glowed like hot coals. There were others with pointed ears—the first bogeymen we'll see when we depart blessed earth if we don't pray to God every day, Franchito. That's what the priest said—devils."

I know she crosses herself in the dark, for I hear her whisper, "Padre, Figlio e Spirito Santo." I know it's all true.

I cover my head with a sheet. I can't get the creature with eyes of coals out of my head. I hear her sheets rustle as she settles into the bed's concavity, and I hear her say, "*Buona notte*, Franchito, good night."

I hear her fanning. It's what all old people do in Ybor City. Children never bother, ignore Florida's heat, never fan or wipe faces. She leaves a trail of fans throughout the house. Advertisement on cardboard fans is common. They're free, given out by Ybor City merchants around New Year.

Lord and Fernandez Funeral Home displays saintly motifs on their fans. Constantino Granite and Marble Co. has photos of headstones. Cacciatore & Sons and Demi grocery stores have *The Last Supper*.

"Sicilians who came on the big boat worked hard," she says. "It was sad leaving my mother and father behind. I was young then, Franchito, and now they're all dead. I knew it was goodbye before I said goodbye, before I went to Palermo to catch the boat. But let me tell you about the beautiful ocean that surrounds Sicily, about oranges, mountains with snow and a volcano. Franchito? Franchito? Are you asleep?"

"*Buona notte*, Ciccio. *Il nome Di Patre, e il Figlio, e il Spirito Santo. Ave Maria, Madre di Dio. Ave Maria.*"

And always Ciccio's name is welded into her prayers, and she will wear black until she dies.

13

My mother's parents live two blocks south of my duplex, on Nineteenth Street. A sycamore tree shades their front porch. Theirs is a separate existence, quite different than life in a duplex. This grandmother is younger than Anna and has been a *tabaquera* since childhood. After work each evening, she sits in a leatherette rocker next to a radio. Leatherette is the finest my grandparents own. Flaking, the chair lets me know it has withstood the test of time. Nonna Sara rocks as she wheezes from asthma. Inside the living room there's the cadence of a pendulum clock. The house is a "corner house," said to be desirable because air circulates on two sides. Along the side there is no space between the sidewalk and the house, so heads bob outside the windows. Following them from living room to kitchen, I wave until they disappear. Most are *tabaquero* and *tabaquera* heads. The leatherette chair seesaws on the floor on the same spot, and its rockers dent and crack the linoleum. Nonna's fingers move, move to the rhythm of a crochet needle. Back and forth, back and forth, the needle hooks the thread.

"*Uno duo, uno duo,*" the old woman whispers, listening to the doldrums of Cuban soap operas she calls *novellas*.

"Nonna," I say.

"Don't interrupt. I'm in the middle of my count."

Always the cadence, never missing a stitch and the litany of "*Uno duo, uno duo.*"

Crochet was taught to her generation like catechism, and it's called *puntina*. *Puntina* spans Sicily with a unifying thread. In short pants, I imagine rolls of thread tossed by Sicilian women across the Atlantic, landing, unrolling on the sacred floor. Her hands finger the thread night after night. Looping it on a hook, she alternates a light stitch with a bold—*uno duo, uno duo.*

I place my fingers inside delicate holes and play with patterns when they roll off her hands, all different and all beautiful. I see the thread unthreading itself, setting itself free in America, shaking itself loose from the confines of the ball.

The to and fro swing of the pendulum makes me conscious of the passage of time. My grandfather winds the clock with the same key at the same time each day. I feel the pendulum pushing them farther into eternity, teasing them back and forth with memories of what used to be, taunting them with thoughts of what now will never be.

The clock's white porcelain face gathers light. Roman numerals X-out the hours and chimes abbreviate half-hours—all lauding irreversible time. Yet the clock can't measure time, can't measure eternity, for it has no beginning or end. It focuses on life spans, keeping track of used up lifetimes.

I sneak up behind her and pick at the dried-out leatherette.

She says, "Stop, Franchito. Stop that."

Arthritic fingers stop, too, but soon they're back in the rhythm.

I smell spaghetti sauce in the kitchen. My grandfather never peels garlic. Cloves float dressed in transparent skins. Nonno Domenico taught my mama to cook, but she's too compulsive to leave garlic alone. She strangles the springtime out of *primavera* sauce. My grandfather, like many Italian men, cooks with a flair, smokes a cigar while stirring the sauce. He's a chef that once cooked for hundreds in the Italian Army, maybe legions, maybe millions—maybe ashes make the difference in the sauce.

My grandparents' table setting is archaic, an abomination imported from Sicily. They eat from opposite ends of a common plate called a *spilonga*—a long dish resembling a serving platter. It brings them together like dancing cheek-to-cheek. They plow through pasta with forks until utensils clash. Their elbows stick out on contralateral sides. It's a coordinated effort, but I'm pleased I'm not made to share.

Their dinner is viewed from the top, same overlook every evening. Face-to-face they face life, swallow it a mouthful at a time. Mama justifies the custom by saying it's a form of oneness like man and wife sleeping in a double bed, and not to continue tradition is analogous to sleeping in twin beds. No one else in the *barrio* practices the insanity.

Nonno grates the cheese with a hand-grater and sauces pasta only once. Cheese graters are made from wood from an apple box that is the shape of a small paddle with a piece of a perforated olive oil can nailed to one side.

"Franchito, don't skim off the top," he says "Cut down on it like *lasagna*, straight down. It will taste good to the end that way."

He says cut down, cut into it, but what he really means is—cut down on the use of sauce and cheese. Everything is measured except love.

"Papa grates cheese twice," I say.

"That's not what we do. We do it like it was done in the Italian Army."

On a day we eat fish he says, "Franchito, when you eat fish don't talk."

"Why?"

"Don't want a spine stabbing your throat. Here, drink wine, not water."

"Why?"

"Water and fish don't mix—makes you sick. Drink *vino*."

"Why?"

He doesn't respond.

I think water revives fish. It's dead, but water is the fish's natural habitat, so maybe a fish can resurrect itself inside my stomach in three days, so I drink wine.

"*Sì*, give me *vino*, more *vino*," I say.

I develop a passion for wine. I raid his barrel when he's not around. On cinder blocks, a couple of feet off the floor it stands. I crawl under the spigot and let it flow, perhaps like farm children do under hanging teats.

When eating soup, he says, "Don't blow on it. It's not nice, makes noise."

"*Sì*, Nonno, but it's hot."

"Spoon it from the edge, away from you. It's cooler there. Don't slurp, *per favore*, Franchito."

"Papa blows and slurps," I say.

"I know." He smiles.

Grandfather Domenico, like most immigrants, never learned English, never did, not one iota, and I, well, I am about as Sicilian as anyone in my family. I will learn my first American words in first grade that coming fall. Reined in by Mama's hand that Sunday morning I crossed a couple of narrow streets and alleys to get to my grandfather's home, two city blocks spanning eternity to a six year old.

In the kitchen, my grandmother wheezed, doing about all she could do when her asthma flared. She stirred spaghetti sauce in a large pot with a long wooden spoon. I ran to the backyard and found him where she said the old man would be.

"Nonno Domenico, *fascesti un bello fuoco!*" I say running up and planting my feet next to his, shielding my face from the heat of the flames. I had one grandfather left, and this one would last me through my teenage years.

"*Sì, un fuoco*, Franchito."

The five-foot two-inch man towers over me.

"It's a beautiful fire, beautiful. I want to watch," I say.

He throws in more wood.

Old bricks prop up termite-infested planks. On the steps sits a kerosene can, and next to it is a pile of folded clothes. The clothes are reminiscent of what soldiers wear—wool khakis—clothes out of character for a man I've seen only wear black trousers. His woolen trousers are my itchy anathema. He wears them year round, pricking my bare thighs when I sit on his lap. My chalky shoes scuff them, agitating his calm demeanor.

These are dark years in America, even darker than black trousers—World War II. The siren of cigar factories tells cigarmakers to switch off their lights during blackouts. Latino men strut down sidewalks to make sure we do. Designated air-raid wardens hold the power, all right, hold it over us as if we're Jews hiding from storm troopers, or something like Spanish foremen lord power over Italians in factories.

In candlelight I make shadowy dogs with wiggly ears on tongue and groove walls, and brown window shades seal us in. Luftwaffe bombs are said to be targeting MacDill Air Force Base. I spring roller shades, pulling down hard on their fringe. It's exciting to watch whimsical flames like the days nameless hurricanes blow in from the Gulf of Mexico and snuff out electricity.

Black is the motif, all right: black market gasoline, black market canned goods, meat, toilet paper, black painted windows and black dresses transform Sicilian mothers into black Pietas. President Roosevelt tells us we're making a difference, and we are. We make it profitable for black marketers. Everything and everyone defaults to the dark side.

I scurry home hanging on to Mama's hand, jumping out of the way of half blackened headlights that look like they have heavy mascara. I watch cars turn into alleys seeking refuge in dilapidated garages. Like cockroaches, they detest light. Sirens scream as we approach the duplex, the second house from the corner, silhouetted against searchlights that reach out like giant flashlights into the sky.

B-17s, P-38s, and Super Fortresses fly low to and from MacDill Air Force Base, and military convoys cruise Columbus Drive. Mussolini betrayed us all. Not only did he cuckold Italy but Ybor City Italians, too. I know Italians have nothing in common with Germans, absolutely nothing, not appearance, style, temperament, food and certainly not Giuseppe Verdi. It is the anti-Semite Wagner Germans tout.

It's a time I listen to off-limit conversations in my home.

"We should get naturalized," Papa had said one evening in our parlor.

"But what good would it do? We're Italiani, can't speak American." Nonno Domenico, with hands locked behind his back, paced in a house that didn't expand for ponderous thoughts.

"Yes, but when the FBI goes through the alien list, Papa, we'll be listed Americans. Might keep them out of our homes."

"But, Filippo, it means giving up the motherland."

"But, we don't want to go back to Italy."

"The government does as it pleases, doesn't matter if it's Italy or America, always the damn government."

When typed envelopes peek out of mailboxes with letters immigrants can't read, thoughts of deportation loom. They never forget America's prejudice and the sham trial of Sacco and Vanzetti. Appalling things can happen to innocent men.

I look up at my grandfather standing next to the raging fire.

"Can I watch?" I say again tugging at his arm.

"Yes, but not near the fire."

"Yes, Nonno, here?"

"*Sì.*" He holds up a jacket.

"Nonno, I didn't know you had a uniform."

"Got it when I was seventeen."

"It's a beautiful jacket," I say.

He nods.

"Did you like the army?"

"Armies kill, Franchito."

"Did you kill anyone?" I say, hoping for a yes.

"I was a cook. I was saving this uniform for you, Franchito, but I decided to burn it."

"No, don't burn it. It's beautiful. Save it."

"It's just a uniform, Franchito, that's all, just a uniform."

"I know, but it's yours, Nonno."

"It's Italian, Franchito, Italiano." He shakes his head.

"So what? It's yours. You paid for it, right? Mama says if you pay for something it's yours in America. You keep it."

He says nothing.

"Keep it, keep it, Nonno, keep it until I grow up."

"It's no longer mine, Franchito."

"I don't understand."

"Someday you will," he says.

I see emptiness fill his eyes as he gathers the rest of the clothes. He picks up a pair of trousers and holds them up against the sky as if searching for moth holes.

"I can hardly wait to wear long pants." I jump up and down.

He smiles.

After flipping the army pants from side to side, he dangles them over the fire and drops them in. He fingers a brass insignia on the collar of the jacket. Rubbing it between thumb and index finger, as if polishing it. He tosses it in, too.

He picks up a cap and puts it on and brings his right hand up to a faded visor. He stands at attention. Well, as much at attention as an old man in his late fifties can. Frozen with eyes straight away, he snaps his hand to his side, removes the cap, places it on my head, straightens it when it slides and covers my ears and angles it skywards when it covers my eyes. Mothballs have kept his memories alive, and their odor makes me realize just how old the uniform is. I, too, stand erect and look straight away. I smell Italy, smell the past in the burning uniform. There is something official in a government issue, isn't any ordinary import. No, not at all, it's something special, something I sense can't be bought, something of merit, abstract yet concrete but not canned pasta *con sarde* or anchovies, Romano cheese, or Pompeii Olive Oil. No, it is something fine, all right, and I know it by the way he consumes it with his eyes.

"Throw it in, Franchito."

"No, I want to keep it."

"I'd like to keep it, too, but we better burn it."

"Nonno, it's such a beautiful cap."

And it is. There is a shiny brass insignia over the visor, which protrudes straight, as if it, too, is standing at attention, defying the sun. It's a most beautiful cap.

"No, we must burn it, Franchito, throw it in."

It's the first time I see tears in his eyes. Maybe that's why I feel close to him, like part of him, like never before. Every child knows how it feels to cry. A child is always alone when he cries, all alone, and Nonno seems so alone with the fire at his side. He'd always been stoic, unwavering, never flinching. I watched him rub my grandmother's arm with an alcohol sponge and plunge the needle of the adrenaline syringe, rubbing off blood oozing from the puncture.

"No, no, Franchito, you're Americano by birth, and someday, no doubt, you'll wear America's uniform, the one with the eagle. You won't need this one. Countries are self-righteous, you know. All have uniforms and play games. All have something to hide."

"I play war games now," I say.

"I know." He resists a smile.

"They won't deport you, will they?"

"What? Where did you hear that word?"

"Papa said he's worried because he doesn't have American papers, and the FBI went to my uncle Vincenzo's last week and took away his short-wave radio. He said if they find anything Italian they'll deport him."

"You don't have to worry, Franchito. You're Americano, Americano, understand?"

"Yeah, yeah, *sonno* Americano, *sonno* Americano." I jump up and down and then spin around. "A real Americano, right? *Tutto* Americano."

Stepping between the fire and me, he says, "That's right, Americano."

I don't understand fear, deportation, confiscation, and I certainly don't understand ambivalence.

After awhile, he says, "Like Italy deserted its people, I desert her. Throw it in, Franchito, throw it in."

He snaps the cap off my head and tosses it in the fire. He stokes the fire with his foot, jumping back when it flares. When the fire dies, brass buttons are all that remain in the carbonized sand.

In the kitchen, he raises a glass of wine above his head as if to say *salute*, but says nothing. We listen to a mockingbird chirp high up in a mango tree.

He was an old man when I met him, always with a full head of white hair, square jaw, and straight nose, not beaked like Papa's or other Italians. His is a ruddy complexion, and he tells me he was a redhead when young. Freckles run up and down his arms testifying to it. Frustrated, I'd given up trying to rub them out sitting on his lap. He's rotund like most Sicilian men who eat lots of pasta. I never see him do physical work, blames reluctance to the outdoors on sun-sensitive skin.

Sometimes I tag along when he goes to Ernesto's café. I love walking down the hill holding his hand, balancing myself on a block fence as if walking a tightrope. I call the slope a hill, but there are no hills where I live. It's a gradual incline in Florida flat land on Nineteenth Street, just north of Twelfth Avenue. There, I watch bicycles zoom with frozen pedals. Inside the café, he idles away the years.

The café fascinates me. I feel its cavernous coolness inside and love the evenly spaced metal poles that support the awning outside. I transform the poles into merry-go-rounds, grabbing and running around each one, ignoring vagrants who sleep on the café's benches.

A radio sits at the end of what to me is a long bar. There are no jukeboxes, pinball machines or risqué calendars or condom dispensing machines. It's an old man's café by anyone's standard. There's nothing inside to disrupt old age. A Regulator clock hangs on a back wall. Each tick is a dot on a domino's face. Oh, it's a hell of a place. The odor of stale whiskey and beer slaps my face each time I walk in. I shake it off and run and skid on sawdust, coming face to face with a stand-up electric fan, and in winter the odor of kerosene fills my nose.

Tables form a maze. The men's restroom is out back where cigar and cigarette butts float in a commode. There is no women's restroom. The men know it's a man's world. A worn bar is robbed of varnish along the edge, and a string of barstools hugs its length. A scuffed brass rail rims the base. Sandwiched between bar and wall is a bald-headed Cuban who pours whiskey into squat jiggers, then wipes the bar down with a dirty towel. He floats shots and beer bottles to customers whose hands go up like first graders yelling, "*Un* whiskey." Behind the bartender are dusty bottles of Calvert's and Four Roses and a few Petri wine gallons. It seems well stocked with more than there is because a wall mirror serves as a backdrop.

Old Cuban cigarmakers prop up sour mash, and some, like my grandfather, wall themselves off behind domino walls. Underneath tables, I watch feet rearrange sawdust soaking up tobacco splats. As humble as the place is, it provides old men respite from spouses who have grown stale on them. Dominoes slap tabletops and argumentative old men scratch shrinking balls. Now and then, one looks at me and says, "*Cómo esta,* Franco?" Oh, it's a hell of a place, all right—a hell of a place.

Nonno grins, unleashing dominoes. I know domino is his game, not because he plays it well, but because his name is Domenico. It's so natural that Domenico should play dominoes. Dominoes are dense and ponderous, a cross between noisy dice and silent cards. I don't know how to read numbers yet, but I count dots. Dominoes are toy blocks I never own, so I build houses and garages when the old men take breaks. Dominoes are smooth, slick and so innately Sicilian.

I love hearing echoes when the men wreck the dominoes, spinning them out of control. Old men dig in, scramble them facedown like over-light fried eggs. A new game begins.

Oh, this grandfather is different, all right, doesn't roll cigars anymore, and my family berates him behind his back. "Doesn't want to work," some say, "…lets his sick wife support him." He's a sedentary man, cerebral perhaps, possessing darker and thicker gray matter than the run of the mill Sicilian. He loves whiskey and drinks straight shots. I watch him slug them and see his face turn red.

The café is Latin with none of that milk toasty stuff I hear exists outside Ybor City. For every action there is reaction even into old age.

My grandfather smokes large-ringed cigars. The diameter of cigars is measured in ring size, the thicker the better. He holds them with a full set of teeth. When pondering a domino move, the cigar hides its burn. Barely visible helical spirals of smoke telegraph it's still alive.

He's a master at slipping paper rings off cigars, too, slips them off without injuring the delicate leaf. Children of the ghetto love cigar rings. It is our cigar experience. I rejoice in the ornate bands of Bering, Perfecto Garcia and Garcia y Vega. I marry into cigars early, in more ways than I know.

My grandfather hasn't worked since fifty. He was fired from the factory for testifying against a *capotasso*. He witnessed the automobile collision and refused to falsify his account. That's what Mama said. The Great Depression hit, and my grandfather no longer rolled cigars, gave up on life, rolled out permanently.

I see him fade physically, and I realize there is no permanency in being a grandfather. Grandfathers go first—introduce children to death. At best it's an evanescent position without tenure, glory or payback.

The day I watched his uniform burn was the day our lifetimes merged, but I wouldn't realize it until I was grown. He never spoke of Mussolini, his uniform or the Italian Army again. He was naturalized an American citizen and went on to teach me the multiplication tables in Italian. There was no internment of Italians where I lived, but we heard some were imprisoned on the west coast—sardine fishermen in Monterey, California.

14

September arrives, acorns turn brown, and V.M. Ybor Elementary School is slated to take me on in first grade. The school passes itself off as an institution of higher learning at certain times of the year. Naturalization classes flourish in the evenings during the war years. Papa says he's going to be an American, but when he's sworn in, I see no difference, no difference at all.

"Who was America's first *presidente,* Filippo? Where is the *capitolo*?" Mama says in broken English. They're all questions I'll soon be asked, too, making first grade déjà vu.

If Papa answers Washington every time, he'll ace the exam, correctly answering: who chopped down the cherry tree; which American wouldn't tell a lie and whose face is on the dollar bill? It isn't much of an examination, and Anglos ridicule Latinos, scoff at our ignorance, but Latinos don't care; it's our Americanization. For immigrants it's the test of a lifetime.

Mama says, "Next week you go to Ybor School, Franchito, *la scola*, understand?"

"Me?"

"Yes, but first you need to learn to say water and bathroom."

In Sicilian I say, "I don't know how."

"Franchito, say it—waaaater—baathroom, say it after me slowly."

I mimic my first words, say them with expression, for that's how Mama believes English should be spoken, with unmitigated feelings, touching every vowel with the tip of my tongue. I'm told to have no fear, for schoolteachers at the school have no problem with accents. All children have one, Spanish or Italian.

"Mama, how about if I forget and pee my pants?"

"We'll practice all week, Franchito. Just make-believe I'm your teacher. Each time you're thirsty or need to go, you tell me in English."

There's no reprieve. I learn words promising to emancipate me, words more practical and more important than Papa and Mama—bathroom and water. Each time I drink or she gives me a bath, water assumes the importance of baptism. It washes the Italian out of me, and it's said I can survive on water alone, and with bathroom it'll be a cinch. I train hard, and it's like toilet training all over again. She assures me I'll make it through.

"Want waater? Go to the baaathrooom?" She hovers at the kitchen sink and lingers in the bathroom after I'm done.

The more waaater I drink, the more I say baathroom, more training she gets in.

"But Mama, I don't want to go."

"You can't get along in America speaking Italiano. What's the matter with you, want to write your name with an X like your grandmother?"

"But, Mama, nobody talks Americano, nobody."

"That's right, Franchito, but you're going to learn. We live in America, so your name is now Frank, not Francesco. That's what Papa put on your birth certificate."

"But nobody calls me Frank. I'm Franchito, right?"

"Well, that's Frankie in Italian, close enough."

"I thought you said I was named after my grandfather?"

"Yes, but not on your birth certificate. There, you're Americano, understand? You're lucky you have an Italian and American name. We did it so children won't make fun of you. That's what your aunt should have done with your cousin Vincenzo."

"So, what's my name?"

"Don't change the subject."

Monday arrives and my cousin Junio runs downstairs. "Ready to go?" he says in Sicilian.

Thank God he's going, too, I think, lends credibility to my fiasco. Grandfather Domenico appears out of the blue like Japanese "zeros" will in Pearl Harbor that coming December, but today I'm the target, and I'm not ready to walk the last mile.

"I need more practice, Mama, more practice."

"You're ready."

I dig my feet into the sidewalk. "Forget it, I'm not going."

She loops a belt. "You're going. Here, sniff it."

My nostrils flare. "I smell it, Mama, put it away."

"You are going, understand?"

"I don't want to."

"See, your cousin isn't crying."

"You want to go, right, Junio?" she says.

He nods.

"Say, no, Junio! You don't want to go! What's the matter with you?" I cry.

My cousin is unaffected, maybe understands Mama has no jurisdiction over him, or maybe his parents preprogrammed him with a belt before they left for work. A combination of a belt whipping and short pants is devastating. I realize my world, as I know it, is coming to an end, and my grandfather is participating in my day of infamy. There is more to fear than fear itself—there's first grade. Tears dry as my grandfather walks us to school.

First day ends and Mama stretches out on the tobacco-colored sofa after work, taking a breather before cooking pasta.

In Sicilian she says, "Franchito, did you like school?"

"I didn't understand the teacher," I say.

"Is she nice?"

"*Sì*, her name is Miss Salas." I play with my Snoopy toy dog on the floor.

"That's nice."

"I learned a new word, Mama." I run to the sofa and stand proud.

"Oh? How nice." She rakes my tangled hair.

"Yeah, now I know three."

"Say them for me, Franchito. I knew you'd learn. Say them slowly."

"Baaathroom, waaater and fuck."

She erupts into the sitting position.

"Mama, what's fuck?" I say.

"What?"

"*Sì*, fuck, fuck, fuck. Cuban boys told me to go around yelling fuck, fuck, fuck. Miss Salas made me stop."

"Don't say that word again, or I'm going to get out the belt."

"But, Mama…"

I learn the little word scribbled in the boy's room and desktops is omnipresent, perhaps even omniscient. It substitutes grammatically for adjectives, verbs, adverbs and nouns. The old school is foreboding, and I fear it like no other, ruining Sunday evenings in anticipation of Mondays. The building stands motionless except for its flag at the corner of Columbus Drive and Fifteenth Street. I look up at the stoplight waiting to cross, and El Reloj Cigar Factory's clock looks over my shoulder, bearing witness to my enlightenment. I know Mama is inside rolling cigars so we can eat.

The school stands catercorner from a filling station pealing off gasoline from glass-gallon pumps. A green Sinclair Oil dinosaur hangs from a stucco portico as motorists sit in cars waiting for shatterproof glass, turn signals and air-conditioning to be invented. Service station attendants wipe windshields clean. Water and tire pressure checks are a given, and oil dipsticks, like fever thermometers, are wiped clean before being shoved underneath hoods.

Walking to and from school, I memorize house numbers, don't know where missing ones go. Numbers fall out between houses, on the aside like Shakespearean soliloquies. Even ones fall out on one side, odd ones on the opposite. I see the same buildings sequence *Day In And Day Out,* and that's the name of my first grade book. People sequence, too, affixing themselves to front porch swings and chairs like numbers.

I believe the school ageless, an Egyptian pyramid. Inside I learn to count numbers imported from Arabia and Rome. El Reloj's clock with its four-sided face follows me everywhere I go: north, south, east and west. It stands sovereign, standing up to the compass winds, thundering on the hour. I learn to tell time audio-visually. In the playground or in the streets, the clock is seldom out of sight. The neighborhood and everything in it is permanent, no one leaves. Old people move on simply because they grow old. Latin cemeteries back up to the *barrio* to pick up the dead. No one really leaves. They merely rearrange themselves.

It's a time when garages stand detached from homes. They stand aloof shading vintage cars. The neighborhood survived a Victorian period that mixed the scent of sweet basil and fennel with the ammonical odor of urine. Outhouses near alleys demanded open door policies, but that is now all part of the past.

There're two schools, tuition laden Our Lady of Perpetual Help, and public or free school, V.M.Ybor Elementary, home of the brave. The latter is the populace choice. Anything free wins hands down. Ybor school is of lesser prestige, lesser academic standing and devoid of religious constraints.

In second grade Mama helps me with lessons, reading about a boy named Jerry, and his sister, Alice. Alice and Jerry live in a home with a picket fence, driveway, lawn and a stay-at-home Mom. There are pictures of apple pies cooling on windowsills. Their dad wears a necktie and cardigan sweater to breakfast and dinner and is slim. He reads newspapers in an easy chair.

They feed a dog, named Spot, and my cousin and I watch Spot run. He lopes across the pages, and every other word asks us to watch, and we do. I'm told we can't afford a pet, so I live inside pictures, and there, I pat my dog and smell apple pies. Brown grocery bags make fine book covers, keeping images fresh and crisp, assuring my parents they don't have to pay for damaged books.

"Mama, will you help me with reading?"

"Only after we cut coupons. Cónte Luna pasta boxes, Franchito," she says.

"But that will take all night."

"No. There aren't so many. I want to pick up a prize Saturday."

She never dumps an empty pasta box. Instead she tears off pieces and sets them aside. We eat lots of pasta, so we go through boxes like smokers go through cigarette packs. There're a couple of coupons on each Cónte Luna box, and I've seen her cut them out late into the night. Cónte Luna means Count Moon, like the villain in Verdi's opera *El Trovatore*. Moon faces are cut out like apples are peeled; except peeled off a cardboard sky. She stacks cardboard moons and binds them with a rubber band.

Pictures of green stamps hang over a storefront where she cashes in her moons, redeems them like later she will redeem green stamps. That's what the store is about, redemption. Prizes from kitchenware to lamps to vases to glass figurines are there. It's how I am taught about redemption.

Mama insists I read with expression, so after the coupons are cut out and stacked, she says, "All right, Franchito, read."

"Alice and Jerry went to grandfather's farm," I say in staccato English.

"Not like that. Say it like you mean it. Don't be unsure of yourself. Repeat after me and don't hesitate."

I repeat the sentence.

"That's better, but you're going too slow."

"The teacher gives us a ruler at school, Mama, so we don't swerve. She says it's like driving. One must stay in the right lane."

"Use a long pasta box," she says.

And I do. The box works. I move in the fast lane.

"Remember when there is action—make it stand out."

I mimic her, sort of like a coloratura soprano out of control, hitting low notes booming. Words growl off the page. I worry I speak broken English like her, but I land the lead role in the class play. I say, "Humbug." A chilling one-liner the teacher says comes natural to me. I'm Scrooge, growling at more humane class-mates in the play.

Mama is my reference librarian, loves reading *Official Detective* and *True Detectives*, but it's Papa I want to emulate. He can't speak English well at all, and he doesn't read newspapers like Jerry's father or sit in an easy chair smoking a pipe or wear a necktie to the kitchen table.

"What the hell they teaching Franchito, Mary?" Papa says in Sicilian.

"Teaching him to read," she says.

"Yeah?"

"*Sì*, he's learning about Americans."

"Mary, blond, blue-eyed, tall, skinny people."

"But he's growing up in another world, Filippo."

"Yeah, but it might turn him against his people."

"Not Franchito."

"No? Look at those Italians who don't teach their children to speak Italian anymore. Think they're American."

"I don't agree with my brother. I'm the first to admit it's shameful his children can't speak Italian."

"See, that's what I mean, Mary."

"What?"

"Think they're hot shit, better than Sicilians."

"Well, moving out of Ybor City didn't help."

"Yeah, go to a Baptist church. Who ever heard of Italian Baptists?" he says.

"But Franchito is pure Sicilian."

"Hell, never know in this country, could end up marrying an Americana."

"God forbid, Filippo, don't think it." Mama stomps out of the room.

V. M. Ybor Elementary School, constructed in 1908, is my legacy, handed to me by my parents' generation. Ybor was a name I uttered early, like Ma-Ma. I join legions of Latins who attended the school, but what will it do for my generation? How will it propel my ascension, into what and where? One thing rings true; it will teach me English, and it does, and it matters, matters gravely.

Why Ybor? Ybor who? Named after someone, surely but whom? Succinct and terse, a four-letter word, so why not clarify the name, define it, do it for me if not for mankind, but do it. I never see a photograph, a plaque or a bust; if there's one, I never do. The name echoes in homes, scissors itself in barbershop haircuts, and bounces off bleachers like foul balls at Cuscaden Park.

Sicilian cigarmakers stress names, simmer them in the rhetoric of genealogy: Decidue meaning ten and two, Coniglio a rabbit, Testasicca meaning dried head and Urso a bear, and on and on it goes. Over and over, I listen to elocution.

Immigrants say, "A name is all one is born with; what he is before he puts on his pants, the pity disguised in the word *bastard* and what lingers after rotting remains." The lesson preached is, "A good name squandered is never retrieved."

But why ignore Mr. Ybor? Not worthy of mention? Wasn't Italian, so what? One thing I know, it isn't the name of a woman. Nothing is named after women. Sicilian cigarmakers aren't like the rest of America. I know that from the start, not blood related to America—like coloreds aren't related to me. I know I'm different—better but poor. My family knows it, too, and they don't need to tell me, but they do.

Late in life I learned Vicente Martínez Ybor was a Spaniard, a cigar industrial-ist. In Key West, he encountered labor unrest in 1884. Ignacio Haya, a friend of Ybor, another cigar industrialist, also encountered labor difficulties in New York City. Martínez Ybor purchased forty acres of swampland northeast of downtown Tampa, and with Haya set out to build a company town. By 1885 Mister Ybor's acquisition totaled 110 acres. The grid map of Ybor City was born.

15

Papa's going to work at the shipyard has turned out to be a landmark decision. He's making what cigarmakers call real dough. He works seven-day weeks along-side Anglos, taking advantage of time-and-a-half and double-time on weekends. There, he breaks the tongue barrier listening to rednecks yell, "Wop, come over here and give me a hand."

Laughing he tells Mama what he'd said to female workers on his first day, "Where do I go? I gotta piss."

Women defense workers snickered and some smiled. He didn't know how to say piss any other way.

Mama asks, "Well, how do you say *orinare* in American?"

Papa says, "Never found out. Piss worked just fine."

Papa's skin turns dark that summer, and his teeth shine white in contrast, reminding me of a Negro flashing a big smile. It's because the sun beats hard on McKay Bay where he works high on scaffolds, and the water below reflects the brightness of the sky. Overnight Papa becomes muscular like Rocky Marciano, not sinuously muscular but the stocky-strong typical of an Italian athlete, one with lots of pasta covering red muscles.

It is a time of Mama trying to rein in Papa's English, and cigar talk at dinner is diluted with shipyard talk, which is redneck talk. Papa replaces factory characters in conversations with American names. A man called Jessie is Papa's foreman at the shipyard, and he oversees the crew. I never learn his surname, and there is also a woman called Pearl. I hear at the dinner table Jessie and his wife and little boy are coming over for Sunday dinner, so Papa can show his appreciation for keeping him on. It's been a big adjustment for Papa after being a cigarmaker all these years and never being among Anglos.

"Fili, think those Americani will like baked pasta with crushed meatballs and cauliflower?" Mama says, stirring sauce full of meatballs early that next Sunday morning.

"Why not, Mary. All Crackers eat at home are hotdogs," Papa says. "As long as I get a bottle of Four Roses, Jessie will enjoy anything you make."

Jessie and his family arrive at noon. It is one of the rare occasions we eat in the dining room, and Papa bought paper napkins, but there are no knives on the table. We don't own place settings, only a mishmash of spoons and forks.

Jessie has a ruddy complexion, blond hair and deep blue eyes, and his eyebrows are so blond, I can't see them. He and Papa talk about shipyard people, and Jessie keeps pouring bourbon and washing it down with Bock beer Papa bought for the occasion. The two women smile at each other and say nothing, and the boy sits listlessly next to me.

Mama says, "Do you like the baked pasta?"

Mrs. Jessie, a redhead with freckles, nods and smiles.

The little boy is too little to play with me, so I ignore him. He's a rowdy kid who looks like an albino and keeps getting up from the table to manhandle Mama's delicate figurines sitting on the parlor table. Mama can't keep her eyes off him. He keeps turning the radio on and off while he fingers her figurines. He's raring to explore the rest of the house, so Mama closes the door leading to the back. She's cut off any circulation to the dining room we might have had. It's hot and muggy, and we sweat and drip into homemade chicken soup.

"I think they enjoyed their dinner," Papa says after they leave.

"You think so, Fili? She didn't eat much baked pasta."

"Mary, I don't think American women eat like Italians."

"But she's pretty plump."

"It's all those hotdogs, Mary."

"You're right, from the way she talks, I don't think she cooks much," Mama says. "Did you notice she had a shot of whiskey and drank two beers? I thought we were going to run out."

"Those American women drink like fish and smoke like chimneys," Papa says.

Mama nods in agreement. "Did you see how misbehaved the boy was?"

"Well, Mary, they live in a trailer near Plant City, so what do you expect? Jessie tells me they go to juke-joints on weekends, so hell, who knows what goes on in Cracker homes."

"He takes his wife to places like that?"

"Those Crackers aren't like Italians. They let the women wear the pants, but he gives me lots of overtime, Mary. He's better to me than many Italians that work at the shipyard."

Jessie was good to Papa. He was the first and last redneck that visited my home, but Papa was grateful to him long after the war was over.

Pearl is a name I never knew was a name. The only pearls I'd heard of were found inside oysters. Papa often talks about her. She is a shipyard worker he picks up in a carpool. Carpooling provides him with extra gasoline stamps during the wartime rationing.

I overhear Mama ask, "How old is Pearl?"

"Oh, I guess a few years younger than you, Mary," Papa says.

"What does she do working around all those men?"

"She's a welder, a good one."

"Those American women are tough," Mama says.

"Yes, she is. Lights a mean torch."

"I bet there is a lot of hanky-panky going on at that shipyard."

"Mary, she's a nice lady," he says. "She's the first one I pick up each morning."

"So she's the last one you drop off in the evening?"

"*Demonio*, Mary, she's married."

"She is? You don't have to say hell because I asked. You know I trust you, Filippo."

"I think we should go visit her husband. He just got out of the hospital," Papa says.

The following Sunday afternoon we arrive at a trailer park somewhere out west of Tampa, off Hillsborough Avenue where tall Florida pines drop pinecones and shade engulfs a doublewide. Outside the trailer, leaning on a tree, is a wrecked Harley Davison motorcycle. Inside, just inside the front door, sits a redneck in a cast up to his hip.

"Nice to meet you," they all say one at a time when Pearl lets us in.

"Philip, would y'all like some whiskey or beer?" Pearl says.

"No, Pearl, we no drink. Maybe Coca-Cola," Papa says.

"I get some. How about you, Honey?" She looks at the man in the cast.

"Just a beer."

She looks at me, too. "Would you like ice cream?"

I nod.

We sit around and grownups sip, and I spoon a bowl of chocolate. A radio plays "Red River Valley" on a drain board next to a tiny stove and sink. I see Mama eyeing Pearl, seeming to have difficulty taking her eyes off her. I've never been inside a trailer before, so I take it all in: the low ceiling, cramped space, funny looking windows and the way it rocks when Pearl walks to the other end, for it seems there are few walls separating space.

"It is so nice of y'all to come by," Pearl says, sipping a glass of bourbon and ice. "Sure I can't get y'all something stronger?"

Mama says, "No, we are okay."

The tall, thin man reminds me of the redneck that sold Papa gladioli on Saturdays, so I stare at him, but it's not him, just another tall, skinny redneck with long sideburns.

"Hope you doing better," Papa says to the man.

"So you that I-talian that takes Pearl to work?" he says.

Papa nods. "How you break your leg?"

"Takes you all a long time to get home, don't it?" he says.

"I drop off three other guys first," Papa says.

"Yeah, it's out of Phil's way," Pearl says and Mama sips her Coke.

"How you break your leg?" Papa says again.

"Can't even make love with this damn cast," the redneck says.

"But you gonna be all right, right?" Papa says.

"Yeah, I be fine the doctor says."

"So how you break it?"

"Long story, long story. Looking out for that hellion." He winks at Pearl. "Right, Babe? Just didn't see that damn bus. Hit it broadside looking back for her."

"Not my fault," she says to Mama. "He just had too much to drink. Should have never let him get on that Harley."

"Well, yes, but you was wrapped with your arms around Rufus pretty damn tight. No man likes that," the man says.

"Yeah, but Honey, I didn't want to fall off. We was doing a pretty fast clip. Besides you know you can trust Rufus."

"Yeah, but it ain't him I was worrying about," the man says.

"You ride motorcycle with your husband?" Mama says to Pearl.

"Started piggybacked on Daddy's at ten." Pearl lights a Camel and exhales a straight jet through her nose. "But Bill is not my husband, Mary."

"No your husband?"

"That's right. Had two of them, and Bill treats me better than all of them."

"That's nice," Mama says.

"Have one?" Pearl offers Mama a cigarette.

"No, thank you. I no smoke."

"You work, Mary?"

"In the cigar factory."

"Mary, you should've seen Phil the first day on the job. Asked me where he could take a leak. It was so funny, so cute the way he said it. Knew I liked him right away. All the gals did. Ole Betsy said to him, 'Want me to come hold your hand?' And he just stood there and smiled."

"Is that right?" Mama says.

"Oh, he's a lot of fun at work. We all love how he talks."

Papa looks at the man. "Yeah, I no know how say *orinare* in Americano." Papa laughs. "So I say piss." He laughs harder.

And that is what Papa does when he's embarrassed or unsure with American people, and the more there seems to be a problem the louder he laughs.

"Well, Mary, when you get a chance bring Frankie over some weekend, and I take him out on my Harley. All kids love to ride," Pearl says.

Mama smiles, nods and looks at me. I know it's a no show. I'll never ride on a Harley—like Italians don't listen to country music or Negro music. It's not what we do.

The ride home from the rednecks is eerily quiet.

After what seem miles of driving on Hillsborough Avenue, Mama says, "She's another American *puttana*, I don't care what kind of welder she is."

"But she fills the carpool and we get gasoline," Papa says.

In my culture there is no gray—"judgment" is not the Lord's. Women are *femmine oneste*, virtuous, or whores, *puttani*. Italian women cut them no slack. I never hear the name Pearl mentioned again.

It is as if there is an understanding between Mama and Papa. He does what he has to do to get gasoline rations and put pasta on the table, and Mama goes along for the ride as best as she can.

When the shipyard closes Papa never returns to work in the cigar factory. He repairs termite-riddled floors in Ybor City homes—becomes the curator of the ghetto.

16

Mama continues at Regensburg Cigar Factory, works in something called a *papori*. The word *papori* in Sicilian means boat, and I learned it not long after I learned to say Mama and Papa. Cigarmakers say they work in this boat or that, with this person or that—this so-and-so or that so-and-so. In time, I meet those I hear about, put faces on cigarmakers. At the turn of the century, it is said cigar factories numbered close to two hundred in Ybor City and West Tampa combined. Now there are less than a dozen or so in Ybor City. It is the result of a shake out in the tobacco industry because of the cigarette onslaught.

Their *papori* or boat is devoid of salt breeze, keels and dry rot. It floats without oars or sails. What cigar workers refer to as boats, in reality are long tables with straight-back chairs lined up on both sides. Hundreds sit side-by-side and across from each other in a factory, and they talk and gossip, telling each other their woes. *Papori* are compartmentalized into workstations resembling cubbyholes with desktops like one sees in libraries and learning institutions, except they're not well lit and are besmirched with tobacco scraps. The room is flanked by rows of windows on at least two sides, so as to create cross ventilation.

Bales of tobacco from Havana arrive in Tampa's port. The tobacco has been aged; allowed to mature, turned brown in field houses in the Cuban countryside. It is then baled and shipped to Tampa where it is stored in warehouses until factories call for it.

Spaniards and Cubans get the better paying jobs. Easy jobs like selecting tobacco go to those who have been taught to grade tobacco leaf. The better-quality leaf is designated for the outer wrapping of cigars, and the lesser grades become filler. Tobacco is stripped in Tampa factories. Once the sticklike stem is removed, the tobacco leaf is pliable and of a size that can be used by the cigarmakers to make the cigars. Strippers are called *despaldilladoras* in Spanish and are paid the least. I hear most are Italian women hoping to become cigarmakers.

Selectors or *rezadores* sit next to large barrels and parse tobacco for distribution to cigarmakers. Those who work the cheap *vitolas* like *brevas* and others get poor quality leaf. Upper-end cigars get premium. The leaf is doled out in amounts of twenty-five at a time. Each time a roller makes a withdrawal he or she presents a ticket, and the selector punches it. It is how factories keep track of where the tobacco goes.

Mama says, "Those *maledètti* Cubani get the best *capa*, Filippo."

"That's the way it is, Mary," he says. "Think they're going to give you the good leaf? They take care of their own."

"But what can I do if it's discolored, spotted or so dry I can't roll it? I feel like throwing it in their face."

"If you do, you better have your *machinetta* packed and ready to come home."

"I know," she says.

All conversations in my home are in Sicilian, and *maledètto* or *maledètti* means accursed or *dannato*, which literally is damned.

"But, hell, why worry about color? The *capotasso* knows you can't change that," Papa says.

"I complained, and the *capotasso* said, 'your work is good, Maria, don't worry.'"

"You're lucky, Mary. He's not a bad foreman like that Mongo at *lo* Paradiso. Mongo doesn't like Italians," Papa says. "And Italians all hate his guts."

"Panchito has been good to me. He gave me my job back after I had Franchito. But days like today give me hives, Fili—look." She bares her neck to him.

Stored tobacco is kept moist in rooms in factories to keep the leaf compliant, pliable. Cigar workers who wet it and cover it with burlap are called *mojadores* or moisteners. I've heard El Reloj's clock tower contains enough space for that purpose. In winter when the air is dry, and humidity drops, tobacco dries and becomes friable and difficult to roll.

Boncheros or bunch-makers create the innards of cigars. A right-handed bunch-maker holds tobacco leaves in his left hand and with his right aligns leaves, tips of leaves all at one end. He rolls it into the shape of a cigar on a wood block that sits on his workspace and wraps on a tobacco leaf, which binds the tobacco. He places the bunch into a slotted wooden mold made up of two blocks of wood. Each mold contains ten slots carved out in the shape of cigars. When each slot or receptacle is filled, the other half of the wooden block is slapped on and tightened with a steel press. There, *bonches* sit for a while. Empty molds are stacked next to the presses, and those full of bunches are made accessible to rollers in workspaces.

Most tobacco is imported from Cuba and is called "Havana." A much smaller amount comes from Connecticut. Cigarmakers say there is nothing better than Havana. It's something about the soil and climate that makes Havana tobacco the best in the world. It is the one they prefer to work with. When cigarmakers speak of Havana cigars they make a distinction. When it's all Havana, through and through—filler and wrapper both—they say, "*Claro, sí sí, claro es mejor*. It doesn't get any better than *Claro Havana*—Clear Havana."

Natural leaf is milder, lighter in color and flavor. There are many variations in color of tobacco. *Maduro* means ripe and is dark brown. Unsightly creases and rips at the edge of the leaf are cut out with broad-bladed knives called *chavetas*. I'm fascinated by the tools and love the feel of sharp edges. When there is a lay off, I find where Mama puts hers, and I play with them. I cut up brown paper bags that substitute for tobacco. *Chavetas* make linear marks on palms. *Chavetas* have no handles and have a bowed edge. They're simply flat pieces of steel.

Rollers or wrappers wrap bunches, and I am told each tobacco leaf adds flavor. Each *vitola* has a specific ring size, shape and length. The types of cigars or vitolas are numerous and include: Coronas, Queens, Presidentes, Rothchilds, Panetellas, Brevas and many more—upper-end cigars to cheapest stuff of all—*cherutos*—all cut to specific length with the guillotine blade of a *machinetta*. Each roller owns a blade. During layoffs they bring their *machinettas* home. The blade of the *machinetta* comes down quick and snappy with a hit of the meaty part of the palm; similar to how one hits a stapling machine. A knife sharpening concession-aire or *chavetero* sharpens *chaveta's* and *machinetta's* blades. It's an out-of-pocket expense cigarmakers incur, very much like Cuban coffee poured into their cups in their work spaces by a *cafetero*.

The cigar heads take up a wrapper's time, for each head must be smooth and rounded to pleasing perfection. After all, it is the head of the cigar the smoker tongues before he smokes the cigar, and the process itself is ritualistic with tongu-ing, rolling and licking even the shaft of the cigar. The head of the cigar is what wealthy connoisseurs snip off with fancy cigar cutters, and men in the *barrio* bite off and spit on sidewalks. Tobacco-stained splats are seen all over the neighbor-hood, common on sidewalks and floors of social clubs and cafés.

Inspection of cigars is random by *el capotasso* who struts down the aisles. Small, U-shaped wooden racks sit on top of their hutches. Bundled in ribbons, cigars in racks wait for pickup and count. Each rack holds a predetermined amount, twenty-five, but it depends on ring size. The standard of measure for the number of cigars rolled is called a *rota*. A *rota* is 100 cigars. The word *Rota* is *wheel* in Sicilian. Spanish is close—*ruda*.

Fifty cigars are called a *meza-rota* or half a wheel. The number of *rotas* made each day determines a cigarmaker's pay. Most put out a similar amount each day as if they are programmed machines and to some degree they are—machines with feelings. Fast bunch-makers and rollers are referred to as being *larga* or *largo,* depending on the cigarmaker's gender. A slow cigarmaker is referred to as *corto* or *corta*. Piecework is a numbers game. A fast roller is one that rolls over 200 cigars a day, and some make in the vicinity of 300. A bunch-maker makes bunches for two rollers.

Fast cigarmakers finish early, and relatives often help out slow ones at the end of the day. It might be a daughter, father, mother or spouse working in the same factory.

Papa told me when he started rolling cigars he rolled them "freehand," from beginning to end is what he meant. He was *bonchero* and *rollero* rolled into one. It was how he learned to make them in 1910. There were no wooden molds—did it all by hand. The introduction of wooden molds created an assembly line of sorts, making cigarmakers keep up—putting pressure on them, pitting bunch-makers against rollers and vice versa. They now had to keep up with each other while factory owners watched profits soar.

Cigar bundles are periodically picked up. Packers select cigars that blend in color, and banders place paper rings on them. Banders in Spanish are called *anilladores*, the Spanish word for ringmakers, and are women.

Prior to the '30s, readers or *lectors* sat in chairs on top of built-up, wooden platforms and read aloud in Spanish to rows of workers below. They read newspapers from Cuba and those published in Tampa: *La Traducción*, *La Gacetta* and *La Federación*. They translated *The Tampa Morning Tribune* and read Victor Hugo, Emile Zola, Alexander Dumas, Cervantes and other socialistic writers, including Karl Marx. Italians enjoyed novels and the daily news, but they could care less about the Cuban revolution.

I only hear about *lectors*, for by the time I exist, the custom doesn't. I was told *lectors* commanded good salaries based on voice and style, sort of news anchormen of their day. There were no loudspeakers, so a stentorian voice was a must, and I was told some read with animation, thrusting themselves into the characters of novels. Workers were assessed weekly for a *lector's* salary, and a committee of cigarmakers did hiring and firing. Readers read two hours in the morning and two hours in the afternoon. In the 1920s factory owners feared incitement of strikes by the readers and outlawed them completely in 1931.

Inside El Reloj Factory, I stand in an aisle holding Mama's hand. *Boncheros* and *rolleros* sit like children in school. It's winter, but inside the factory it's warm, more like Havana. Cigarmaker faces are lit by overhead incandescent light bulbs. The dreariness of the factory makes me focus on wood floors and redbrick walls. Overhead wood beams, water pipes, and electric wires run exposed. These wires terminate in ceramic light switches. And, oh yes, tobacco—brown leaves, selected and stacked, straddle rims of barrels like cowboys straddle horses in movies.

I watch the machinations of cigarmaker hands from low down and see armpits sweat. I see why my relatives smell like tobacco, know why they smell the way they do. The pungent odor of tobacco stings my nose. There is no air-conditioning and body odor mixes with the tobacco aroma. There is no deodorant in our medicine cabinet. We have no medicine cabinet. Perhaps it is a time before deodorants exist, but the combination of body odor and tobacco is a smell I know anywhere.

Story telling and gossip is the art of the fast workers. Those who are struggling to make their *rotas*, roll and listen. Getting cigars out is what it's all about—piecework. On a good day, when tobacco moisture is just right, they make more cigars than they anticipate. They call these extra cigars *pico* and set them aside. They turn them in on a day they have reason to leave early. They are given no breaks, paid vacations or sick days. It is the ultimate quid pro quo.

Mama's laid off and she stops and chats with a woman rolling cigars after picking up her brown envelope in the front office. I'm used to seeing Mama count dollar bills and loose change on Fridays—dollar bills and cents.

She asks the woman if she's heard when those who have been laid off are going to be called back. Notification is done by word of mouth, and it works. No letters arrive, and none of us have telephones, yet no one misses a day's work. The word goes out like the pony express with cigarmakers stopping at coworker cottages on their way home from the factories.

I see Mama's workspace and see the black apron she brings home to wash. I see my godfather's moth-eaten sweater hanging on a straight-back chair. My godfather makes bunches for Mama and another roller who visits my home. Her name is Margarita. The team has been laid off for three weeks. A team is what a bunch-maker and his rollers are called. The bunch-maker is the leader of the team, for without him there would be nothing to roll.

There aren't many cigarmakers working in the factory. It's more than half empty. The New Year has brought a slowdown. It always does. Layoffs are common around Christmas and New Year's after factories fill orders. It means Mama is home for a while. I feel comfortable inside the factory, heard all about it, so it's déjà vu.

I imagine what it's like when it's running full blast. I see my mother rolling cigars in her workspace, and I listen to cigarmakers talk.

"*Hoy*, Peppino,"A *tabaquero* says to my godfather.

"*Sí*, Pedro, *che*?" he says.

"*Vas a ver los* Tampa Smokers Sabado? It's the home game."

"Hell, the Smokers are shit this year, not worth the money. Got no pitchers. I rather go see the Italian Club play the Cubans Sunday."

"El Circulo Cubano is better this year, Peppino, much better. Your homerun hitter, Joe Schiro, won't see a Fernandez fastball."

"*Sí, sí*, but Centro Asturiano hit the hell out of him last Sunday—lost 10 to 3."

Sunday afternoon at Cuscaden Park is legendary. Cigarmakers attend the Latin baseball league, which consists of the Italian Club, Centro Asturiano, the Cuban Club, Loyal Knights and MacDill Air Force Base. Each ethnic group is represented—even Anglos. The park isn't fancy with hotdogs and popcorn, but it seems big to me. It is there I see my first dugout and slurp my first ice cone doused with colored syrup.

The men in the tin-covered bleachers argue plays and root for their team, which in reality is all about nationality. They stand and scream at Freddie the empire, a Cuban, who is trying to put nationalities aside. And, when one of the younger players comes to bat and gets a base hit, a man yells, "*Esse mi hijo!*" That's just how it's said. "That's my son!"

And it's always in Spanish, even if the man is Italian and, if the young player gets a homerun or makes an outstanding play, he screams his claim to fame louder. My dream is to grow up and play for the Italian Club—beat the hell out of the Cubans, Spaniards and Gringos that play for MacDill, but for now catching foul balls in the street is the best I can do. It allows me to enter free, and that makes me proud. Those of us from the *barrio* avoid admission fees at all cost. Sneaking in is the ultimate satisfaction.

"Peppino, *sonno tutti duri*," Mama whispers in Sicilian to my godfather. Bunches are packed too tightly she complains. "If the *capotasso* smokes one you're going to get hell."

"All right, I'll ease up." Turning to the other roller, he says, "How are yours, Margarita?"

"The last ones were better, but still tight."

"Peppino, you're lucky to have Maria. She's a hell of a roller. Covers your shit, and nobody is the wiser until they smoke the turds." Pedro laughs.

"*Hoy*, what about me?" Margarita says. "I cover up his shit as much as she does."

Pedro glances over the hutch that separates him from the team. "*Peros tu sabe,* I don't have to tell you, Margarita. You know you're the best roller in all of Ybor City, maybe *el mundo.*"

Margarita slaps the *machinetta* hard, chopping off the end of a cigar. "That's what I'd like to do to your tongue, Pedro, or maybe something else."

"My wife would never forgive you."

Peppino bursts into laughter. Mama looks away.

Peppino fills the last empty groove in the mold with a *bonche.* He tightens the steel press and allows it to set. Mama gives him the same look she gives me when I'm misbehaving. Mama goes back to cutting out the frayed edge of a leaf with her *chaveta.*

Mama is focused, speaks little. Her stream of consciousness runs deep. My godfather embraces gab, loves to joke, and men smoke cigars ad lib—don't give a shit. None of the women care. No one cares or complains of secondary smoke. Without smoke there'd be no jobs—no Ybor City—maybe no Tampa.

Peppino raises his hand, and the *cafetero* brings a large, enameled coffeepot, a commercial coffeepot.

"Three coffees, Santiago."

Santiago starts to pour. The *capotasso* walks up and holds out his cup. His gets filled first. "Peppino, need to fill a special order," the *capotasso* says to my godfather. "It's for a man who says he doesn't care what they cost, wants five hundred of the best, *bien?* You and your rollers will get paid extra. All Coronas in Havana *maduro*, understand?"

"Of course, *peros* all *maduro?*"

"*Sí, sí,* all *maduro.*"

The women smile, but they hate working *maduro* tobacco. Very few women smoke—only a few Cuban women do—no Italian woman that I know does. *Maduro* is more apt to make them sick.

"Who is *el gaucho grande?*" my godfather asks.

"A Mister Siberling. He owns Goodyear Rubber in Akron, Ohio. Called the office this morning." The foreman walks away sipping coffee.

"*Caramba*, can you believe that, Pedro? We're going to get paid extra," my godfather says.

Mama and I start to walk out of the factory. She has what she came for—the brown envelope. A *tabaquera* stops Mama. "*Hoy*, Maria, take some smokes to your father. With you and your mother laid off, he must be in short supply."

Men are allowed to smoke "on the house" during the course of a workday. They can smoke as many as they wish while they work. Each is also allowed a take-home quota, several *fumas,* depending on factory policy. *Fumas* are rough smokes with twisted ends. The cigar's head is not smooth nor is its distal end cut off. It is the smoke of *tabaqueros*—rough and without pretense. Non-smokers and women take cigars home to relatives who are smokers. The time will come when cigar factory owners see their bottom shrink, so they abolish take-home smokes. It is then I see the cigars inside men's shirts, bulging their sides, and when the men walk down the factory stairs at five, the cigars bounce like love handles.

"*Gracias,*" Mama says, and stuffs the cigars in her purse.

Walking home on Columbus Drive, I ask, "Mama, how come I didn't see any paper rings like Nonno Domenico gives me?"

"Oh, they're put on out back where the cigars are packed in boxes."

"Do all cigars have rings, Mama?"

"No, usually the cheaper ones don't, Franchito. Do you know the story about rings?"

"No, what?"

"I heard centuries ago cigars were banded with fine fabrics, silk and satin," she says with the uppity tone of a schoolteacher. "Royalty smoked them, even queens, Franchito. The ring or band kept tobacco stains off their hands."

Mama works in three factories in her lifetime. Her first and longest stint is at the Regensburg factory—twenty years. From there she goes on to roll cigars at two other factories—"La Pila" and "The King Bee."

The clock tower gave Regensburg & Sons Cigar Factory its identity. The city block long building was nicknamed *El Reloj* by Hispanics and *Lo Rogio* by Italian cigarmakers. Its bell, pealing on the hour, insisted I learn to tell time. Sitting on the factory's white terrazzo steps in late after-noons, I waited for Mama to come out. The chatter of *chavetas* and *machinettas* inside told me I was the son of cigarmakers. Today, the building is the home of the J.C. Newman Cigar Company.

A 1950s cigar factory with long tables called "*paporis* or boats." Mama was still working in factories then—rolled cigars for over forty years. Cigarmakers were confined to tight cubicles and hard chairs. Rows of windows created badly needed ventilation in Florida's heat and humidity. Wood beams, electrical conduits and water pipes were exposed. Women wore skirts and dresses to work, never slacks. Some men wore dress shirts. A man wearing a *paglietta* is seen in the foreground and several other straw hats are seen hanging on vertical wooden supports in the background.

A bunch-maker presses a mold, keeping the "rollers" on his team sup-
plied with the long filler of cigars. My impression was that most, if not
all, bunch-makers were men.

A roller or wrapper rolls on the outer leaf on a cigar. Her tools are a flat
steel *chaveta, machinetta* and a glass container of gum for sticking on
the leaf. An empty wooden mold is seen leaning in the upper left of the
photograph.

17

Entertainment is cheap where I live. A weekend movie is as good as it gets, but there are other things to distract my parents from cigar factories before the weekend comes.

A hot summer evening, my father says, "Mary, let's go get a Coca Cola. It's too hot in this house."

Short car trips are a respite from the heat. A Coke is always a treat, and an ice cream cone is even better. Even after they own a refrigerator they don't keep either in the house. It's a luxury perhaps they feel they don't deserve.

"Franchito, you stay with Nonna."

"No, I wanna go, Papa."

Papa parks the Chevy and walks inside Los Hilados on Fourteenth Street. He carries out three ice-cream cones, so-called triple-deckers, mixing flavors like *sapote*, mango and coconut. We never go in and sit at the Cuban greasy spoon. We take out our ice cream like Negroes do, and we lick and drip them on our clothes. He drives over a rickety Palmetto Street bridge slurping and says, "It's time to catch the bay breeze."

They sit in the car with doors open, inviting the breeze, but mosquitoes invade. I run up and down the shore catching fiddler crabs.

On the way home, in the back seat, I play with fiddlers, and I hear Mama say, "Fili, you know Olio Di Rigio, Castor Oil."

"*Ma suu,*" Papa says.

Ma suu is a combination of an Italian "but," which is said *ma*, and an American "sure." So what the immigrants are saying is "but sure." It is an early sign of Americanization, but, of course, I don't relate for a very long time.

"The *capotasso* said his work was *mierda*, shit. He smoked a cigar in front of Olio Di Rigio. It was so embarrassing to see the cigar burn so unevenly."

"He's always been a poor bunch-maker, Mary. I worked near him at *lo* Paradiso."

"I was afraid the *capotasso* would stop and look at mine, but *grazie* Dio he kept going," Mama says.

"Mary, you worry too much. Everyone should make them like you."

Mama smiles.

The thought of foremen inspecting her cigars is an affront to her dignity. It's fear of humiliation, of being reprimanded in the presence of peers. She often says, "In public, Filippo, in front of everybody."

Spaniards and Cubans practice nepotism, keep top *vitolas* among themselves. I never hear of Italian foremen—never. I hear about lots of reprimands, favoritism and gossip about women having affairs with foremen. Considering the number of men and women thrown together in factories, affairs are not a common occurrence. The women—so-called honest women—as they refer to themselves—scorn those who cheat. Being an adulteress is worse than being a murderess.

"Papa, tell me about Oilio di Regio," I say.

"Olio di Regio, oh yes. It was my brother Pedo who gave him the *juria,* the nickname. Pedo fought with him all the time as a boy, scarred his face. Pedo was little, but he didn't take shit."

"*Mischa*, Papa." I let out an Italian wow, for my uncle is short and pudgy, and it's hard to imagine him winning a fistfight.

"Yes, Franchito." He grins. "Beat the shit out of Olio Di Rigio."

"But how come you call the man Castor Oil?" I say.

"The man's tough to take." Mama cuts in. "Has a nasty personality, *brutto, brutto.*"

"Do we have a nicknme, Papa? Do people call us something ugly behind our backs?"

Mama says, "Us? No, no, not us, Franchito. We're likable people."

I sigh.

She continues, "*Jurias* or nicknames are terrible, Franchito. Look at Peditada. She's such a hardworking woman. She can't help it if she's homely. That's no reason to call her Little Fart, but people do. But Velma, oh, that Velma, she's another story. Velma deserves to be called Para Palo. I just know she puts horns on her husband. I see how Cubans look at her. Honest women don't dress like that or smile back when men look."

"What's Para Palo?" I say.

Mama dodges my bullet. A convoluted explanation ensues. I'm a fool to ask.

Castor Oil, Little Fart and Para Palo are nicknames—two Sicilian—one Spanish. "Little Fart" is a spinster, and Velma is sensual and dresses provocatively. She is called Erector of Sticks or Para Palo in Spanish, for it's said, when men gaze at her derrière, penile erections take hold. That's what *para palo* translates to—something akin to an Erector Set. It seems no one escapes. Between Cubans, Spaniards and Sicilians every one is a target for a nickname.

Most *jurias* are not complimentary and are common. They're pinned on a victim while he or she sleeps. I think it's all part of becoming American, and my people are no different than Native Americans who name children after attributes and events—Crazy Horse, Red Cloud and Sitting Bull. I shrug off *jurias*, but if my family hangs one in a closet I never know.

I look forward to Friday nights, for they have potential to link me up with America, learn more Americano. Movies play at the Casino Theatre, the second floor of Centro Español, the Broadway Theatre, the second floor of the Italian Club, and the Ritz.

Picture shows are Mama's distraction. She prefers American movies, rarely goes to the Spanish ones at the Casino playing during weekdays. She understands enough English to get by. There are no Italian movies, not even at the Italian Club's Broadway Theatre. Italian cigarmakers who don't understand English are forced to view Spanish movies.

A weekly wash sometimes interferes with movies. Mama drags a two-legged washboard from behind the gas stove and leans it inside the claw-footed bathtub.

"Mama, I thought we were going to the picture show tonight?" I say.

"We'll go this weekend, Franchito. Got too much wash to let it go until tomorrow."

"But Gene Autry is at the Ritz, and Charlie Chan is at the Broadway."

"We'll see if we can go Sunday."

The issue resolved, I play on the floor and watch short legs bend over the washboard in the tiny bathroom next to the alley. Sounds of running water and slopping clothes fill the room. There is never a washing machine or dryer in the duplex, or a faucet labeled hot and cold. A bar of Octagon Soap rubs back and forth on the corrugated wood, and, looking up, I see Mama's cellulite thighs shake, thrashing the wash. Sweat rolls down her cheeks onto the washboard. The tiny window above the toilet sweats, too, and I hear breathing. She breathes synchronously with the rub bouncing off the tub, as gray water, swirling, forms a vortex pinpointing the drain.

Upstairs, a naked clothesline awaits the wash, looping across a tin-roofed garage. Mama pulls on the clothesline, and a pulley squeaks and moves counterclockwise as if unraveling time. She flies Papa's shirts and khakis over the garage and, with wood clothespins clenched between her teeth, she peers into airspace and catches her breath. I know cigarmakers all shake and dangle like wash.

It is dollar bills and loose change she counts and recounts after spilling a week's wages out of a brown envelope with her name written cursively on a straight line. It's always counted on the oilcloth covering the kitchen table. Each

Friday evening the envelope brings out her smile, and each morning I'm reminded beauty is indeed more than skin deep, as I watch her sitting in front of a 1930s dresser powder puffing up a smile.

That Friday morning I had high hopes of going to a movie that night.

"We'll try and go tonight, Franchito," she'd said. "What's showing at the Casino?"

"*Cantinflas.*"

"Don't care for that Mexican."

"Me neither. I'd rather see Abbott and Costello."

"Me, too, Franchito. Costello is Italian, you know."

Movies are reasonable at the Casino. It's our first choice. The Broadway Theatre at the Italian Club plays old movies. The Ritz Theatre features movies trekking down from downtown, but it's more expensive by a few cents, so it's third choice.

It's cool inside theaters. In summer, children camp in for nine cents a day.

"Mary, what did they say?" Papa says to Mama while watching a movie.

Mama keeps him abreast of what's happening. Hushes in Spanish quash Papa's desire for the plot.

After the movies, Papa drives us home, and Mama translates the movie in detail.

"Oh," Papa says. "I couldn't understand it because those damn Cubans were making so much noise."

I understand American movies, understand their plots, but I never quite understand my people's struggle. I accept my relatives are all cigarmakers, accept it for what it is, the way it is. I never see the assault to their dignity. It's illiteracy pushing them through wide factory doors.

18

It's never Mass Papa attends on Sunday mornings, but it's a sanctuary nonetheless. Facing north, the building stands on the southwest corner of Seventh Avenue and Eighteenth Street. It boasts no pews, holy water, incense or bell tower to rein in its flock, yet I see the faithful gather en masse, rushing as if they're late for nine o'clock Mass. My father holds my hand, and we hurry along a narrow sidewalk leading to a set of double glass doors. From the sidewalk, I get a glimpse of the *cantina*, a dugout subbasement below street level. There, I see men lined up at a bar as if awaiting the Eucharist, but no priest ever comes.

I'm six years old when I start going to L'Unione Italiana or the Italian Club with Papa. I go as regularly as any six year old can be expected to. The club molds me early, defines my existence—lets me know how I am to be when I grow up. I stretch my eardrums and hear the chatter inside.

It's a four-story building made of brick, and the windows in the *cantina* face east, look out to Eighteenth Street. Behind the building, a stretch of coal-laden tracks run east and west, and a little behind the tracks shacks rattle to the rumble of trains. Up front, at the main entrance, four white Corinthian columns hold up a Pantheon parapet, and from the face of what looks like first century Rome protrudes a gaudy 1920s neon marquee. Above the marquee, riveted into brick, protrudes a large, vertical neon sign. It reads BROADWAY THEATRE. The movie theatre shares a common entry with the *cantina*. It is there Papa parks me for nine cents on Sunday afternoons, and I watch a double feature, serials, cartoons, and an RKO newsreel while he plays billiards downstairs in the *cantina*.

Men socialize in the *cantina*, organize their thoughts and shoot at what they call "shit." Standing next to Papa in short pants, I watch men stand at the bar, sit at card tables and rim billiard tables.

Men stand out front, too. Some lean against the building, and others sit on window ledges, dangling legs like their lips dangle cigarettes. Others treat themselves to Negro footrests, homemade wooden shoeshine boxes that hang off black shoulders with slings made from discarded black belts. I listen to the taut rag of a barefooted black boy pop again and again as if he's playing ragtime. His knees protrude through torn jeans and scrape on dirty cement. He taps on the man's shoe when he finishes the first shoe. Leaning back, still kneeling, he waits for the shift. He gets no response, so he taps on the man's sock. When that fails he taps on the pant leg as if afraid to touch white skin. The man shifts his feet, and when both shoes are shined, the boy says, "Shined them up like new—yess, surr, Mister, yess surr, yess surr—like new."

The boy looks up and puts out his hand.

The man says, "You missed a spot, boy. Hit them again. Hit them good this time."

The man grins.

The boy looks down at the man's feet, and I see him grimace, but he revs up and pops the rag again and again, and I smile thinking it all grand.

That's what the club is about, hanging around, hanging loose and scratching balls. Some spit pinpoint between their front teeth, spit downward, between knees. Others suck up succulent postnasal drips and bazooka them at the street. Inside, those playing *scopa*, a Sicilian card game, lift their heads. I hear them yell out numbers I don't understand. Some say, "*Porco* Juda." Take Judas' name in vain. Some sip Coca Cola, but most drink Cuban coffee. I realize most are lifers watching me grow up.

The Italian Club is similar to the Spanish and Cuban clubs farther west on the business strip: Centro Español, Circulo Cubano, and Centro Asturiano. Not all are on Seventh Avenue but in the vicinity. All have *cantinas*, and are places cigar workers go to slap dominoes, flip cards, miss urinals and hit defenseless restroom floors. Papa goes to the Italian club after dinner and weekends, making me think that's what all men do. It's a manly place and smells like men.

Papa and I walk up to a game table. A grandfatherly man grins. I smile back.

"Filippo, is the boy in school yet?" the man says in Sicilian.

"*Primo grado.*" Papa prods me front and center—between him and the man. I grab Papa's hand.

"Learning to be Americano, eh?" The man folds his cards, folds his hands and shifts to English.

"You talk Americano, *pechoto?*" he says to me, stressing the word *pechoto*. His English is thick with an accent that in time I learn to ignore.

Boys are *pechotos* and girls are called *pechotas* when adults don't know our names.

Papa squeezes my hand. I turn to the man and say, "*Si, signore.*"

"Tell me what school you go to, boy."

I say, "V.M. Ybor." I look up at Papa.

"What is the matter with you? Look at me when you talk. No you like school?"

"Yes."

"Yessa? Is that all you know how to say? What your name is?"

"*Mie nóme* Frankie."

He parks his cigar in an ashtray. He's not just running in and running out. I know I'm being interrogated, so I scribble on sawdust with my foot and avoid eye contact.

"*Sonno* in first grade. My *maestra* is Mrs. Salas."

The old man is a fixture at the club, always sitting at the same table. He reaches into his trousers and hands me a nickel. "Go get yourself a cold drink, Franche. Keep up the good work."

"He's gonna be *differente* than us, eh, Filippo?" The man shakes Papa's hand, and I finger my nickel.

"*Sì*, but it's all up to *la ventura*."

Ventura is a word from the stem word *vento*, meaning wind. Cigarmaker lives hang out like wash in the wind. It's left to *la ventura* or wind to give direction. *Ventura* also means fortune. Italian cigarmakers pray for good luck, *buona sòrte* and *fortuna*. They hang their dreams on randomness, knowing Lady Luck deals from a stacked deck. Papa hopes life will be different for me, but I am just another roll of the dice, and I'm too young to know—too young to understand the meaning of snake eyes.

"Filippo, want to play a few hands?" the man says in Sicilian.

"*Grazie*, but I'm going to play *bigliardo*, billiards."

Papa and I walk over where a man shoots solitaire pool.

The man gathers balls and places them in a triangle when he sees Papa.

Slotted cue sticks cling vertically to a shellacked wooden rack, and long lamps illuminate green tables that simulate lawn. Papa selects a tapered stick and chalks its tip as if he's sharpening a pencil. He leans over the table, aims one way then another. He slides the smooth stick through his hooked finger resting on the table's bulky edge. He slides it back and forth like I do my pencil in school. Satisfied, he stretches, cocks his head and breaks the triangle. The report startles me, and I watch electrified balls scatter, bounce off each other—three sink, but the eight ball survives. Papa racks up as I sit on a bench against a wall and drink a very good Coke.

The Italian Club is more than a social club. It provides health care to its members. Medical clinics are held above Lodato's Pharmacy next door. Cuban and Spanish doctors show up several times a week, mostly Cuban. It's where Mama takes me when I'm sick. I climb with old cigarmakers and immigrants who were too old to make cigars when they emigrated from Italy. Women and men climb up the steep flight of stairs, challenging old hearts that beat next to mine. At the top I see them catch their breath and slide their buttocks on burnished benches. In the hallway they sit under a skylight. They wait to be seen by a doctor or to get a shot from the nurse. They look up at the skylight and see what's left of blue skies.

Waiting for medical verdicts, I hear a man say, "What was your blood pressure, Gaetano?"

"240 over 110."

"Hell, that's what Vito was running before he died."

Another breaks in. "Could be worse. I got the sugar."

"Yeah, but I got the chest pain. These damn steps bring it on every time. But I got to come get my nitroglycerine, helps me cope with the *capotasso.*"

"You better cut back on pasta."

"I rather die."

And they do.

The club members compare symptoms waiting for Jesse, the nurse. She calls out numbers like a fishmonger, "*Cinco, sette, diciassette.*"

She's not a registered nurse, but she wears a starched uniform and a white cap and gives shots. Numbers are handed out when the patients check in. They're written in pen on cardboard squares. The card I hold has number eighteen and is frayed. They all are.

Italians are asked to urinate in glass jars and are examined behind frosted glass doors. I see shadows undressing inside. The same doctors, *medicitos,* "little doctors," make house calls. They're not thought of as legitimate like American doctors. Italians know they're not getting first-class care, but Cuban nationals come as a package deal with the cost of the club membership. The mustachioed men, in flowing Cuban shirts, drive Cadillacs and bounce in and out of *casitas* and shotgun homes with black bags at their sides. Hospitalization occurs at Centro Asturiano and Centro Español Hospitals, and if a doctor's therapy fails, plan "C" kicks in. The cemetery plan, a consolation prize—a free cemetery plot at the L'Unione Italiana Cemetery. Plots are dug up on a first come basis. I'm a card-carrying member of the Italian Club since birth, but I don't worry, for it seems it's a day that will never come.

There are times I run fever.

"Got a sore throat, Mama," I say in Sicilian.

"Let me feel your forehead."

"Got the *maledètto* fever again."

"Do I have to stay home?"

"I'll give you a dose of castor oil before I go to work."

"Do you have to?"

"You know it makes you feel better."

"But that stuff is terrible, Mama."

"You've missed too much school with those sore throats. You're going to flunk first grade."

It takes a week or so of missing school before Mama gives up on home remedies. Then Papa goes next door and phones the Italian Club to send a doctor. When the Cuban comes, and I fail to improve, Papa calls Doctor Torretta, one of our own, one of a kind.

Doctor Joseph Torretta is pudgy and soft. I can tell he eats lots of pasta. He wears a dapper pencil-thin mustache on his leonine face and dyes his hair. I see red hues in the waves of black hair and white flecks at the hairline. He smells strong of Old Spice. He's my father's age, and he grew up on Eighth Avenue, too, but men in the *barrio* don't color their hair and don't wear aftershave. Lo Dottóre, as my parents call him, is first generation and graduated from Tulane Medical School. He lives in a fancy part of town, Davis Island, where suburbanites drive over a short bridge and park Cadillacs in driveways. He sports a big M.D. logo on his car tag, and he and his wife appear in the society page. Italians marvel at the expansiveness of the American dream. "Did you see Dottóre Torretta and his wife at the Gasparilla Ball? They had a picture of them in *The Tampa Morning Tribune* on Sunday."

"Did you see her gown?" another says.

Torretta is a general practitioner but performs surgery, delivers babies, sees kids, too. He's a hell of a doctor. He has no limits—turns nothing down. He comes to my home after office hours. A tongue depressor sticks out of his vest pocket. It stands tall and mute—wooden. And the low-set ears of his stethoscope dangle like a hangman's noose. His fingers on my pulse are viselike.

He sticks a mercury thermometer under my tongue and asks me to say ahh.

I say it in the key he demands, for if he isn't satisfied he'll roll me over and ram the thermometer up my ass.

"It's forty-one degrees, Mary, real high, and probably higher at night," he says. "Frankie, say ahh. That's right, ahhh," he lifts my chin.

"Aaa-ahhhaaa," I say, looking at his thin mustache.

"Dottóre, it's been high for over a week. I gave him castor oil twice," Mama says.

"That's good, Mary."

"Ironed his chest once."

"What do you mean?"

"Rubbed Vicks Self and Musterole on his chest and back, then pressed with a hot iron."

"You got to be careful, Mary."

I never understand Vick's Self, and it is years later I hear the radio advertise Vick's salve.

"I'm careful. Only nicked him once, Dottóre. See the scar on his throat?"

"Only once," she said to Torretta, but there are close calls when I'm on my back like an ironing board with eyes glued to the ceiling and nose stinging from Musterole.

Watching the two of them, I relive the experience while lying in my bed. How can I forget being branded?

Mama says, "You're going to get a treatment for that cold, Franchito. Stop it from going into pneumonia."

"Do I have to?" I say.

Mama plugs an electric iron into a socket next to my bed. She loosens the cap on a Musterole jar.

"Okay, on your back," she says.

The odor of Musterole stings like Chinese mustard. Mama smears it on my chest then places a woolen cloth over it and picks up the hot iron.

"This will get the congestion out—break up that phlegm."

I lay still, afraid to move, looking up at the shiny face of the iron coming down, landing on my chest. Its tip swerves this way and that. It's hard to see the iron from my vantage point, but the penetrating heat betrays its location. The cloth is protective, but, if she pauses, the heat breaks through. I sense wide turns under my chin—cocksure and more reckless—she drives the iron.

I say, "Mama, you're awful close to my neck."

"Don't worry. Be still!"

"It's hot, Mama, please."

"Got to be hot to do any good."

She presses on. The cloth is all that separates me from her branding iron. She continues to iron out congestion like wrinkles, so I say, "It's real hot, Mama."

All I see is a determined face.

I sizzle, feel pain, and I inhale burnt flesh. I yell, can't grab her hands for fear of burning mine. I can't sit up.

She freezes. My pain intensifies. She regains composure and places the iron on an asbestos pad on the seat of the cane back chair next to the bed.

She's beside herself, apologizes to the Virgin and her mother. "Madonna—*Mama mia—perdona.*"

Then I lie on my stomach and she presses my back.

Three weeks later the scab falls off, and I feel like I sport the sign of Zorro.

"Yes, it was only once she nicked me, but I fear the iron after that. However, her enemas and laxative treatments are even worse.

She greases a black nozzle with Vaseline and sticks it up my ass. She holds an enameled can above her head. It's filled with soapy water that runs down a rubber hose into my ass. When the water level drops to near empty, she says, "Hold it, Franchito, hold it."

"It hurts bad," I scream.

"A little longer. Just a little more to go."

"I can't! I can't!"

The chamber pot waits bedside.

I hope Doctor Torretta will intercede, and be my Savior.

"I don't know how much good ironing does, Mary. Maybe it's better to stick to laxatives and enemas," he says.

I don't know if I should cry.

"I gave him two enemas with Octagon Soap," Mama says.

"Lux Soap works as good and is gentler. Octagon is abrasive, made to take out grime. But you have to do it until it comes out like spring water."

"I think he cleaned out," she says. "He held close to a gallon, but I stopped when he passed out."

"Mary, has the boy been eating?"

Food at last, I think.

"Not since the fever. Give him water and Coca Cola."

"That's okay," he says. "Starve a fever."

"I stir castor oil in orange juice and add baking soda. It makes it fizz," she says.

"That's good, gets the job done."

"This morning I gave him Milk of Magnesia to refresh his stomach," she says.

"That's good. When the fever breaks, start him on broth—later add baby pasta, *pastina.*"

Body language terminates the house call. Doctor Torretta closes his bag and leans back in the chair as if he's the one who's had a hard day.

Papa pulls out his wallet. "*Quanto*, Dottóre?"

"For you, Fili, *Cinco scutti.*"

Papa hands him a five. The doctor sticks it in his pocket and shakes Papa's hand.

"*Grazie*, Fili. Wish all my customers were like you."

"Dottóre, if the fever doesn't break should I give him Epson salts?"

He nods in her favor.

The Italian Club on the corner of Seventh Avenue and Eighteenth Street
was more than a sanctuary for Italian men—it housed the Broadway
Theatre, always operating "in the red." There, I watched old movies
while Papa played billiards in the *cantina* downstairs. During early teenage years I snuck in and saw live burlesque. The theatre's marquee and
neon sign defaced the club's Greco-Roman facade for decades. In the
adjacent building to the right, Cuban physicians held medical clinics on
the second floor above Lodato's Pharmacy. The trolley was a way of life
in the 1930s and 1940s.

The Italian Club today. A plush ballroom rents out for wedding receptions. Low window ledges where Papa and other Italian men sat and "shot the breeze" are freshly painted white. The stage where Enrico Caruso sang is still inside. The Broadway Theatre's garish neon sign and marquee are forever gone.

19

"What the hell you mean? You want to go out with a damn Cuban." I hear my Uncle Pedo yell in Sicilian.

It's summertime, and only a screen door separates me from his parlor. I see movement, but not detail, so I place my face against the screen in a way it smudges my nose. My eyes adjust, and I see a blurred white undershirt pacing inside.

Papa looks at Mama as if he's about to do an about-face, but Aunt Maria opens the door, and Pedo, in his undershirt, pauses. My aunt disappears into the kitchen after we walk in.

"*Vaio fachu lo café*, I'll make coffee," she says. "Want sugar?" she screams from the kitchen.

That's what women do—make coffee. Fresh Cuban coffee in demitasses is routine. Italians drink it black. In the morning they add scalded milk, yet it's never called *cappuccino*. I never hear the word. My parents sit on the edge of the sofa and ease back. I watch body language take over. It telegraphs their thoughts. Sitting on the edge means a short visit—leaning back means we're here to stay. Coming back to the seat's edge signals they're ready to leave, that is, if they don't filibuster on their feet. Discussion as to the merit of Cuban coffee's taste and price is common. They don't make a big deal about caffeine. No one mentions it. After all, it's what makes coffee, coffee. I enjoy tasting something other than Mama's Naviera brand. It's like having Pepsi instead of a Coke. All coffee brands lubricate Sicilian tongues—all speak at once. They're always intent in getting it all out, but today there is trepidation inside the room.

"Fili. *Uno momento*." Uncle Pedo acknowledges Papa with, "Just a minute."

"It's just a school dance, Papa." My cousin Frank grips the sofa's armrest.

Pedo says, "All those nice Italian girls and you want to go out with a Cuban. What's wrong with you? You've been taught better than that. *Porco* Juda, open your eyes."

"But she's only half Cuban; her father is Italian—Russo." Frank's head is cocked, measuring distance and trajectory. His eyes implore my parents, but there's no intercession.

"Doesn't matter. The mother is Cuban, and the girl will be like her. When you look at the girl you should see her mother. The whole factory knows about her *querido*." Spanish kicks in.

Querido is the Spanish word for paramour.

"What?" Frank says.

Frank's mother cuts in. "*Tu che sa,* Pedo?" my aunt says Pedo knows nothing.

Pedo's eyes aim at Frank. "Next, you're going to tell me you want to go out with *una* Americana."

"Papa, I'm just taking her to a dance, that's all. You're so old fashioned. Just don't like Cubans or Spaniards, that's all. They are not whores like Americans."

Frank wipes his face on a sofa pillow. My cousin is taking a hell of a stance. I didn't know high school boys cried, too. I take it in stride sitting next to my mother. Mama's hand eases over and pinches my thigh with steel fingers. I know what her sign language means—"Don't you ever ask to go out with a Cuban."

Her hand slides back and forth as if she's soothing me. Short pants provide endless opportunity for her to penetrate flesh, so I don't move. She never looks down. That's how it happens, on the sly, under tables, when people look the other way, leave the room, or anytime she has something to tell me covertly. I say nothing no matter what. I better not wince and give her away. I know it's Mama's way of objecting to whatever it is I'm doing, saying or thinking or whatever it is I'm not doing, not saying or not thinking. It's hopeless if I'm within reach, for it's an arm's length transaction she engages in.

"If I find out you take her, I'll break your legs." Pedo takes off his belt and loops it like all Sicilian parents do. It is just the way discipline is dealt out. Pedo's eyes blink as if he's trying to decide whether to open or shut them or stay in between. He flushes and beads of sweat gather on his brow. He ceases to blink, firing and fixing stares, glares at Frank. My cousin senses the inevitable and jumps over the sofa's armrest, running out of the parlor. Pedo gives chase, and I hear a door slam. "I'll break your legs," he'd said—the ultimate threat. It's an Italian tradition, a form of kneecapping children for their own good.

Aunt Maria says, "Filippo, talk to your brother."

Pedo's rhetoric escalates in the hall outside Frank's bedroom door. "You *figlio di puttana, somma ama bitcha,* come out." And, of course, it makes no sense, for Aunt Maria is a hell of a nice lady, definitely not a whore. I hear Pedo kick the door and sense the firestorm's back draft heading towards the parlor.

Pedo coughs a wet one, as if he's coughing up lungs. Gasping for breath, he says, "Where are my cigarettes, Maria?"

There are tons of Marias in my family and in the culture. It is just that way. There are two Franks and two Marias in the room.

She points to the china cabinet in the dining room.

"Maria, where are my damn cigarettes?" He crushes an empty pack he picked up and tosses it across the room.

"On the buffet, on the buffet. Try the buffet—look there," my aunt says.

He lights up in two shaky tries. Smoke whizzes out his nose, and the cigarette ash glows. My aunt looks at my father, and Papa and Mama exchange glances.

Papa shakes his head. "Pedo, he's just a boy, take it easy. Talk to him when you cool off. Come drink your coffee. Sit down, *reposo te.*"

"Fili, you know those Cubans. They're no good, no damn good. They're not honest like Italians. All have Negro blood. Don't forget the Cuban who married Vincenzo and then ran off with a Cuban bunch-maker. Left him with a dark-skinned boy." Uncle Pedo punctuates his feelings with his hands; a *va-fa-goo* gesture they all understand.

Papa puts his arm around his brother's shoulder. "Pedo, we don't know what went on behind closed doors. The woman married her lover and has not been heard of ever since. So maybe she made a mistake. That's life."

Pedo snorts smoke. His eyes calculate trajectory and aim at Papa.

"So, you take up for the Cuban? *Porco* Juda, against your own flesh and blood," he says. "Thank God Papa is not alive."

"No, no, Pedo, I just don't think all Cubans are bad."

Frank is still locked in his room. I hear him whimpering like babies do after a hard cry—three short inhalations followed by a prolonged sigh.

Aunt Maria walks to Frank's bedroom. "Franche, let me in. *Per favore* let me in."

Every time she says Franche, I react, think it's me she's calling, but I catch myself. Mama gives me the look that says—"Don't you dare move."

Mama repositions her hand on my thigh.

Pedo and Papa go out on the porch, and the fragrance of Pedo's cigarette lingers. I stay inside, for the human vise is playing tiddlywinks with my thigh.

The brothers return laughing, and my uncle has finished smoking his cigarette or maybe two or three. He seems relaxed—nicotined up. Pedo scans the room. The conversation shifts gears. They discuss factory characters and an Italian who was fired at the factory the previous week.

"That Mongo thinks he's hot shit, but he's a *come mierda*," Pedo says.

Papa nods, "I bet he wouldn't have fired him if he was a Cuban."

Come mierda literally translated means a shit eater, and Italians adopt the Spanish cliché, which covers all kinds of inappropriate behavior.

We don't stay long, and soon we're back in the Chevy. I have a front row seat in the back. From there I get wide-angle views in the rearview mirror. I see their faces in profile—his right, her left. I listen to one and then the other. The seat cradles me. I feel sorry for my cousin, for he never reappeared, but I bet he got it, got it good before we rounded the corner.

"Your brother has some nerve saying your nephew is dark skinned. Doesn't Pedo ever look in the mirror?" Mama says, avoiding Papa's gaze.

"When Pedo gets that way he can't think straight, Mary. That's the way short people are."

Papa is the tallest of his brothers at five feet six. Being short among Sicilians is not a stigma. Papa often reminds me it's the size of a man's balls that count.

"There are many that are dark in your family," Mama says looking out the window.

"Yes, my mother's side is dark," Papa admits.

"Well, your mother is very dark and your brother Stefano, too. Oh, and Ninida, your mother's sister, can pass for a Cuban and her daughter Lilia, too."

"I know, but the Cuban woman, my nephew's mother was especially dark, so it's not my family's fault." Papa looks in the rearview mirror at me.

"I worried when I was pregnant, Filippo. Worried the darkness on your side of the family might shade our baby. I knew there was a chance of us having a dark one, really dark. So, I prayed, but I always said as long as it's healthy, Dio, I don't care if it's dark, don't care. 'Dio, just send a healthy baby, don't care if it's a boy or a girl' I said. That's all that matters as long as it's healthy, and God blessed us. Right?"

Mama smiles before Papa can answer. "Filippo, my father had such beautiful red hair when he was young. He was not bright red but auburn, you know—a rich red. You wouldn't know it now."

"You're right, Mary, but Judas was a redhead. That's why Italians don't like redheads." Papa searches for me in the mirror, finds me and smiles.

Mama is silenced by the Judas comment.

A few blocks later, she says, "Why did your brother Vincenzo marry the Cuban? Did he have to?"

Cigarmakers intermarried, but it was not acceptable at the time of my parents' generation. A number of them lived neither in Ybor City nor West Tampa. They settled in a neutral area along the Hillsborough River called Roberts City. Diversity was never a Sicilian game.

20

At V.M. Ybor Grammar School Spanish and Cuban children outnumber Italians. Spanish words slide on the waxed floors of hallways, as I stand mute, practicing the Sicilian code of silence. In classrooms teachers insist I speak English. It's the hardest language to learn because, unlike Spanish, it has no similarities to Sicilian, and there is no place to practice it except in classrooms. I don't like how I sound, so I pantomime The Our Father and The Pledge of Allegiance to the Flag. I stand in an aisle next to a desk whose seat flips, sticks and squeaks like a stubborn toilet top. Each morning with eyes lowered in prayer, I stare at a blank floor, and out of the corner of my eyes I figure out who's present, who's absent, who doesn't wear shoes and who didn't take a bath the night before.

"Our Father who art in Heaven." Miss Salas leads the class.

"Hallowed be thy name." I have no idea what "hallowed" or "thy" are. The rhythm picks up.

Miss Salas takes no breaks. After prayer, she moves inexorably onto the flag. "I pledge allegiance to the flag…"

I can't say "A—lle—giance." It short-circuits my tongue.

"And to the republic for which it stands"—sounds good, so I lift out my heart and hand it over to America.

English words are meaningless, but I stare like a tin soldier at the stars and stripes and say, "United States of America."

The class doesn't hear me, so one day I say with enthusiasm, "Thy will be done on earth as it is in Heaven."

I do the same with the pledge of allegiance, except louder. "One nation indivisible with justice for all." I come down hard on "all."

I realize speaking American links my balls to my fist, and the prayer and the flag are indivisible in my school. My parents never pray at home, but they say they believe in a God, but whether they do or not, parents are not about to tell teachers how to do their job. I am indivisible with justice for all, so I clench my fist at my side, ready to swing if anybody calls America a whore. That's how fights start in first grade, you know—someone calls somebody's mother a *puta*, a whore, and Cuban children are always calling somebody's mother that.

School is full of catchy childhood diseases, and some children have parasites. I see ringworm and head lice commonly. One evening Mama says to me, "Franche, this is going to sit overnight on the kitchen table. Drink it when you come home from school tomorrow."

"What is it? It smells *brutto*," I say in Sicilian.

"It will rid you of any worms."

"Worms?"

"Yes, worms."

"I got worms?"

"Well, you don't know for sure unless you see them, but I know there are children with worms in your school. That's how it was when I went to school there. Worms make children listless and give stomach aches, and lately you've been listless."

"Did you ever have worms, Mama?"

"Coming home from first grade, I felt something dangling between my legs. I rushed home, and went to the bathroom. I saw a long, round worm sneaking out of my *culo*. I pulled it out."

"Yuk. I'll drink it, Mama, I'll drink it."

Culo is the name for ass, and it's pronounced and spelled the same in Spanish. It is a unisex word without male or female gender.

Mama had pureed onions like she does tomatoes when making spaghetti sauce, poured in tons of sugar, covered the jar tightly with a screw-on lid, vacuum packed a concentrate of onion breath. It takes me days to gulp the concoction. Each day she pours a glassful, and I swallow it without breathing. It will drive out the worms, I think, but I never see one. I worry about it; fear they'll start marching out of my ass in class.

In third grade I discover my falsetto voice singing "America the Gem of the Ocean," and scream my heart out to "Stout Hearted Men."

I sing at home, too, and my Uncle Vincenzo says I'm a tenor.

"What's a tenor?" I say.

"It's in the blood, Franchito, in the blood."

Uncle Vincenzo speaks of the throat as a gift. "Listen to the sweetness," he says. "Listen to how it soars, *dolce* like sugar."

"But how come you say it's sweet like sugar? It's loud." The radio is blaring.

"It needs to be loud to be felt by the audience. If Caruso hadn't smoked all those cigarettes, he'd still be around for you to hear today—the greatest voice of all time. But maybe you'll get the gift. It's your voice that must make the sound, and you won't know until it changes."

"Changes?"

"All boys are tenors, but when they get to be thirteen some become baritones, some basses, but it's the lucky ones who remain tenors."

He listens to the Texaco radio broadcast with Milton Cross from the Metropolitan Opera each Saturday afternoon, sitting in a small parlor upstairs, staring at a radio. It is from him I learn about beautiful music—the ones never sang at school. He listens to Gigli, Jussi Berling and to Mario Delmonico. He loves Italian operas—nothing German. Verdi, Puccini, Donizetti and Bellini are his favorites. Gesticulating, he stretches his neck as if it connected to his toes. I imagine the hanging light bulb in the room a microphone, and I just know he would have been a hell of a tenor if he had been discovered. I know I won't be like him, for the Italian in me is being watered down. The best I hope for is to be a weak Italian-American tenor like Sinatra or Como.

My uncle loves *Il Pagliaci* and narrates the story while Tonio's baritone voice booms the prologue, addressing the villagers in the opera as Signore e Signora.

"It's a story about a clown, harlequins in a traveling carnival. A slice of life," Tonio says in the prologue.

Zio Vincenzo hums *Vesti la giubba*, and like the white-faced clown tears as if he is the cuckolded husband of Nedda, the woman who sings, "Beautiful birds are vagabonds of the sky." Tonio sings the last line, "*La commedia e finita.*" And I see blood drip from a dagger on the linoleum.

My uncle says, "Wasn't it beautiful?"

"The man said it's a comedy, Zio?" I say.

"It is, it is the comedy of life, Franchito, *la comedia di la vita.*" He messes my hair.

I laugh with him but don't know why.

It's the way stories with beautiful music and voices end. It's the Italian way, so I learn about horns or *corni* early. Horns are worth killing for because they pierce a man's honor, which is worse than goring his heart. He says adultery is something American men take lightly and forgive.

"Americanos have no honor, Franchito, no honor at all."

Americano is a word said with disdain, and although I live in America, it is Italian morality and chauvinism I'm taught.

Downtrodden garbage men or *basurerros*, as they're called in Spanish, are examples of honest men earning their daily bread, picking up *basura,* garbage. Garbage men are Mama's props to keep me in school.

"Never quit school or you'll end up a garbage man," Mama says, but I wonder what treasures garbage men find in a rummaging day. I see them inspect garbage with a serendipitous eye. They rip off stench like gift-wrap as gentle smiles scale garbage heaps, and now and then, a man yells to his partner, "*Mira*, look what I found." And it seems like a chance of a lifetime to me, better odds than playing *bolita*.

Cubans drive garbage trucks. Rarely is the driver Italian. It's a four-man crew including at least one Negro. Dangling a cigarette from his lips, the driver, mustachioed and with kinky hair and tattooed, lackadaisically steers the truck over weeds. Weeds grow between tire paths in alleys, paths reminding me of narrow landing strips in the Belgian Congo. The driver is Bwana, all right, el Honcho, the cigarette-smoking *capo* in charge of the expedition. He is white, or at least quasi white because he is, after all, Cuban.

A man stands knee deep in garbage in the truck's bed while two groundlings follow. They keep up with the truck, tossing garbage cans up. The man on top catches the cans and dumps them. He scans and stumps the contents, scattering, looking it over, and then, rhythmically, without missing a beat, flings the cans back empty. He sings and whistles on top of the heap as garbage cans fly back and forth. Cans sound off, too, smashing to earth with a clang, and an all-white dog chorus in backyards joins in until truck and Negro disappear.

"Doing an honest day's work is better than robbing, Franchito. Better a garbage man than a criminal," Mama says.

"You don't care if I become a garbage man?"

"No, no, I don't wish that, but I'd rather see you a garbage man than a convict."

The line—"I'd rather see you a garbage man than a convict"—punches me to sleep after the bedtime stories she tells me.

She quasi reads detective stories from magazines she buys at La Económica drugstore. They are great stories, better than scripture. She doesn't actually read them, but it's her way of telling a story in black and white—black and white photos display compelling evidence that crime does not pay.

"No job is below a man's dignity," she says, as if scolding me because I'm unemployed.

"Mama, would you have married Papa if he was a garbage man?"

"Doesn't matter what kind of work he does."

"Wouldn't mind it if he came home smelling like garbage?"

"Might not like it, but I love your father."

Official Detectives and *True Detectives* magazines are replete with stories. I see her flipping pages and picking out exhibits. She's determined to make her case on me.

"Maybe nobody wants to be a garbage man, but there're those that do that work; someone uneducated that can't add and subtract. It beats robbing banks and killing innocent souls."

"Mama, I'm going to go to high school, you'll see."

"Look at this pathetic man, Franchito—killed a grocer. That's his picture at the top of the page."

I grab the magazine. "Where, where?" I say in Sicilian, always in Sicilian.

"Found two dollars in the register. Took a man's life. He thought no one would find out, but this little boy saw him. What do you say to that, Franchito?"

"There's no perfect crime."

"Right." She smiles as she drives in the nail. "Say it in Americano just like I say it," she says, so I repeat, "CRIME DOES NOT PAY."

I cut it off at "pay." The phrase seems like one of the Ten Commandments, at least, the killing and stealing parts. I derive omnipotence in self-righteousness, as if I know all there is to know about crime. She points to photos of the victim and a plainclothes detective talking to a boy. On the floor lies the body of a fat grocer in a pool of blood next to a cash register. It'd happened the way she said it did.

"Wouldn't it have been better if the killer worked for the city? He's going to get the electric chair for two dollars. Can you imagine—for two dollars? God, help us all."

Ybor City Sicilians don't know about the Ten Commandments and Moses, don't read the bible. They weigh the risk/reward ratio, and some are involved in a sundry of illegal activities, particularly *bolita*. Taking a life is unpardonable, but defrauding the government and insurance companies is not a black and white issue. Ghetto circumstances justify a sense of entitlement.

Men in the *barrio* become naturalized. Naturalized citizens qualify for Social Security, and some work strictly for cash and do not report their incomes on tax returns. Breaking the law is not always a crime, for it never is to people below the poverty line. The brutality of the haves toward the have-nots justifies petty crime. It levels a rocky field—just can't kill anyone along the way—that's all.

I never see Mama volunteer extra change given to her by an inept clerk. Instead she smiles and pockets the dime or the quarter and walks away. She tells me the purchase turned out to be a hell of a deal, so I understand some things in life are relative.

She closes the magazine.

Switching off the light, she says, "Garbage men work hard, and they do better than cigarmakers. They retire and get a pension from the city. Cigarmakers get nothing."

I am convinced it's better to be a garbage man than a killer. I really am.

21

Every Italian boy gets into fights. In my neighborhood it's endemic. Oh, fistfights in grammar school aren't main events resulting in cut knuckles, puffy eyes and broken noses, but they are fights nonetheless.

Latin children stick together, yet we fight with each other. It is a form of nationalism. Italians pit themselves against the Spanish-speaking bunch and vice versa. I make no distinction between Cubans and Spaniards—don't know how. Oh, I guess if the person is dark skinned, it is a good bet he or she is Cuban, but that isn't foolproof. Many Sicilians are dark complexioned.

Augustine Fraga is my friend. We started first grade together, and although he isn't Italian we spend hours in the playground and walk home from school together. I don't know if Augustine is Cuban or Spanish, but I make the assumption he's Cuban. It doesn't matter. He is my friend.

On a Friday, we walk home from V.M. Ybor School. Augustine and I argue. He makes his point by calling me—"*Hijo puta*," calls me a son of a bitch and flashes his middle finger at the sky.

"No, your mother," I say.

It never matters what's been said, or how close the friendship is. Once the word mother is interjected, discussion stops and fists fly.

Puckering his lips, he makes the sucking sound of a drawn out kiss. It's a sound Cubans learn to make early. It's a sound implying one is queer. And even at that young age, that implication is justification to swing.

"You bastard," I say.

We fly at each other. I knee him and send him into a dilapidated fence, sagging it further, but that's no sin, for fences stand rotten and propped up where I live.

Suddenly it doesn't matter that a six-inch scar scrolls down his cheek. It doesn't matter I'd pitied him when others called him scar-face, and there'd been times I'd seen him fingering the scar in class. I'd seen him surreptitiously looking in the mirror in the boy's room, and I saw it while lying in bed trying to sleep. I imagined the scar alive, open with glass protruding from its jagged edge.

He'd told me he was asleep when glass from the car wreck penetrated the back seat, slashing the right side of his face. But none of it matters as we tear tee shirts, scrape elbows on a sidewalk and street curb. It's a matter of honor, and I'm merely doing what my godfather said I should do, so I hit him with a barrage of punches to the midsection and fold him over like a wilted Cuban sandwich.

"Augustine, you got no chance against a *wop*. Black beans and white rice ain't no match for the power of sauce."

And black beans are the Cuban staple in my neighborhood. It seems Cubans eat them daily.

"*Conyo*," he mutters.

I catch him with a right on the side of his head.

"*Hijo puta*." Another son of a bitch stings my ears.

Insulting Italian mothers is blasphemous. Mothers are icons like Santa Maria, sacrosanct, above the flesh, sleeping with our fathers solely to keep warm. Mothers screwing are reprehensible thoughts. Stray dogs on neighborhood street corners teach us what the word really means, perhaps like Socrates taught logic to the youth of Athens. Italian women are held to a high standard, almost like the Immaculate Conception. I'm told Italian girls don't screw around, but depravity finds them in playgrounds, too. At one time or another, Italian girls learn the ways of the world.

Conyo is sandwiched in Augustine's words like commas. *Conyo* is the Cuban slang word for "pussy" and Cubans in my neighborhood can't carry on a conversation without it.

At home, my grandmother Anna says everything is God's will, but my godfather solves issues differently, says there are ways to bend God's will, even His word.

He'd said, "Don't be a sissy, Ciccio, if they don't listen speak with your fist. Leave words to God. That's His job. That stuff is okay for when you're ready to die, but for now, do what you gotta do and get in the first punch."

I didn't forget, understood it, and I loved it when he called me Ciccio like my dead grandfather. He told me life was all about big balls and family honor, so it seems it isn't me thrashing Augustine, but my nationality demanding justice. It doesn't matter Augustine is a friend, doesn't matter at all, so it's as if Lady Justice blindfolds me, and I let fists fly that Friday afternoon.

After the fight, Augustine and I walk to our respective homes not speaking, like prize fighters go to neutral corners—Augustine to Cuban parents and, no doubt, to white rice and black beans and me to leftover meatballs. We don't realize we're parting forever, never to giggle again as we often did in the school's lunch line where gray-haired ladies encouraged us to stuff our mouths with American mashed potatoes and gravy. No, no longer will we eat American turkey with cranberry sauce the day before Thanksgiving. Augustine and I created our own big bird last Thanksgiving. We pasted tons of color paper, and Miss Cusumano, our fourth grade teacher, tacked it up on the bulletin board. It was the biggest turkey made that day. Oh, it was a beautiful bird—a bird pilgrims in tall black hats shot in New England woods. It was a bird I never saw in my home. I tasted turkey the first time in school, for Thanksgiving was never a Cuban or an Italian holiday. My parents worked Thanksgiving Day.

No, we'll never be pilgrims again. No longer will Augustine find me hiding behind the stout oak in the playground playing hide-and-seek. No longer will I take small or giant steps toward him on soft Florida sand, sneaking up playing Mother May I. No, no longer will we assassinate boring classroom time playing tic-tac-toe, for the following Monday morning his desk is empty. A young Miss Cusumano leans piously over hers and unleashes a hideous tale.

"Children, there's something I need to tell you before we pray and pledge the flag."

She bites her lower lip and pushes her dark hair aside. "Augustine will not be coming to class anymore. There was a terrible accident this weekend. Augustine and his sister drowned."

The class goes silent. I hear myself breathe and look at Augustine's empty desk.

"We'll always remember Augustine, won't we?" she says.

"SIBLINGS DROWN IN LAKE." She reads aloud from *The Tampa Morning Tribune*.

I scan the room, repeatedly scan rows and desks, searching over and over for a pair of mischievous eyes. The imagination of a child is beyond the comprehension of adults, so how can anyone say I don't see him? Did not the apostles see Jesus when no one else did? It was what my *nonna* told me happened after the entombment, told it to me each Easter. Apparitions happened in ancient times, so why not at V.M. Ybor School? I find him hiding in a back row, slouching, making a smart-ass face. I smile letting him know I'm still his friend, but he picks his nose and flicks me off.

"You, Italian bastard." His voice crisscrosses the room, but no one hears him, not even Miss Cusumano.

"Augustine, let's be friends," I yell back.

"Sorry, can't do it."

"Why not? We're friends," I say.

"Because of your pride…you kicked my ass you no good son of a bitch. For no fucking reason, Frankie." He shoves his finger in the air.

"But, Augustine, you started it."

"My Papa says you're gonna grow up and be a Mafia boss like all *dagos*. Got it in your blood."

"No, Augustine, I ain't ever gonna be no Mafia boss, not me, besides, if I did, I'd be your godfather, take care of you, protect you, honestly."

I see him gasp for air like hungry groupers do. His feet suddenly turn into a fishtail, and his eyes cloud over like the not so fresh fish at Tony Labruzzo's Fish Market, ones Mama instructed me never to buy. A dead fish delivered to your doorstep or your classroom is a bad omen, a real bad omen. All Sicilians understand the prophecy of a dead fish.

Fingers fuse and wet flippers flip me off, but no longer can he make the bird fly, but he tries. He flips and flops in his seat, screaming, "*Conyo, máricon and hijo puta.*"

The Cuban trinity is upon me: pussy, queer and son of a bitch. He puckers his lips, lets out bubbles and shakes transparent scales onto the aisle. He's hoping I'll slip, screw up and make an ass of myself, for that's his inscrutable style. Next, he stretches his neck, and I see froth filling pink gills. Augustine submerges himself beneath his desk. As usual, Miss Cusumano doesn't see a thing. She says we should all be sad because we'll never see our dear, dear Augustine again.

"Augustine and his older sister fell out of a rowboat." The teacher blots a tear.

But I know Augustine capsized the boat, know his antics, and know the lake's bottom is too deep for outstretched feet, so he and his sister no doubt floated like chum-bait. Soon, like pebbles tossed into a lake, I see them sink.

He surfaces twice.

"That's two out of three. Swim like a fish, Augustine," I say.

Widely set eyes wink, and shredded water lilies close in over his head. I lose sight of him in the macabre lake. The struggle turns the water murky as white water lilies seal its fractured surface. Moments later, silence awakes to the odor of gasoline, and frantic motorboats skim the lake. By evening, all is quiet. The lake is placid and beautiful as it is each evening when bullfrogs croak, crickets sing and fishes jump uninhibited, unabashed and unafraid.

It's Monday morning, a hell of a never-ending Monday, and I'm the so-called survivor needing to survive. Augustine, like the sun, has been eclipsed, and I'm the big, bad moon. It's Monday all right, a day that should reflect a hint of blue, but it's black—black—pitch black. There are no psychiatrists, psychologists, school nurses or garrulous counselors keeping V.M. Ybor fourth graders afloat. We're learning about death in what is said to be a peripheral way, like children at parallel play, minimally involved in a comfortable way, a non-intrusive way. After all, he was a non-relative, non-blood, just a school chum, and he wasn't even Italian.

I search for priests selling dime dispensations to wash away my sin, but there are no black cassocks in public school. Only the Devil, in the form of the Devil Crab Man, appeared early that morning before the school bell rang my death knell.

Oh, the morning began glorious, all right, with Mr. Miranda bringing his white box full of deviled crabs strapped on the handlebars of his old bike. He parked in front of the school bright and early that morning like he always does, but I didn't notice Augustine wasn't there to try to outrun me. I was just happy to see the Devil Crab Man.

"How many?" Mister Miranda says.

"*Uno, por favor, señor.*"

"Want *salsa?*"

"*Sí.*"

"O right."

With a flick of his wrist red liquid squirts. Upside down the bottle pours the red blood of Satan, Miranda jerking it on target. The slim Tabasco bottle dips again and again, gouging open crust and exposing claw and back-fin crabmeat.

"*Bastante?* Enough?"

It's hotter than hell, but it's how I love crabs—hot—real hot.

"*Un poco mas.*"

Wrapped in wax paper, Mr. Miranda's dark hand gives it over in exchange for a dime. The sauce makes my eyes water, and it feels as if resurrected crabs pinch my tongue.

It's always a great morning when Miranda brings crabs. A great continental breakfast, for all I eat at home is day-old Italian or Cuban bread dunked in Cuban coffee with scalded milk. This morning hadn't started out any different, no different than all those other Mondays I dreaded going to school, but it is, sure is. Soon, I'll stagger into infamy and be known as the Judas of the watery crucifixion. I will understand how Judas felt the day he hung himself, for I sold out my friend for less than thirty pieces of silver, much less—for nothing. That's what they'll all say, for nothing, and Augustine is now walking on water. Being Italian made me bad, just like he'd predicted, inexorably bad.

After the announcement, Miss Cusumano instructs us to say the Our Father. I know the class bows reverently to a new martyred saint. Why not a saint? He has the name of a saint, an outstanding one, so sinful he wrote an X-rated book for Catholics called *Confessions*. I know from my grandmother's teachings Saint

Augustine was a big-time sinner, so why not my Augustine? He fulfills all prereq-uisites, and I just know in a last ditch effort he made the sign of the cross under the boat and made a deal, a deal of a lifetime—life in exchange for sainthood. I know Jesus has special ways of dealing with children, water and people in boats, so if Jesus walked on the Sea of Galilee, lily pads made it a snap for Augustine to walk on water.

Miss Cusumano keeps saying Augustine is dead, and all my classmates, except me, bow their heads to a new patron saint. I'm a tough *wop* with Black Hands in my pockets and Mafia in my blood. That's what Augustine said, but my lips soften, quiver, and I protrude a stiff lower lip, as I bite down hard trying to hide it. Next the class pledges the flag in unison, and it never seemed so large, its stripes so bloody and its blue so blue. I follow Miss Cusumano's lead, mouth every word, but no one hears me cry.

I miss Augustine, but time pushes me forward. I notice desktops take on new meaning. Nudes, placed there by previous generations tantalize me. The draw-ings are varied and probing. Gilded in ink, they are etched deeply with pocket-knives, and I admire women who pose on their sides, stomachs and backs with legs spread apart, and they spread them all right, spread them as far as they'll go. I peer as far as my eyes will see, and many seem to say, "Frankie, come and play, grow up. Oh, yes, hurry up, Frankie, please, it's what school's all about."

Urinating into short urinals, I come face to face with frescoes. I unzip to con-temporary art, and inside stalls, I sit and ponder life-size anatomical DaVinci detail. It's a rough school, and the boy's room reflects modern-day culture. Porn is written in English and Spanish but never Italian.

It is the fall of the year and the air is no longer humid. Acorns drop from live oaks and bounce like brown ping-pong balls. The air smells different as I sit with my family eating pasta one evening.

"Papa, a bunch of Cubans chased Junio and me today…"

"What did you do?" Mama says.

Papa sloughs me off, breaking off a hunk of bread.

"Got it all over the floor, Filippo." She grimaces. "The cockroaches are going to have a feast day." Pursed lips tell me she's perturbed.

I say. "Cubans called Junio a 'Mussolini lover.' They started to beat up on him, so I jumped in. The teacher broke up the fight, but Cubans passed me a note in class saying they'd get us after school."

"That's the way Cubans were when I went to school," Mama says. "I remem-ber my brother always fighting Cubans. They picked on him because he was a redhead. I kept hearing, 'There's a fight.' I'd ask, 'Who?' 'It's Red.' They turned him into a fighting machine."

"That's because he's a redhead, Mary," Papa says. "Has nothing to do with Cubans."

"But it doesn't help."

"Yeah, Mary, yeah."

He slurps pasta and dips bread into *sugo*, the Sicilian word for sauce. Mama sees he's scraping bottom. She gets up and places meatballs in a bowl. Papa goes for another plate of spaghetti, his third.

"Filippo, you're going to need bigger shirts. Seventeen necks no longer fit."

"Can't you alter them?" he says.

"If you ate less pasta it'd help."

"But, Mary, if I had diabetes or something, okay, but I'm healthy."

She looks at Papa and then me. In Sicilian, she starts to say something but refrains. But she can't hold back. "Filippo, maybe you should go talk to the teacher."

"Papa, they were waiting for us, so we ran out the back, but they spotted us. We ran until they almost caught us, so we ran into somebody's house. We stood on the porch first, but the boys walked inside the yard. I noticed the screen door unlocked, so Junio and I walked in and stood just inside the door. The owner never saw us."

He looks up from his plate.

"When the coast was clear, we took off never making a sound," I say.

Mama says, "Madonna, don't you know you could've been shot. It's safer to face Cubans."

"The Cubans believed we lived in that house, so they took off, Mama." I smile.

I never tell them that as I stood protected by a screen door, I gave the boys the finger and pantomimed motherfucker.

"Franche, you don't want me to see the teacher, do you?" Papa says.

"No, don't come to school, Papa, please."

"Well, you need to straighten things out with the boss of the gang."

"Papa, he's a mean guy, older, flunked fourth grade a few times. Everyone's afraid of him, and he's got muscles."

"So, you need a plan. Pick a time and place. Remember, you're Italian. Just because he's got muscles doesn't mean he's got balls. Balls are what count."

"Fili, he's just a boy," Mama says.

His fist slams the table, rattling my plate. "You need to catch him off guard. Hit the bastard first and don't stop. Keep thinking why you're doing it, why it is you're in the fight and don't worry about getting hurt. But you need to catch him by surprise, doesn't matter if you win. What matters is he understands Italians don't take shit."

"But, Papa…"

"You let the *somma ama bitcha* have it. The boy's restroom is a perfect place. Maybe you catch him with his pants down." He laughs a sinister laugh.

"The boy's room? I don't want to roll around on that floor, Papa."

"Well, you pick the place. If you don't, he'll pick on you because he thinks you're a sissy." Papa laughs harder anticipating the next line. "With pants down, he'll be a pushover."

"Really, Fili, he's just a boy."

"You can sit him on his ass," Papa says.

He's serious, for I see how he looks into my eyes. His eyebrows narrow into a V—a V for victory. His fork takes a recess. It usually gets no rest from pasta until he's done, but tonight he makes exceptions. He sighs, looks at Mama and picks it up and digs in with renewed vigor.

Sure, it's easy for him—it's no big deal. It's easy since he won't be in harm's way. Papa knows a first blow often determines outcomes of fistfights. It's the one thing my godfather and Papa agree on, a first punch, particularly if you're a small Sicilian. I know he's right, and I have probably made things worse flicking off the Cubans. Mama knows Papa's right. She never says a word, doesn't say her usual, "Eat more meatballs, Filippo." Papa said to hit the son of a bitch with a first punch, do it in cold blood. It's one thing to lash out in anger, but to do it in cold blood is not my style.

The problem solves itself a day I swing fists idiotically in a mock fight with a friend in the playground. Unsuspecting, the bully comes around the corner of the building and runs into an unmeasured uppercut. I hit him squarely and deck him. I never have an opportunity to follow up like Papa said. A crowd gathers anticipating a fight, but he doesn't get up. Mrs. Jones places wet paper towels on his face, and he sits on the bottom fire escape step. Mrs. Jones glares at the blood he spits out.

He shakes his head, sort of twirling it. "*Hijo puta, hijo puta.*"

He's weak, dazed, and his speech is slurred, but he's calling me a son of a bitch. It's his usual response, *hijo puta, hijo puta*. Even in Spanish his vocabulary is limited. He spits out more blood. I see a gash creasing his tongue. The teacher insists in shoving paper towels inside his mouth. She stuffs it until he's mute. His eyes remain uncoordinated as classmates watch Mrs. Jones prop him up by the arm. She leads him inside to his desk.

I explain, but she doesn't believe my story.

"I know you're Italian, Frankie, but you must never take matters into your own hands."

"But it was an accident. We weren't fighting."

"Weren't fighting? What do you call it, Frankie?"

The bully chimes in, "An accident my ass."

"But honestly, I didn't see him, Mrs. Jones."

"Sure, Frankie, sure, it's your kind of playing, I know." She waves her finger in my face.

Papa is right. The bully has no balls, and the teacher doesn't understand.

22

All Italians aren't gangsters, and Ybor City Italians aren't either, but all look for ways to buy things cheap.

Uncle Giuseppe or Pedo sits on our front porch swing and sips Cuban coffee.

"Fili, want a new refrigerator?" he says.

"Got a good price?" my father says.

"Know a guy who sells them wholesale. Less than half price, so if you want one, better tell me."

"You sure it's not secondhand?"

"No, no, brand new—in the box."

"In the box?"

"*Sì*, others in the family are getting them. I only do it for family and close friends."

Mama and Papa discuss the proposal after Pedo leaves. Cigarmakers are coming into their own, getting away from iceboxes and kerosene stoves. Fancy Italians are putting Venetian blinds on their windows. I have no idea the word Venetian comes from Venice—don't know the word "Venice" either.

"Fili, just think we can keep leftovers longer. Nothing will go to waste, nothing, even bread will keep, and there will be no more ice to buy," Mama says.

"*Sì*, but it uses a lot of electricity," he says.

"That's not what Rose Frisco says. Besides there's a light inside, so when you open it at night, you don't have to turn on the kitchen light. It's very economical when you consider everything."

The cake of ice sits in the top compartment of my icebox. Cold settles where milk and other perishables sit at the bottom. In time, ice melts, but the iceman knows when the ice is about gone, so there's seldom a crisis. Occasionally, if he does fail to show up in time, and we sustain a meltdown, Mama says, "Run to the iceman's house and tell him we're out of ice."

It's simple and clean, and meltdowns are without fallouts, always a twenty-four hour turnaround time, all cool, all state of the art, and ice water flows downhill in a rubber hose that snakes its way into a hole drilled in the pine floor and drips under the house.

Uncle Pedo returns days later.

"Pedo, you're sure the refrigerators are not hot?"

"Would I do that to my own brother? *Porco* Juda, Fili, what's the matter with you?" He laughs and lights a cigarette. Smoke pours out of his nose just like it did Nonno Ciccio's nose when he said fireworks were not to be feared. "A half a dozen relatives want them. Don't think I'd screw them, do you? Give me some credit, Fili. I am your flesh and blood."

Days later, two men deliver the refrigerator when my parents are getting ready for bed.

"It's kind of late, but we were in the neighborhood, so we thought we'd drop it off. Is that all right?" A man, speaking Sicilian, says to Papa at the front door.

"Sure, bring it right in," Papa says.

"Kitchen in the back, right?"

"All the way back."

"We'll bring it through the alley. You go open the back door."

"*Sì.*" Papa rushes to the back of the duplex.

Two men bring it in on a steel dolly. The short man is talkative, the tall one quiet. Mama can't wait to wipe the refrigerator down, rushing around with a wet rag in her hand.

"We'll dump the icebox for free," the short man says.

"Yes, yes, take it away, please," Mama says. "Please watch that ash. It's awfully close to the finish."

The man's cigar ash falls on the linoleum. The man glances at Mama. "*Mi dispiace,* sorry."

"That's all right. Just don't burn the finish."

"Maybe we can use the old icebox as a backup?" Papa says.

"No, the wood is rotten, look." The short man rams his fist through the bottom.

"You fellows always work so late?" Papa says.

"Yeah, we're busy. Can't unload them fast enough. They're nice units. Not a bad price," the short man says in Sicilian.

"Are you from West Tampa? Don't believe I've seen you at the Italian Club before," Papa says.

"Naw, naw, New York."

"New York! You come all the way to Florida to deliver refrigerators?"

"Why not?"

"You speak Siciliano a little different than us," Papa says.

"We came over from Palermo."

"Always nice to deal with one's own people. There are lots Italians in Tampa, you know."

"Yeah, we know. We're trying to branch out. Haven't found a place to rent yet, but we'll have an outlet in town soon."

"So, how you know Pedo?" Papa says.

"Yes, through Leo's sister." The man points to the quiet one who is doing the grunt work. "Pedo is doing a good job of getting the word out. Good man that Pedo."

"Yeah, he's my brother."

"Is there any guarantee? In case it breaks," Mama says.

"Sure."

"Who do we contact?"

"Let Pedo know and we'll make it right, *capisci?* Nothing to worry about, should last twenty-five years. A Frigidaire, *signora*—it's a Frigidaire."

The other man smiles.

"You want it where the icebox was, *signora?*" the short man says.

"*Sì,*" Mama says. "Got to cover the icebox hole. Wait a minute. Let me stuff it so rats won't come in." Mama takes a small rag off the kitchen drain board.

The men pause, and Mama stuffs the hole in the floor where the icebox drained.

"See, Filippo, we'll have less rats in the house now. I told you there are advantages to getting rid of that rotten icebox." Mama looks at the men. "Cockroaches come in through there, too. I've seen them," she says.

"You should have the driver help you with the lifting. It seems heavy," Papa says.

"Naw, that's all right. He waits outside—has a bad back. It's nice you have an alley to unload from. Neighbors won't know your business."

Papa nods.

"You paid Pedo, right?"

"Oh, yes, in cash."

"That's what we take. You all have a *buona sera,* and say hello to Pedo. You got a great brother."

"*Buona sera, buona sera,*" my parents say. The men leave.

Mama keeps food neatly stacked in the unit, and when Papa goes to drink cold water or milk at night, he doesn't switch on the kitchen light.

After work, several weeks later, Aunt Felicia comes over. "Did you hear the news? Police went to Rose Frisco's house and took away her refrigerator. It's all over the factory."

"What?" Papa says.

Mama and Papa look at each other.

"Pedo sold it to them," Mama says.

Papa stands. "*That figlio di puttana,* my own brother. I'll kill him."

"*Calma te,* Filippo, *calma te.*" Both women urge Papa to stay calm.

"I gotta get a truck. Mary, shut the door and don't turn on lights. Franchito, hear? Play like it's a blackout. Keep the house dark."

Papa takes off and reappears driving a pickup truck.

"Where you going to take it, Filippo?" Mama says.

"Don't know."

"Just don't scratch it, Fili. Whatever you do, don't scratch it."

"Nino and Stefano bought one, too. Can't take it there, and the rest of the family lives too close," Papa says.

"Take it to my brother's. The police will never go there. It's only Pedo's relatives they'll check," Mama says with authority, after all, she's the one that reads crime magazines.

"Okay, Mary, okay."

"Franchito, help Papa."

I try, but I'm not much help at nine. Papa single-handedly cat walks the refrigerator across the kitchen, slides it down the back steps, and cat walks it to the alley. Like a dead body, he leans it on the tailgate, sighs and flops it on its side. He pushes it to the hilt. Mama comes running with a blanket. "You should have wrapped something around it. Here, cover it up and drive slowly. Don't want a policeman stopping you tonight."

Papa, the refrigerator and me are off, driving through the alley without headlights, knocking down garbage cans as we go. On surface streets Papa focuses on the rearview mirror, makes unnecessary turns, asks me to see if anyone is behind us. Uncle Tony helps him unload the refrigerator and hide it in his garage.

We drop off the truck at Papa's friend, pick up our car and drive home. He's silent. I know he's thinking.

Mama is sitting in the dark on the porch when we arrive.

"Well, we're rid of the damn thing, Mary."

We walk into the kitchen. They're somber. It's as if we return to a crime scene.

"Fili, what we going to do if the police come? We don't have a refrigerator or icebox. That will look suspicious."

"We'll tell them we use Felicia's refrigerator. Besides, it's a duplex, one house. We say we share it. That's how Americans think we live anyhow, like rats," Papa says.

"Did you put the food in Felicia's refrigerator?" Papa says.

"Oh, yes. There was lots of room. It'll be tough running over there all the time."

"Well, we have to, Mary."

"But how about if police see the hole in the floor from the icebox?"

"Should have kept the icebox," Papa says. "We got to cover it."

"We can move the table," Mama says. "If the police come I'll make Cuban coffee, and they can sit at the table. I'll put a large tablecloth over it, so it hangs over the sides."

And that's what she does. The word is out, and relatives shun Pedo. Refrigerators take vacations, and plain clothesmen visit relatives and ask about Pedo, show them his picture. Pedo drops out of sight. His name is synonymous with *somma ama bitcha* for a long time, and Mama curses each time she runs next door to my aunt's refrigerator.

Zia Felicia is a trailblazer, has no fear, so I know she'll cover for Papa. She's on the cutting edge of the *barrio*, has a hot water tank for bathing, a big electric fan in her kitchen, and she's one of the first to install Venetian blinds. She takes me to a Christmas party on a Saturday. I ride the trolley to the Civic Auditorium. Alongside a large tree on the stage, a tall, skinny, missionary type lady plays a piano. American children are gathered around her singing Christmas carols. Santa Claus is there, too. He drops toys into paper bags children hold out filing by him in a long line.

The toys are scratched and dinged, but I'm comfortable with that. It's the year I'm blessed with more than one or two toys. Santa Claus, without fail, brings me one present each year, and Zia Felicia, my godmother, the other.

Grandparents don't give presents for Christmas or birthdays. I've never had a birthday party. Oh, until about age nine Papa brings home a cake on my day of all days, but there are never presents to puff me up or help me puff out the candles. Adults never celebrate birthdays. I assume birthdays are an American thing like Mother's Day and Father's Day. The latter are days my relatives say Jewish people invented to make money. So this is a flush Christmas, as good as it gets. But it's a once in a lifetime experience, for when Papa finds out it's a Christmas party for underprivileged children, he says, "Italians don't take handouts."

Eventually refrigerators and Pedo reappear. He never admits guilt, says he knew nothing about it, but Mama glances at him and at the marred refrigerator finish each time he visits.

I turn ten, and things aren't going well for me either.
"I hate Mrs. Edenfield," I say to Mama.
"She's just trying to make sure you learn, Franchito."
"Yeah, but she paddles hard."
"I'm sure you deserve it."
It's my year of intro to poetry, and my first poem is not an epic poem like Dante's *Divine Comedy* with Virgil, the loquacious Italian, guiding me across the River Styx. Instead, it's a Longfellow poem with Mrs. Edenfield, the tour guide, holding fifth grader hands across an American inferno.

And it isn't just me fearing Edenfield. It's all of us, including goody-goody girls who sit in front rows, fill buckets with water and wash blackboards after school, and tough Cuban boys who don't mind spending days sequestered with principal "Shorty" Wilson.

The poem tells a story of an American patriot riding a steed, slicing through the dense curfew of midnight. Mrs. Edenfield, embroiled in vision and verse, hypnotizes the class with the catchy phrase, "one if by land and two if by sea…" Ad nauseam she recites it to the sleepy afternoon class explaining how farmers sought destiny in flaming lanterns from the belfry of the old North Church.

Revere is his name, and Edenfield's is the class, and I'm determined to become American, but the whole affair about minutemen doesn't fit the *barrio*, so I imagine cigarmakers striking against totalitarian factory owners.

I recite the poem over and over at home. If I memorize it, I'll surely be American, so I study hard, read every line over and over aloud.

From the second story classroom, I peer out a window and watch cars flowing down Columbus Drive making wakes as if it's the River Charles. Though I've seen snow only in Christmas cards, Spanish moss hanging from Florida's live oaks crystallizes into icicles. El Reloj Cigar Factory's clock tower stands a short city block east like the old North Church, the highest structure in the *barrio*, holding up colonial lanterns with two black hands.

Edenfield recites the poem as if she lived the experience, languishing inside stanzas, braking at line-breaks. Oh, she is one hell of a teacher and a master disciplinarian, too; the best there is. The class abhors her like colonists abhor Red Coats. No doubt, she's pure British stock steeped in bitter English tea, detesting the laissez-faire attitude of Latino students.

She's wiry and middle age and lipstick anchors down her pale Anglo-Saxon face. She protrudes nowhere except at the nose, having no gut, no butt, no tits, and thin thighs scissor across a waxed floor.

She shoulders a three-foot stick with a rubber tip. Like a U.S. Marine Drill Sergeant, she motivates us with her prod. She calls it a pointer, but I know it's a musket with blood on a bayonet's tip. Stridently, back and forth, the she-General struts as my eardrums stretch awaiting a drum roll from the picture in my book of the *Spirit of 1776*.

"Was the battle at Lexington or Concord?" she asks.

It doesn't matter. I imagine punched out entrance wounds and blown out exit wounds. It's obvious to a second language student we're no match for English piercing verses. Under each breath it's Longfellow I curse, but Edenfield I fear.

Gold-rimmed spectacles bounce on the saddle of her nose, keeping cadence to meter. Caught up in the rhythm, I tap my foot.

"Left, right, left, her left, her right, left, right, left…and my Mama was there when I left—your right." Mesmerized, I gaze out the window.

"And your Mama ain't here." Like a helicopter, she hovers over my desk.

Her nose flares, and I look up into hairy caverns dividing steel eyes. I blink and look at sleepy George hanging on the wall. Not knowing what to do, my pupils fix and dilate on his wig. The whites of her eyes are upon me, and an earth tremor shakes my knees, and my bladder sphincter warns, "Hold it, Soldier."

"Frankie, recite," she commands.

I stand at attention in the aisle, always to the right of my desk. The radiator's valve hisses as if it knows it's a public hanging, and I know it, too, for all eyes focus on my face like adults do at viewings at Lord and Fernandez Funeral Home. The aisle is my scaffold, and like Sacco and Vanzetti, two poor Italian immigrants hung by a prejudiced judge in 1927 for being Italian, I, too, will never see Mama again.

"Yes, Ma'am."

"Well, what are you waiting for? Don't you want to be American?"

"Yes, Ma'am."

I clear my throat. With hands locked behind my back, I fix my eyes on a crumbly ceiling.

"Listen, my children, and you shall hear
Of the midnight ride of Paul Revere,
On the eighteenth of April, in Seventy-five."

Words flow like winged angels. Then all goes blank.

"Well, we don't have all day," she says. "Get on with it."

"Ah, ah,…Hardly a man is now alive
who remembers…ah,…the day and year.
ah,…" I'm mired in colonial words.
"Ah,…ah,…" It won't come.

I sigh and think, dear Lord, the Bible says you're the word, so please send one now.

Lynched or shot? It doesn't matter. There'll be no clemency or divine intervention. Suddenly, to my right, an open book snails across a desktop. Margaret Charavella, my first grade heartthrob, still at my side, nonchalantly points to page nine. The poem mushrooms into view.

Should I risk treason? I ask myself.

The decision made, I invoke Santa Lucia, the Sicilian patron saint of vision as my eyes twist and strain. In the back of the classroom my cousin Junio raises his hand.

"Mrs. Edenfield, may I go to the boy's room?" he says.

I know the gang is mobilizing. When she turns, a spitball plasters her right ear, and a blackboard eraser whizzes by her nose. Stunned, she plunges across enemy lines, walking down one aisle and up another as if students are would-be assassins. She does an about face and, with chalk screeching and squealing on a slate blackboard, she writes names of those who will stay after school, hoping a traitor will squeal, but there are no yellow canaries sitting in my nest. Only names, class and room number do students volunteer. During the debacle I slither into my seat forfeiting my bid to fifth grade hall of fame forever, and, like any good Sicilian-American, if anyone asked why, I would have pleaded the Fifth Amendment.

23

"Nonna, I recited in class today," I say, crawling into bed.

"That's good."

"Everyone stared at me." I say in Sicilian.

"Aren't you sleepy?"

"No, I'm scared."

"Of what?"

"Mrs. Edenfield."

"Why?"

"I didn't finish."

"Finish what?"

"Reciting. I know she's going to call on me tomorrow."

"Go to sleep."

"But she's mean, real mean, Nonna."

"What did you recite?"

"*Paul Revere.*"

"What?"

"It's a poem about an American who sent signals to his friends."

"So it is about a good man?"

"Happened during the revolution."

"What revolution?"

"He liberated America with his horse."

"What horse?"

"Liberated America from Europe, from *gli inglesi*."

"Ah, yes, I know Europe, and there is an England."

"Don't turn on the lights, Franchito, I need to relieve myself."

"Yes, Nonna."

I hear her waterfall. Women piss differently than men. Then I hear the lid rattle, sealing itself on the *orinale*, as it is called, and I hear her crawl back into bed. It happens in the middle of the night, too, but most nights I don't hear a thing. But when I do, it's the unmistakable sound of woman. The *orinale* or chamber pot is a relic from Sicily, but it serves my family well, for my home doesn't have central heat, any heat at all, and winter nights are cold in the middle part of the state, dropping to below freezing many nights. It's tough to get out of a warm bed and go to the toilet. And the bathroom is in the north face of the home, next to the alley. I keep a chamber pot under my bed, too.

"Do you know we had patriots in Italy, too?" she says.

"Sometimes Papa talks about Garibaldi."

"Not him, Franchito. There was sort of a revolution in Sicily when the family came to America."

"Did you have a North Church in Sicily?"

She laughs. "We had lots of churches in Sicily. Alessandria della Rocca was just a village, and it had two. After all, it is the land of the Pope."

"Tell me, Nonna, tell me more."

She pauses, always does before starting her story, clears her throat before the *racconti*. It sounds like "count," recounting the past. I can't see her face in the dark, but the roughness in her throat cracks the silence in the room. I hear her swallow twice. I know she's about to begin, so I close my eyes.

"Everything in Sicily is old," she says. "Old is Sicily, Franchito. The young grow old prematurely, and adolescent boys work in the fields. At puberty girls marry—emancipate themselves from puritanical fathers. Squalor begets squalor, and the only lines *contadini* move up are confessional lines, and there, too, the *feudi* squeeze in front of the poor. Life is anchored in the land and the church. Churches are old, some converted Greek temples and mosques—centuries old."

"I see it, Nonna, I see it, but what are *contadini* and *feudi*?"

"We were *contadini*; villagers who worked the fields. *Feudi* were the landowners."

I can see Sicily from my bed. It's a mixture of old—everything old. Time is not measured in years but in millenniums. Everything is crumbling, yet buildings stand, and old priests say Mass and don't die. There is no quaintness in old, only misery. I see faces in the dark and hear voices in the *piazza* on the village's main street, Via Roma, and the old stone church with stone steps near Via Bellini. There's a watering trough at the top of a hill near a cemetery and cobblestone streets. Clotheslines are strung in backyards and along narrow streets. Mules are housed in liveries and some in fields and others fenced in yards.

I see spoons on one side of a rickety table. A loaf of bread sits next to a crock of black olives floating in brine. My *nonno* spits out pits. He's alive and well, and each time he reaches for an olive he bumps the table with his knees. He breaks off a hunk of bread. It's bread Nonna baked that morning in a brick oven outside.

It's called a *forno*. Ciccio chews and doesn't hide his chew nor insulate the sound inside his mouth. A half-gallon of red wine sits in front of him.

"I spoke to my mother today, Ci. I told her we might go to America," Anna says.

He fills his glass with wine.

"She broke out into tears," Anna says, laying pasta on the table, scanning it between fingers, searching for vermin that hatch in summer—tiny, black dots against white *semolina*. She gathers the strands, bunches them in one hand and breaks them into small pieces. She waits for the boil in the pot on the wood burning stove.

"Was your father with her?" he says.

"No, but Mama will tell him. Go wash up, Ciccio. The pasta will be ready soon."

"Does she know your sister Ninida is planning to leave?"

"Not yet."

"Why not?"

"Don't know. That's her business. I feel badly though." Anna pushes hair away from her face and reconstitutes her expression. "If they weren't so old they could join us." She sighs.

He puts down the glass, stands and stretches, arches his back and walks out the door. He walks to a water pump and pumps its curved handle stamped *facto en* Italia. He pumps it until pressure builds, holds, and water flows. Cupping his hands, he catches it and splashes it on his face.

He dries off with a towel that hangs on an olive tree branch.

"It was an oven out there today, *un forno*," he says and runs his hand through wet hair when he walks in. He hugs Anna around a swollen waist.

A child runs in. "Papa!" She grabs his hand and pulls him away.

He turns around. "*Bada*, give me *uno baccho*."

She hugs and kisses him. He slaps her buttock, and she runs off.

Smiling, Anna stirs the pasta, knowing Giovanina loves to be called *bada*. It means beautiful.

"Ciccio, I don't know what to do," Anna says.

Fragmented noodles roll and tumble in the boil. She pours salt into a cupped hand and tosses it in, quelling the boil momentarily.

"Mama said to me your place is with your husband, Anna. But I know I'll never see you or the children again."

Ciccio walks up to the stove and fishes out a few noodles, slurps them as if inhaling them, mixing pasta with air. He tries to speak, but the heat immobilizes his tongue.

He pauses, then says, "The fields are burning up. The grapes will not be sweet if it doesn't rain soon."

"Mama, can I help?" Giovanina says, tugging at Anna's dress.

"Get the colander from under the sink," Anna tells the nine-year-old. "We're going to be taking the pasta down any minute."

Anna stacks the plates on the drain board. "So, I said to my mother, 'We're not sure we can go. We don't have money for passage.'" She glances at Giovanina. "Quit picking at the cheese."

"That's God's truth, Anna. How can we book passage?"

"Mama told me Vincenzo said now that he's twelve he wants to go work in America and send money home for passage." Anna puts spoons on the table. There is no utensil trilogy of knife, fork and spoon. Spoons will do.

"Need those Americano *dollaros*. The *lira* is worth nothing," Ciccio says.

"Giovanina, go see if the little ones are still sleeping."

Ciccio samples the pasta again. "*E perfecta.*"

Pasta is not cooked *al dente*, *al dente* refers to teeth, and many *contadini* lose them early, so many peasants eat pasta overdone.

The head of house is served first. Ciccio hand grates Romano cheese on the *minestra*. *Minestra* is pasta mixed with one vegetable or another, with or without a spoonful of sauce and olive oil—definitely no sauce if the pasta is mixed with fava or lentil beans.

The hilltop village of Alessandria della Rocca, is nestled in the Magazzolo Valle in the Madonie Mountains, in the province of Agrigento in Western Sicily. The countryside boasts vineyards, almond trees and olive orchards. Ten kilometers north is the sheep-herding and cheese-manufacturing village of Santo Stefano di Quisquina. The *lana* or wool produced there, like most things, is sent to Palermo. All roads in and out of the villages are primitive, traveled by *carretta*s pulled by long-eared donkeys and mules. It is *carretta*s the villagers decorate and paint with bright colors on festival days.

It is from the villages of Santo Stefano di Quisquina, Alessandria della Rocca and, to a lesser extent, La Contessa Entellina that Italians come to Ybor City in the 1890s and early twentieth century. Those from Santo Stefano, Stefanesi, make up sixty percent of Ybor City's Italians and those from Alessandria della Rocca the rest. The numbers from Contessa Entellina, Gheg-ghegs, and from mainland Italy are insignificant. The Gheg-ghegs originated in Albania centuries earlier and still speak the language. The surrounding villagers are illiterate and know little about Albania and Albanians. They hear the foreign sounds of the language, and it sounds like *gheg gheg*, hence the name.

The Magazzolo Valle is hot and dry in summers with rains in winter.

Contadini live a life of serfdom, sharecroppers. The land is pastoral, and the harvest bountiful for the *feudi*, rich land owners, and clerics. Wolves inhabit the countryside, so *lupo* fairy tales are told to children by grandparents, but the *contadini* know who the real wolves are, the real *lupos* whose fangs ravish the poor.

Contadini make their living off the land, and sing rustic songs in the fields where shirts rot off their backs in the blazing sun. Substantial land holdings are in the clutches of engineers, judges, lawyers, politicians and businessmen in Palermo.

The rich purchase more and more land in the Magazzolo Valle stuffing pockets like children stuff candy. The land is cheap and labor cheaper, so they glut themselves, and stomp the land, stomp the poor and feel no remorse. It's the time of the haves and have-nots, the time Bolsheviks are rattling sabers in Russia, and socialism is inhaling its first breath.

The *feudi* yield no ground and dejected *contadini* shout to each other, "We live in order not to die." It becomes their battle cry, and labor leagues feebly organize. In *piazzas* villagers meet, secretly draft modest labor reforms.

Lorenzo Panepinto, a Santo Stefano proponent of socialism, leads the quivering movement. The moderate Italian government of Giolitti fails and is replaced by the clenched fist of Francesco Crispi. In 1894 Crispi pounds his fist, vowing *contadini* will have no voice in government, no voice in Italy. He promises land barons he will crush labor uprisings and deal with the *contadini* with a language they understand—brute force. In Santo Stefano, hometown of Santa Rosalia, the embroiled Stefanesi patriot Panepinto visits labor camps, incites strikes, organizes villages and publishes *Viva La Socialismo*. The publication praises socialistic ideology decried by Rome as revolutionary. The *contadini* band and call themselves *fasci*, followers of Panepinto. These are not Mussolini's *fascista*, but Panepinto's *fasci* who attempt to educate peasants. *Panepinto*'s name is revered in Sicily, and the *contadini* began to believe labor reform is imminent.

In a small loft, Ciccio takes off his clothes, hangs them on a chair. Dust laden trousers dangle.

"Don't be so hard on yourself, Ci." Anna turns off a kerosene lamp.

Ciccio says, "Don Gaetano didn't pay us today."

"Don't fret, he'll pay. He may not be a nice man, but he provides work."

"It's not that. You know the size of his vineyards, orchards, and he won't pay our pittance on time."

"I know, but he eventually does."

"My brother Antonino wants to organize. He talks about bringing the wealthy to their knees. It's out of control in Santo Stefano. There have been beatings and killings. I told him it's a sure way to get killed."

"What did he say?"

"He's hotheaded, doesn't understand, but we're going back to work in the morning."

The loft traps the heat of the day and overlooks a clay roof through a small window. A lace curtain hangs limp. The home is centuries old.

"Mama's right, you know. I'll never see her again, won't see her or Papa in their caskets." Anna rolls over in the bed, away from Ciccio. He slides closer and places his arm around her waist.

"Anna, few villagers return. If your parents had a chance when they were younger, they would have left. I know they understand."

She turns to him. "Don't you think I know that? But it doesn't make it less sad. I hear women in church talk, say many from Santo Stefano are leaving."

"Look at the children, may get the low blood and die. I break my back like a dog, and we can't accumulate a thing, not even debt."

"Don't fret," she says.

He sits up. "From sunup to sundown sweat to earn *una lira*, and the *maledètti* priests want the fireworks for nothing. That's what the demons of God say. They say, 'Ci, come and shoot the fireworks for God, for the glory of paradise, for the saints, and you will be assured heaven.' They slap my back, throw me bones like a dog, for that's what I am, a lap dog, but the real dogs feast inside the rectory. The dogs of priests eat better than people. Anna, tell me, am I wrong?"

"Ciccio, try to sleep. It does no good to lament."

"Priests say the poor are Jesus' favorites, and the meek will inherit the earth. The church's interest is common with *feudi*. Meek, that's how they want to keep us, so they can nail us to the cross, and let the *feudi* kick in our teeth."

"It's a two-faced church Saint Peter founded, Ciccio, but we don't go to church for priests."

From underneath her pillow, she slides out a rosary. She starts on beads as if lamenting in Braille, rolling them between thumb and index finger. Ciccio sees a furtive tear reflect the dim moonlight. He thinks of happier times when he serenaded her, when the moon lit up her dark eyes, and he sang to her the Neapolitan song *Te Volgio Bene Asssje.* He reaches for her hand, says nothing—simply squeezes.

"It will work out, Ci. We have faith in God."

"God, God—what God? Anna, I used to look up to Padre Giorgio when I was a boy. He was educated and kind. Now he abuses wine. He eats and drinks like a pig, yet there are things he cannot have—things more meaningful—things like children. He has women, I know, sneaks them in, and I understand. After all, he is a man, but I do not understand him turning his back on his people."

"Maybe you exaggerate."

"No, no, listen, Anna. Yesterday, he said to me, 'These are hard times for priests, too, Ciccio.' But I see through his lie. He thinks because I can't read I'm ignorant, but I see him for what he has become."

"Calm yourself, Ciccio."

"Priests are despots who use vows to further their cause. Churches, rectories and monasteries are fit for kings. When I go inside I see all I need to see."

"They let you in?"

"Yes, when I bring the wine to him. I see servants dress priests. Don't need to lift a *maledètto* finger, never bend over to put on their shoes. Servants clean the rectory and cook meat at all their meals. Don't you see how fat they are? *Feudi* own the priests, help them change the definition of sin. Priests genuflect to the almighty *lira* and confessionals are nothing more than corrupt cubicles."

"Ciccio, calm yourself. You'll wake the children. Let's go on the roof until you're ready to sleep."

They slip through the window onto the roof and sit on a wooden bench that is sandwiched between warm clay tiles and a stone wall.

He puts his arm around her, yet it's his gaze she feels. She squeezes his hand.

"Maybe we should leave the little ones with your mother until we settle?" Ciccio says.

"No, no, Ci, together. We all go and never look back, eh?"

Ebony is their mantel, and flickering stars reflect ambivalence. Village streets are dark, prophetically black. Electricity is unimaginable in the village in 1904. Their bench wobbles like they wobble. They lean on the wall, and feel the roughness of stones impinge on their backs, so they lean on each other. They sit like the rich sit out a dance, wallflowers waiting to join the immigrant dance to America.

"Anna, did you hear Lorenzo Panepinto will be in the *piazza* Saturday?"

"Maybe it's safer to be in America."

"I hear there is a place near the ocean. Stefanesi and Calabrizzi are settling there."

"Where?"

"Tampa. It's a city with lots of cigar factories. They say there is work there."

"Ci, let's go to bed? You need to get up early."

He steadies her and guides her through the window and to the bed.

"*Te amo,*" Ciccio says.

"It will be fine, Ciccio."

"*Buona sera,*" he says.

She kisses him. There is a promise tied to each kiss in the unspoken language of fidelity. He smiles an abbreviated smile. Her tenth pregnancy does not matter. Tonight, nothing matters, nothing shows under the sheets.

"Franchito, are you still awake?"

Cars on Columbus Drive flash headlights into our bedroom. I see nothing.

"*Ave Maria—Gratia plena…Buon reposo,* Ciccio."

Alessandria della Rocca, Sicily—Via Roma, the town's main street today.

Alessandria della Rocca—clay roofs are forever.

The Sicilian countryside evoked tales of bandits and wolves told to me by
Nonna Anna.

A memorial to Lorenzo Panepinto stands in Santo Stefano's tiny piazza. The labor leader and socialist was shot-gunned Sicilian style at his door-step in 1911.

The author (right) and University of Palermo Professor Vincenzo Libici Alfio stand next to fava bean fields in the Sicilian countryside during the author's visit.

24

In sixth grade I'm made to place my head on my desk when I disrupt the class. My eyes bore into blackboards, and their bleakness forces me to count stars and stripes, for I know it's easy for flag manufacturers to cheat. Well, Papa didn't really say that, but he'd taught me something about the flag, something my classmates didn't know, something American teachers didn't perceive, perhaps something Betsy Ross didn't anticipate.

After school the previous week, I'd found him in the alley, a handsaw balancing on a garbage can, a hammer hanging from his belt. An American flag, constructed from rattan, is nailed to a huge wooden frame. Malleable rattan had been bent into wavy stripes, and slivers of bamboo into wheels. Brown bags of explosives hung from the wheels like hand grenades. Some lay partially hidden among weeds.

Ground pieces are Papa's artistic designs. First, he sketches on paper, then on sand and finalizes them in rattan. Red, white and blue candles, connected by a sleeved fuse, would give birth to an apparition on Halloween night.

"Papa, you made a mistake," I say. "You got six red, five white, and way too few stars."

He waves me off like he waves off flies.

"Why put more?" he says in Sicilian, steps back, removes his cap, scratches his head and counts stripes, pointing to each one.

Papa wears a cap when he works, a tan cap with a stained sweatband.

"Papa, it's not the American flag."

I get a quizzical look.

"Supposed to be seven red and six white, thirteen colonies. You got eleven."

"Coli...what?"

"Colonies, you know, Papa, states, United States?"

"Okay, but I bet you don't know the flag is a *spirito*?"

"A spirit?" I say.

"Yes, a spirit."

I'd heard of the *Spirit of '76*, imagined myself ducking musket balls, but Papa doesn't know about the American Revolution, surely not the *Spirit of 1776*.

"Papa, people don't care about spirits. They count stripes."

"Franche, you know how many times I've used this flag?"

I can't believe he's committing fraud, and he doesn't care, doesn't bother him in the least, and he doesn't consider defaming the flag a serious offense.

"Franche, people don't know how many stripes unless you tell them, *capisci*?" His eyes implore me to swear our secret.

"But, Papa…"

The Sicilian code of silence has just wrapped itself around the flag.

"Now, the Statue of Liberty, that's different," he says. "People who came through Ellis Island know the torch is held with the right hand. He raises his right arm. "Can't fool them with the left, not the American Madonna."

He finishes implanting hundreds, perhaps thousands of colored candles. Each is interconnected with a sleeved fuse, allowing fire to travel like lightning inside the paper sleeve.

"Don't worry," he says. "The public is too busy listening to 'O Say Can You See.' Look around; you'll see them watching each other, watching to see who's not standing, who's no placing their right hand over their heart, who's not taking off their hat and who's not singing. By then the flag disappears like a spirit. So you see, recognizing the flag is what counts, not the number of stripes."

"But, Papa…it's wrong, still ain't right."

"Why? I make it big and beautiful."

The flag is a staple in his armamentarium, built once upon a time, before I was born. He keeps it in the garage with rats and resurrects it each show. Pyrotechnics are his avocation, inherited from his father and his father before him in Sicily. Papa's face lights up brighter than his intricate designs. I see no need to pursue the numbers of stars, can't count them if I try.

Friday evening at Cuscaden Park, he gives me a last minute pep talk.

"Franche, do it my way, understand? And don't tell Mama."

"Yeah, Papa." I look up smiling.

"Don't laugh. This is serious business."

Responsibilities are granted gradually. I need to prove myself before advancing in his battlefield. He is Rommel, the fireworks fox, wearing his desert cap.

"When you see me wave *la candela*, light the statue then the flag, *capisci*?"

He allows me to light aerials, too, the most dangerous of all.

"If a bomb doesn't go up, don't go back," he says. "The mortar can split, or it may be a delay fire. Once the fuse is lit, stay away."

Papa is excited, for tonight he's an actor, and the show is about to go on.

"And never take the *candela* to the box where aerials are stored, *capisci*?"

I nod knowing he's right, for it's happened to relatives in Sicily, and it'd been like walking up to a gasoline pump with a lit cigar to pump gas.

Candela, a long candle used to torch fuses, telegraphs our positions in the dark. He needs me for the finale when we repetitively light fuses as fast as we can, load and reload aerials to overpower the sky. The Statue of Liberty and the flag hide in the darkness. There are no electronic igniting devises to lean on, so Papa leans on me.

Maintenance men construct a makeshift stage. The carnival is held on Halloween night, and stadium lights transform a softball infield into an outdoor stage. Classmates sing, dance and play musical instruments in talent reviews. The outfield is overrun with people holding hot dogs, candied apples and cotton candy. Loudspeakers pick up the clap of castanets from Flamenco dancers, and a classmate zing, zing, zings a Jeanette MacDonald song into slatted bleachers.

At nine o'clock, costumed children drag parents and hot dogs and popcorn across the softball outfield to a fenced off area, a portion of a larger baseball diamond. Aerial salutes keep beckoning the crowd, exploding inside a mantle of asphalt. Papa runs back and forth like a trapped base runner between third and home base as he ignites the crowd. They love his rattan artwork staked along the third base line, and the wild bunch, Crazy Wheels and Devil Wheels, wind up on the pitcher's mound. Near the third base dugout, rows of cast iron mortars sternly aim at the sky.

Papa smears paint on the dark canvas above, and streamers corkscrew luminously down. Some aerials chase infinity, and others whistle as if trying to wake up the moon. The Devil Wheel, like infantry, rattles the ground, and the crowd, deafened by explosions, covers its ears. The Crazy Wheel muses, spins one way, then another, unpredictably pausing and starting up again. The crowd, mesmerized, screams for more.

Sandwiched between torrents of explosions, Roman candles ejaculate potently. Soon they lose their pizzazz and squeeze out the last bit of their fiery existence. A blazing waterfall scorches the left field grass, and children, squealing, hug parents trying to escape the intimacy of earth shattering sound. A red fire truck and white ambulance are parked nearby.

The crowd awaits the finale, the seminal event. It's an overpowering barrage of unprecedented explosions. The fury of Technicolor rivets tired feet, and the crowd applauds, applauds loudly my father.

The battle raging, I ignite the Statue of Liberty and torch the flag, a one two punch against Hitler and Mussolini. The band plays Sousa's "Stars and Stripes" and without pausing, launches into the national anthem.

The wind picks up smoke and marches into the crowd, sweeping across the outfield. Infield clay mixes the odor of hot dogs, onions and yellow mustard.

All of Papa's displays are patriotic. Anti-Italian sentiment runs high in the Anglo community while Italian-Americans die on paper, yellow telegrams mailed by President Roosevelt.

I walk off the field like a twenty game winner. Papa replays the extravaganza at home. He tells Mama how well he'd timed it, how well it was received, recreating it with his ebullient voice. Late into night, I hear him. "I tell you true, Mary, it was grand."

Mama says, "*Dórme*, Filippo, *dórme*."

But he can't sleep, for it's been the moment he lives for, and it comes but once a year.

There was no trick or treating in the *barrio*, but Papa pulled off his trick, and the crowd got their treat. The number of stripes remained unchanged, remained our secret, and we never spoke of it again. His flag was a spirit, all right, his spirit, and when I see a flag I still think of Papa and count stripes.

Papa teaches me other things in sixth grade. I've heard my relatives speak disparagingly about police, heard how crooked they all are, but I don't know just how far their dislike of law enforcement goes. I don't really understand it's a cultural thing dating back to the days of the *carabinieri* in Sicily.

"Papa, the teacher said I can join the safety patrol."

"Sì?"

"Have to be a good student to join," I say.

"What would you have to do, Franchito?"

"Cross children at the corner and make sure they observe school rules."

"What about when it rains?"

"The school gives us raincoats and hats. I'd love to have a raincoat, Papa. They're bright yellow, so beautiful."

"What else would you wear?"

"You've seen it, Papa—a white belt around my waist, a strap over my shoulder, and a badge."

Papa continues to eat. It's not his favorite, nor mine, but even collard greens taste okay when I'm thinking about the shiny silver badge.

"Joaquin Campo will be our captain. He lives near the Martinos, Papa. Gaspar Martino is going to join, too."

"Campo? The Spaniard who lives in the big two-story on the corner of Twenty-first and Thirteenth?"

"That's his father."

"His son is a cop?"

"He's in my class," I say.

"Franchito, what do you do if someone breaks the rules?"

"Well, turn in his name to the teacher."

"Even your cousin?"

"Well, if he breaks the rules."

"You'd turn in your blood?" He pauses and looks at me from above a steaming spoonful of *minestra*.

"As a safety patrol, I have to be honest, Papa."

"Honest? At what cost? You want to be stoolpigeon? It's not right," he says. "You're never to turn in one of your own people."

I realize our conversation is hung up like a badge.

I envy those who wear badges. I never become a safety patrol, but later I realize Papa has insight. I hear some safety patrols show favoritism, float in school halls with swollen heads, and children on the outs fear being turned in. Power dissolves friendships, and one fat boy starts to resemble Mussolini—acts like he owns the school.

25

I'm now liberated. I own a bike, and on a Saturday morning Mama sends me out to buy chicken. I lean handlebars on the flaking white paint of Tony Labruzzo's Fish Market. It's an old two-story frame on Twenty-First Street and Columbus Drive. The store sits a block west of Ybor City's Mason Dixon line, Twenty-Second Street's black strip. It isn't black people making me uneasy; it's Mama's request hiding under my tongue. It lies there ashamed, yet ready to spring, be done with it, get it out, say it as fast as I can, say it before I forget, say it when the timing is right, so it won't be obtrusive, misunderstood, be natural like, but it makes me feel like a beggar.

I wave at Tony when I walk in. He's gesticulating with cigarmakers in the front section of the store with an apron wrapped around his waist. The day's specials are scribbled on storefront windows: mullet, red snapper, grouper, shrimp, cigarettes, and fresh crab. Market prices are posted up front with dollar signs and crescents representing cents. All of it is scribbled in red ink. Stacks of Coca Cola bottles, canned Progresso tomatoes, bags of oregano, and skinny Tabasco bottles frame a counter refrigerator. Peering through its glass face, I see fish iced. They are cloistered as if trying to stay warm. All are pale except red snappers. Even in death, the red fish retains a regal blush. All sleep segregated in rows with dilated and fixed pupils and off to the side, next to mullets, piles of crabs, so-called Florida blues, are covered with a blanket of ice. The refrigerator's motor hums, and a slow-moving ceiling fan pushes fishy odor out the front door.

In the back, Tony's wife slaughters chickens. She stands on a skid, keeping her feet dry above the rivers of blood flowing into a central drain. Black boots hug her tight up to her knees, and red chickens in wooden crates outnumber whites. All look out with piercing eyes.

"Mama wants a three pounder, Frances," I say.

"Does color matter?"

"No, but that's all the money I got."

"Some people want only whites, you know, Frankie?"

"Mama doesn't care. 'Chickens are chickens—not people.' That's what she says."

An old cigarmaker interjects, "Frances, I need a big fryer."

"Just a minute, Nina. The boy was here first. You next."

Frances is fair. She could have ignored me, but she didn't, and she's fair with the scales, too. I never see her finger rest on the scale's pan like some grocers do—no, not Frances. I'm small for twelve, so she seems tall, not fat by Sicilian standards. On the skid she looms larger than life, but there is something about the way she manhandles chickens that bothers me.

Beady eyes inside wooden crates stacked to the ceiling follow her around. It's a messy place, and chickens wipe their beaks on vertical slats smeared with hard dried chicken shit. So between blood and shit the place doesn't smell good.

Frances sticks her hand inside a crate stuffed with chickens and grabs a pair of skinny legs. She places the chicken on the smooth enameled cradle of a scale. The needle on the scale vibrates back and forth as if unsure what to record. Perhaps it even records the chicken's emotions. I watch her coach the chicken not to panic—be still and not jump off. The chicken stares at me mesmerized, as Frances lets go of her slowly. I know the scale intimidates chickens, for no chicken wants to be sitting there all alone. I don't know what freezes chickens up, but maybe they believe behaving on the scale spares them the death penalty. Frances' hand moves away cautiously. It is as if her outstretched arm is giving the chicken the silent dog command—stay—all the while, Frances is reading the scale.

"Three pounds," she says. "Okay, Frankie?"

I look away. The chicken's eyes are no longer beady but large and friendly.

"Frances, Mama said, 'don't wring the neck, cut it.'"

Frances assumes an omnipotent stance, holding down and bracing the chicken with her left hand just above her left knee. Statuesque and bending at the waist, she eyes the chicken's neck. With the knife in her right hand, she slices, and the chicken, trying to shake it all off, stiffens, flaps, but there's not a chance in hell of breaking out of such competent hands.

Most chickens at Tony's go out of this world with wrung necks. I'm the rare customer requesting a chicken's neck to be slit, something akin to a kosher kill, drains all the blood.

"Mama says it makes broth clear," I say.

Frances nods. "It does."

Chickens with wrung necks leave this world with heads wayward bound—twisted, cockeyed and with blood gorging their necks. They look every which way but straightaway, often back at their tails. I've watched Frances wring chicken necks before with a similar stance, bent over a bit more, firmly yanking heads down toward the floor. A quick tug and a grunt lets me know snapping a chicken neck isn't easy. If it doesn't feel right, she yanks harder, again and again. Once I asked, "How do you know when the neck's broken, Frances? I can't hear a thing."

"Oh, it's all in the feel, Frankie, all in the feel—something in the wrist." And she smiled.

Frances is humane, for I know she feels the chicken's pain, but I'm grateful I'm not her son. Before my chicken figures out what's gone wrong, Frances tosses her inside an oil drum. The chicken does a thrashing dance, making a cacophony of bruising sounds. I peek inside, hoping to see the chicken die, but blood splatters my face, so I look away.

When the chicken goes silent, Frances reaches in and grabs it by the feet. An upside down neck dangles and drips blood on the cement floor from its beak. Frances walks over and dunks the chicken headfirst into a bucket of boiling water sitting on a two-burner gas stove. She dunks the chicken like I dunk Cuban bread into Cuban coffee until it's soggy. She turns on a motorized contraption full of stubby hoses that protrude from a cylindrical steel drum. They look like rubber quills coming off the back of a steel porcupine. Oh, Frances is prepared all right. It's an annihilation machine that strips all her chickens clean.

The cylinder spins and the stubs blur, whiz fast, digging into the sopping chicken. Feathers fly from the carcass as she presses one side of the chicken and then the other until a naked bird with rudimentary wings and a more rudimentary tail emerges. Wet feathers and blood plaster the wall behind the machine.

Fine feathers are singed off on a gas burner, launching the pungent odor of burnt flesh into the room. She slides the slippery bird on a drain board next to a sink. Eviscerating the chicken releases the unmistakable stench of intestinal gas. After a final rinse, she chops off the head and feet with a cleaver, and me, feeling the timing is right, clear my throat and say, "Frances, do you got any extra feet?"

I hated to ask, but it was something Mama insisted I do each time I buy chicken.

"Let me see, Frankie," she says, wiping her hands on her bloody apron.

Rummaging through carcasses on a stainless steel drain board—flipping gizzards, livers, hearts and slithering necks, Mama's coveted chicken feet appear.

"Sure do," she says. "See."

"That will make Mama happy," I say.

"Feet do put flavor in soup, thickens it, too."

I nod.

"I got extra livers, hearts and gizzards. Want them?"

I love livers and hearts, pick them out of soup while it's still cooking, but not gizzards, never gizzards. I hate seeing Mama chew on the chewy things. But I don't want to appear picky, so I say, "Sure, Frances, sure."

She gropes through body parts, flipping organs like women straighten desks. I know the more extras I bring home the happier Mama will be.

Chicken feet are covered with a scaly skin that strips off like stockings, and toenails and spurs, well they're chopped off before Mama dumps them into boiling water. There, stubby toes tumble and reach out of the boil. There isn't much to chicken feet, but they have rubbery pads, and I enjoy chewing and sucking stringy toes.

Chicken feet secure, I stroll into Tony's side and peer into the long refrigerator. Tony is unshaven, but waking up to smelly fish doesn't make shaving a priority. He's middle age with dark hair, standing stocky and tough. I've seen his temper before, lashing out at customers, so I approach him cautiously, for there're lots of knives on his drain board.

Italians own grocery stores and bars in colored town—don't have to speak good English to do business with blacks. Some say it's better than dealing with Cubans.

"How is you, Mr. Tony?" says a Negro with thick hands fixed on his hips, allowing back muscles to bulge under a skintight shirt.

There's nothing high brown about this Negro. He's pitch black with biceps as big as a white man's thigh. Bulky Negroes work cement jobs in my neighborhood. They lift heavy cement blocks and bricks, and push wheelbarrows full of dense cement and slap plaster overhead on ceilings, broadening neck muscles beyond belief. It all has to be laid on fast, before setting up. White men refer to it as nigger work. I see the dried cement on his work boots and a few splats on his belt, and his meaty hands are cracked from the drying effect of lime in cement.

"Doing good," Tony says. "Ain't you working today?"

"No, sir, not today."

"Where you been working, Jackson?"

"All around, little here, little there."

Tony grins.

"Think you can find me a big mullet with a *roll?*"

"Whatever you want."

Tony slides the refrigerator door open and digs into a pile of mullets. Fish faces gape with open mouths. Brushing off the ice, Tony grabs a big mullet by the crotch and lifts it. Twirling, the slippery fish eludes him like a ballerina skating on ice. Finally with a firm grip, he holds it over the counter.

The Negro sniffs the mullet twice.

"I look more, if you want bigger one?" Tony says in broken English.

"Naw, long as it got a *roll*. Gotta have a *roll*."

Tony tosses the mullet on a spring scale. "Two and a half pounds, Jackson. Okay?"

The Negro nods. "Be fine."

Under running water, Tony slices midline—gills to tail. An orange roe falls out with the innards. The Negro's eyes widen. He paces in place with a pulsating beat, sort of an inner rhythm needing to be released, something jivey and innately Belgian Congo.

His white teeth contrast a beefy red tongue when he looks down and smiles at me. "Getting mullet, too?"

"No, chicken," I say.

Tony scales the fish, chops off the tail and is about to chop off the head.

"Mr. Tony, leaves the head on," the Negro says.

"Yeah, yeah, almost forgot."

"Mr. Tony, you sure picked one out with a nice *roll*."

"Need bait? Got cheap shrimp if you going fishing."

"Get all I needs at the bridge."

Negroes perch like black pelicans on the Palmetto Beach Bridge about six miles south of Tony's Fish Market. They scan the bay for dinner like white folks scan restaurant menus, fishing morning and evening tides. Most don't use fishing rods. They use a line with a hook, lead sinker and if not bottom fishing, a bobber. Their tackle box is a newspaper weighed down with a rusty knife, and if lucky, a string of catfish dangle into the water below.

"Jackson, where is Lila Mae? I don't see her for a long time."

"Wells, she gots a new dude."

"No shit."

"He drives a Cadillac."

"So, you gonna put up with that shit?"

"Got to, Mr. Tony. Got no steady work."

"So you gonna let the bastard take your woman?"

"I ain't suffering as long as I gets a good mullet to share with a good woman, Mr. Tony."

They laugh, and the Negro looks at the floor as if he just blushed. But, of course, he didn't—couldn't.

Life is uncomplicated in and around colored town—real simple. I think it's representative of America and maybe it is.

"There you go, Jackson," Tony says.

"Sees you when I's flush, Mr. Tony—promise."

Tony glances at me as if saying, "*Grazie* Dio, for paying customers like Sicilians."

The Negro sashays out the door with the wrapped mullet under his armpit like a fullback protecting the ball on an end-run. With his spirits lifted, I admire his stride as he carries the great mullet, the largest one in the refrigerator, perhaps the largest one in town—one with a hell of a roe. He knows Tony's mullet is live bait for a Saturday night on the Twenty-second Street black strip. It'll surely hook one of those big, fat, hungry mamas no questions asked—one that won't be lost to some young buck offering her a full rack of barbecue ribs or fried chicken wings or the plush back seat of a niggered-up Cadillac. Fish is number one bait next to whiskey, for without whiskey a Saturday night fisherman won't get a nibble.

Tony scribbles in his ledger and says, "Got fresh crabs, Frankie."

"No thanks, Mama said chicken."

"We close late tonight, so tell her about the fresh crabs."

I learned about chickens, fish and mullet roes at Tony's, and I don't remember when it all ended. But at some point, it did, and I grew up and left Tampa, and when I did, I never ate chicken feet again.

26

It is a time before unisex hair franchises in strip malls, and before women cut men's hair. Appearance to Italian men matters. The Italian Renaissance had taught Italians that man was the center of all things, and what could be more self-centered than a haircut and shave. Italians are touted for style, whether it's Ferraris, Armani suits or Bali shoes. So it is not surprising ghetto men look up to their barbers.

Valenti's barbershop juts out of a row of *casitas*. It stands catercorner across the street from my duplex, and next door to the barbershop is a yard lush with hibiscus and lantana bushes. The barbershop is an extension of a home built in the '20s. Like the other homes it's constructed of wood. Columbus Drive runs east and west in front of it, and customers parallel park on both sides of the street. A trolley track runs down its center. However, most men walk to the barbershop.

Mr. Valenti is a wiry, olive skinned Sicilian who smokes Lucky Strikes and Camels with the same intensity he cuts hair. He appears militaristic when his scissors snap at my head, or perhaps it's when the short man drops down two steps into the barbershop from his living room as if he was the U.S. Calvary rattling sabers coming through the rye.

A double door allows cigarette smoke to flow out to the sidewalk where a barber's pole hangs. On white tile sit two large barber chairs, and Mr. Valenti often occupies one or the other when there are no customers. There, he hides behind *The Tampa Morning Tribune*, smoking and flipping pages with nicotine stained fingers.

On Saturday nights men gather at Valenti's because it is the place to be. Customers, sitting in straight-back chairs, are lined up against the small room's white plastered walls. They argue baseball scores and political issues and which is the best—Pompeii or Filippo Barrio olive oil. Discussions rage late into the night, long after I'm made to go to bed. I love staying up Saturdays when after dinner Papa takes me with him to get haircuts. I listen to full-strength man talk, and rarely do Cubans or Spaniards patronize the place.

Customers interrupt conversations only to light cigars and cigarettes, or to do a two-step to the door and fire a bolus of phlegm out into the street. When Valenti calls their names, customer tongues are cut short, but a few continue from under white drapes covering them down to their knees. Customers hang around long after ears protrude, and men, mixing emotions with smoke, are never willing to let go of an issue.

"You don't know shit," a cigarmaker says, says shit in Sicilian. He says *marda* almost like Cubans say *mierda*.

Conversations heat up, and Valenti says, "Please put your chin down, so I can cut." Or, he smiles and says, "Look straight ahead, *diritto, per favore, no te remena la testa.*"—"Don't move your head."

He twirls the chair and rearranges faces in the room. He swivels it three hundred and sixty degrees with the flip of his wrist. It's exciting to see the intricacies of manhood surface in the room. Men on their backs, getting a shave, seem disqualified, but those not under the razor continue to shake fists.

"Loose cannons" shake the room. Italians never forget putdowns, never forget what *va fa culo* means. It says go be an ass or give your ass, for who or to whom, I never know. It takes me years to get linguistics down, but get them down I do. No one tips Mr. Valenti. No one tips anyone where I live except maybe with the flick of the middle finger.

On a Saturday morning I sit in a chair next to a table with strewn comic books. I'm old enough now to go to Valenti's on my own. Mama helps me across the street.

"Don Giovanni? I hear you believe Il Duce should rule the world?" a swarthy man says to an old man waiting in a chair with a cane leaning on it.

The cane fascinates me, always has. I've seen the cane before, seen its carved figures of dogs with bulging eyes and canine teeth. Tortuous serpents snake all the way down to the cane's shiny brass tip. I often see the old man swinging the cane, strolling sidewalks, see him threaten unleashed dogs that approach him. He doesn't seem impaired, doesn't really need a cane. He's agile, walking tall, taller than most Sicilians, with a rose bud pinned to his lapel. He inspects all happenings as if he is a member of a neighborhood watch. He interjects himself into street repairs, sewer connections, fender benders, wakes and cockfights in dilapidated garages. He's everyplace and everywhere. He's every man's man.

He wears the same pinstriped suit in summer and winter, and a food-stained necktie lies on his chest. He lives a lonely existence with his wife, Paolina, having no children and few relatives. I've heard the old man colors his wife's hair, and it looks like he does, for it's brassy black. It is a time few women in my neighborhood color theirs. They are nice people though, and I learned he'd once been a cigarmaker but faded into leisure. He's one of the few Italians who I know that reads Italian novellas while his wife rolls cigars at El Reloj cigar factory. Neighbors say he lives off the land, and in his case, his wife is the land. He's nice to me, stopping me on sidewalks, asking me to play checkers with him on his front porch.

"Why do you ask? Don't you like Mussolini, Primo?" the old man says.

"So you admit it, Don Giovanni. Have you no *vergogna*, no shame at all?"

"Mussolini was a fine journalist, and made the trains run on time."

The conversation shifts to Sicilian. "Yes, but Mussolini is Hitler's puppet," Primo says.

"No, no, Primo, you're the puppet, Roosevelt's puppet." The old man smirks and unfolds *The Tampa Tribune*, but I know he can't read English.

"You call me a puppet, eh?" Primo springs the finger.

The old man grabs his cane. "You stick your finger up your ass, Primo."

"Mussolini is getting Italians killed, and you defend that son of a bitch?"

"*Americani tutti sonno stupido, pazzo.*" The old man grips the cane after calling all Americans imbeciles.

"Don Giovanni, you live in America, not Italy."

"So what if I live in America? I say whatever I want. It's a free country."

"So what? Watch your tongue, old man, or somebody is going to stick it up your ass, *capisci*? And it's no going to be no Americano who does it," Primo says in broken English.

"America is free country. I say whatever I please." The old man's accent is even thicker, but his words are unmistakable.

"It's not free when Italian-Americans die, not free at all."

"*Marda.*" The old man invokes Sicilian shit as if it's one of the noble truths.

Valenti calls out, "Don Giovanni, you're next. Come *siediti*, sit, *per favore*, come and sit down."

"You're an ungrateful *figlio di puttana*." Primo stands when the old man stands.

I pretend to read Captain Marvel.

Valenti waits for Don Giovanni to sit in the barber's chair and says, "Forget all that stuff. Does no good to take words to heart, *signore*."

The old man walks to the door, and sucking out a tenacious post-nasal drip, he spits out the barbershop door. "I spit in your face, Primo," he says and sits in the barber's chair and crosses his legs.

Valenti drapes the old man, lowers the back of the big chair and begins lathering the old man's face as if he's hoping to smother his tongue. The old man is unflustered, smiling under the thick coat of white. Primo is fidgety, looking around with visibly labored breathing. Valenti is trying to defuse the situation by sticking to his routine of flapping the white drape in the air between each customer like a waiter does in resetting a tablecloth on a table.

The old man shuts his eyes, anticipates the razor and the tingling aftershave and the vigorous facial rubdown Valenti adroitly performs. Primo stands and tightens his belt and walks to the wall mirror behind Valenti. He spreads his legs, coming down a notch or two in a spread eagle position, dropping his image on the mirror. He combs his hair off his ears and looks at me. Suddenly he reaches into an assortment of neatly aligned straight razors on Valenti's shelf. He shoves the barber aside and latches on to the old man's nose, twisting it and holding the razor in front of the old man's eyes. "You fucking *fascista*, stick out your tongue, or I'll slice up your face like Capone's," he says.

It's a hell of an option, and Mr. Valenti stands gowned in his white smock like a surgical assistant waiting for the operation to commence.

Valenti backs up, knocking his cigarette off the shelf. "What the hell you doing, Primo?"

The cigarette flips and hits the floor. Valenti instinctively puts it out with his foot.

"Primo think of your family," Valenti says. He invokes God, "Dio, *aiuto*."

Valenti's voice is tremulous asking for God's help. "Primo, look, people come here to relax, lie back and get some peace, so why you no take it easy?"

Primo ignores Valenti.

"Say you're sorry, old man, say it, or so help me you're never going to spit out of your mouth again." Primo, too, invokes God, "*Perdona me*, Dio, *no sapo che facco.*"

Primo seems in control, but he just said, "Forgive me, God, for I know not what I do." He grinned when he whispered it into the old man's ear.

The old man's eyes tighten, and his lips quiver like a supplicant's. I've never seen three grown men invoking God at once—all for different reasons. Valenti is going the extra mile, crossing himself over and over again. It reminds me of how he straps the razor on leather that dangles from the barber's chair.

Two older men in waiting chairs against the wall seem unperturbed. They look at each other and raise their eyebrows. One is heavyset and in a pinstriped suit. The man stands and says, "Primo, are you *pazzo*?"

Primo looks out of the corner of his eye and keeps one hand on the old man's nose and the other on the razor. The fat man, in his seventies, just called Primo *pazzo*, imbecile, without a wrinkle in his voice—said it to a man wielding a straight razor.

"No, I'm no imbecile, Don Salvatore. This old man is giving all Italians a bad name."

"But, Primo, he's old, senile, a man of antiquity, past his prime. He doesn't know better, let go of his nose and give me the razor."

Primo squeezes the nose tighter. He isn't about to let go.

The fat man's friend, still sitting, smiles, as the fat man walks over to Primo and places his hand on his shoulder. "Listen to me, Primo, too many witnesses, this is no the place. Forget it. How can Valenti say he saw nothing? You're going to shed blood on his chair and for what? The tongue bleeds like hell. Maybe the old man bleeds out, then what? *Mori qua?* Forget it, forget it for today, Primo. The young boy is here, and Giovanni will pick you out of a lineup without a tongue. Stop the craziness, Primo, I understand. You are right," he says. "Make some sense, use your head. There are other ways to skin a black cat."

Primo casts his eyes to the floor, moves away from the swivel chair and sits down. Valenti walks over, and Primo hands him the razor. Valenti folds it and parks it on the shelf.

"Don Giovanni, go make your peace with Dio. No one saw anything." The man who'd intervened says in a consoling voice. "I see to that. Go, *va, va.*"

Valenti looks at me—doesn't blink. "Right, Franchito, you no saw nothing, right?"

"I'm here for a haircut. That's all, a haircut, Mister Valenti."

He wipes the lather off the old man's face. Unhooking the drape, Valenti tells him he'll finish the job another time, on the house, for free. Valenti stresses free, *gratis.*

I run home, and ask Papa, "Do you know a fat man called Don Salvatore?"

"A fat old man with a bald head?" Papa says.

I nod.

"Was there another man with a bushy mustache with him with a flower in his lapel?"

"*Sì,* Papa."

"*Mala fama, mala fama,* Franchito," he says. "That's one of the Trafficante brothers."

"Santo Trafficante's father?" I say.

"No, his uncle."

I know Santo Trafficante Jr. We all know Santo. He lives a few blocks from my duplex. He's first cousin to my Zia Giovanina's children, and they're my first cousins. Santo lives in a *casita* like most cigarmakers, but he doesn't roll cigars. He's waiting for his Assumption, a climb up the ladder to infamy. Although his name means saint, he'll be the next Cosa Nostra boss—in power when John Kennedy is assassinated.

Mala fama, bad reputation, was how my father characterized Mafiosi though his sister married into the family at sixteen.

The years fly by, and when I'm about twelve, I encounter young Italian men at the barbershop. They're what Americans call dandies, so-called *chulos* in Spanish. These are men who patrol the night and sleep away the day, have reversed their circadian rhythm—flipped days into night. In the afternoon, after buttered Cuban bread and demitasses of Cuban coffee, the pale men emerge like moles. Many have slicked down black hair, puffy eyes and thick mustaches or pencil-thin ones. They stroll into Valenti's for shampoos, razor cuts and shaves. Most smell strong of cologne.

They bask in Valenti's big chair, like sport models of sorts, for it's what they liked to refer to themselves as—sports—big spenders, but I know they're *chulos*, a Spanish word transcending cultures, the word transfixing itself to Sicilians. I'm afraid to call them *chulos* though, for they're more than big boys. They're ultimate alpha males.

Chulos talk a good game and looking down at me, chidingly mess up my hair. It's their way of being charitable to those of us who, because of age and size, pose no threat to them. To them it's all about acting like big shots. Most recline in Valenti's barber chair, puffing up like blowfish washed ashore on Clearwater Beach.

Chulos wear black trousers and long-sleeved white shirts without neckties, but some sling ties around their necks. They stress the casual, for that's how they face life, or that's what they want me to think. They're sports all right, examining every sign and symptom of a horny ass, for to them, the scent of woman is hard to resist. They jump into rumble seats or back seats and drive to Courtney Campbell Causeway for rendezvous, but in reality, the Casanovas are dressed for work. Most *chulos* work evening shifts in greasy spoons, hotels and bars. Those with hairy chests open their shirts widely, and buttons search for buttonholes across bravado necklines. Most eat well, so belts are let out a notch or two or three, contrasting their love for pasta with masculine necklines.

"Hey, Frankie, learning anything about girls in school?" the *chulo* says.

Before I can answer, Valenti calls him to the chair, so I move up to the on-deck position. He sits down. Valenti drapes him, and I'm glad he no longer sits next to me.

"He's too young to know about girls, Vito," Mr. Valenti says.

"How old you are, Frankie?" Vito grins back at me from the big chair.

"Twelve."

"Yeah, but you is thinking about them, right?" he says in English.

"About girls?"

"What else?"

"I guess." I bury my eyes in a Spiderman comic book.

"Know about rubbers?" Vito says.

"I guess."

"No embarrass him, Vito." Valenti smiles at me.

"I won't, just talking."

"Yeah, yeah," Valenti picks up the scissors. "Stupid talk."

A second *chulo* sticks his head in the doorway. "How long a wait, Valenti?"

"Just the boy. You next, Mario."

Mario sits next to me. "How you doing, Vito?" he says to Vito sitting in the barber's chair. "Give me the sports section, man."

Vito throws a section of the newspaper to Mario, who catches it in midair, crosses his legs and spreads it in front of him like he owns the barbershop. "What the fuck's new, Vito?"

"Just getting my ears lowered," Vito says.

"Saw that redhead of yours at the Cuban Club dance last Saturday. Thought she was your gal?"

"Used to be," Vito says.

"Is that right? You mean no more?"

"Yeah, it's a long story, Mario. You no wanna hear." Vito smiles. It's like my fake smile when photographers come to school to take class pictures.

Valenti keeps coaching Vito's chin down, trying to keep his head still. Now and then, he gives him a break by taking a drag.

"Well, she sure was shaking her ass on the dance floor. Damn, if I wasn't with Rose, I'd given her a ride home, but she left with a Cuban."

"A Cuban?" Vito lowers the newspaper and looks into space.

"Yeah, she's the redhead with freckles, right?"

"Ain't that some shit. So, hey, you still going with Rose, Mario, right?"

"Yeah."

"Still work for her father unloading produce at the farmer's market?"

"Yeah, yeah," Mario says. "Same old."

"You ought to marry that gal, be set for life. A hell of a deal, *la dolce vita*." Vito laughs.

"Yeah, yeah." Mario flips to baseball scores as if he's interested.

"Hell, I wish I had your chance. I wouldn't think twice," Vito says. "Be on easy street."

"But I ain't ready to be tied down and all that. Lots of screwing out there."

Vito raises the newspaper.

"Anyone who marries into that family goes out feet first. Honor and all that crap, you know," Mario laments.

"You right. I know her brothers. They're tough as nails. Just like the old man," Vito says.

"Yeah, if they ever got a whiff of my whoring around they'd come after my ass fast."

Vito smiles.

"I get along with them okay, but she's their baby sister, you know, and they're getting tired of waiting, keep asking if we've set a date," Mario says.

"I think you got yourself married, Mario. No hope for you, man. It's just a matter of time before they drag your ass to the altar, but Rose would make you a good wife."

"Yeah, I'd have to leave this town, all right. They'd be after my ass in a flash if I dumped her now. Expectations her mother keeps saying."

I see movement inside Vito's Italian loafers resting on the chair's iron footrest.

"You want the sides long, Vito?" Valenti comes around and pulls the newspaper down, and goes face-to-face, eyeballing sideburns for symmetry.

"Yeah, long—square off the back, kind of low and don't use that damn machine, Valenti. Make it into a duck's ass."

"You know I no use no machine, Vito," Valenti says.

"So, Vito, since you're done with Gail," Mario says from behind the sport's section. "You mind if I take her out?"

Vito's newspaper comes down then goes up fast.

"I thought you just said you and Rose was on for life?" Vito says.

"Yeah, but you know how that goes," Mario says. "Always room for one more in the stall."

The newspaper hides Vito's face.

Valenti finishes trimming the sideburns and is now clipping the top, placing hair between fingers cutting with snappy scissors.

"Shit, Mario, I don't give a fuck, but as a friend, I gotta tell you that Gail gave me a dose of the clap. Can you imagine what would happen if you took the clap to Rose? You'd have to leave the country. Sicily wouldn't be far enough."

"Sounds like you still got the hots for that bitch, Vito."

"Naw, I just don't wanna see a friend get the drips."

"I won't."

"Do what you gotta do, Mario. You don't have to ask me."

"But I don't want to hurt your feelings, Vito."

"You won't."

"I know Gail is just a Cracker, but I know sometimes guys get attached."

"Not me, Mario. Take them or leave them. No big deal, just another piece of ass."

"The drips eh?" Mario lowers his newspaper paper a bit, looks over it at Vito who is now scratching his balls under Valenti's white drape.

They're eyeballing each other. Both newspapers are down, and Valenti is eyeballing them.

"Yeah, a bad dose. Burned like shit for two weeks. Each time I took a piss I saw stars."

Mario, smirking, fixes his eyes on the tin-paneled ceiling. "What you expect from a Cracker? When American women get drunk they fuck anything in sight, even blacks. That's why you can't take no chances. Gotta use a rubber or you gonna get burned." Mario laughs. "Burned. Get it?"

"Yeah, yeah, you're quick, Mario, real quick." Vito looks at me. "That's what I was about to tell the kid, but Valenti collared me. Gotta use them fucking rubbers, can't take no Goddamn chances."

Mr. Valenti smiles at me as if assuring me he won't tell my father a thing.

They're all looking at me, making me feel guilty, and I hadn't done a thing. I'd only seen Trojans inside La Económica Drugstore on a back shelf.

Valenti breaks the momentary silence. "Frankie is Filippo's boy, you know him, live across the street, next door to Peppino in the duplex."

I'm being introduced to the big boys, but I'm not sure I like it.

"Peppino's nephew, ain't that some shit? Nice to meet you, Frankie," Mario says.

"You don't look like Peppino."

"Peppino is my godfather. Married to my Aunt Felicia. He's not blood."

"Oh, that's right. Hell, my father used to hit juke joints with Peppino when they was young. Peppino ran the speakeasy on Eighth Avenue, The Tambourine. Yeah, that's right, and your cousin Frank ran around with that bunch, too. Lots of Franks in your family, right?"

I nod.

"That godfather of yours can tell you some stories, Frankie. Good man Peppino." He winks at Valenti. "Say hello to Peppino, hear?"

"Sure," I say.

"Yeah, kid, gotta use them *prophalaxatives* if you wanna stay clean." Mario slaps my back, and I see Valenti take a drag.

Mario stands and pulls out a comb resembling a black stiletto from his hip pocket. He combs his hair in a spread eagle position in front of a backsplash mirror. *Chulos* can't resist mirrors. It's an inbred weakness that won't let them pass up a mirror.

Valenti drapes all his customers with an oversized bib and tucks it around their necks, covering and isolating shirt collars from clippings. It hangs to just below their knees, so cut-hair rolls down a white slope onto the tile floor. He sweeps hair into a dustpan, mixing the gentle white of old age with the dark flair of youth. He lathers stubby faces with a stiff brush he dips into caked soap inside a mug. Valenti tells me the straight razor is made of German steel. I watch the razor glisten in the sunlight when he strokes a cracked leather strap before every shave. He pours aftershave into his cupped hands and dabs it on faces in a coveted style. Following the stinging aftershave, vanishing cream rubs faces into soporific oblivion.

I associate scratchy sounds with a razor's edge, and Mr. Valenti tells me a barber's shave resembles life because of scrapes, nicks and bleeding points, but no one tells me about a novel written by Somerset Maugham—*The Razor's Edge.* Comic books are as literary as it gets in the barbershop.

There is no Siddhartha leading the way. I never hear of Herman Hesse, Tolstoy or Franz Kafka or any of the greats. I don't delve in the meaning of words or life. Hell, all I know is Ybor City, and it's east of downtown Tampa like perhaps east of Eden.

Later I learn Maugham's book is about people who can't extinguish the "self," and, of course, it was never meant for *chulos.* There was no way they would have allowed anything to extinguish the self—too Italian for that. The self in *chulos* was always ablaze. So, I guess I was being fashioned after *chulos*, and Valenti's *Razor's Edge* was as close as I came to reading the novel, but I did see the movie at the Ritz Theatre on Seventh Avenue with Tyrone Power as Larry, the enlightened one, and Gene Tierney misjudging life and losing the love of her life. But what the hell? How could anyone not enjoy her, materialistic or not? There wasn't one *chulo* who'd turn her down.

27

The Negro Catholic School across the street provides my cousin and me a built-in playground. We're still twelve or so, and there is only Nonna Anna to keep an eye on us after school. The two-story brick building empties out early, and it is then, after school, we sneak inside to taste a slice of Negro life. We tiptoe in when the janitor is upstairs sweeping the floor. The school's halls are foreboding, and echoes amplify our voices. We open desktops at random, and pull out desk drawers where black-hooded nuns sit during the day. We see crucifixes on walls, a picture of the Pope, and Jesus looks at us from a big cross.

"Boy, it's scary in here. We better not go any farther," my cousin says.

"Well, how we going to know what's in here if we don't look around?"

"Did you hear that?"

"Hear what?"

"Don't know. Something. Everything echoes in here," he says.

"Yeah, it feels like a mausoleum."

"Don't say that."

"I think you're right, better get the hell out of here," I say.

We run outside into the playground, which is really a sandlot. Two paint-starved outhouses, boys' and girls' restrooms, sit off to one side under a large oak. Green vines snake on the roofs and their backsides are engulfed with dense vegetation. We open rickety doors and see black widow spiders framed in delicate webs. We marvel at the hourglass emblems on pear-shaped abdomens. They're the real things and don't care if the skin they pierce is black or white.

The playing field is worn barren. Negro children have pounded it clean of vegetation. On Saturday and Sunday mornings, the playground is a haven for winos that sleep hung over under lantana bushes, so we play muted, fearing they'll wake.

It doesn't matter the playground is for coloreds. I play with coloreds and see nothing wrong with it, but I hide it from my parents. It isn't because it's the Deep South, but because Negroes have so-called "no families." That's what all my relatives say—Negro children have no fathers. Sure, somewhere, there are blacks that are God fearing, responsible and marry and are moral, but there are no Booker T. Washingtons or Marian Andersons in my colored town. Most blacks are not Catholics, even the ones that go to the school.

On my trips to the Italian Club Cemetery with Papa and Anna, I see how Negroes live. I see fat and skinny women in white dresses gadding about Sunday mornings. White carnations hang on embroidered bodices, and wide brimmed hats shield the flowers from the noonday sun. The women laugh and gesticulate, holding bibles, standing on Baptist church steps.

I see them from the back seat of the Chevy, see them in a different light. I hear Negro spirituals when Papa drives by names like Calvary and Trinity and Jesus Saves. I see Negro ministers dressed in black garb with white collars—men of all ages, sizes and shapes. Some are sober, some awfully heavy, and some possessed by the spirit, smile and welcome the sisters. Widening their grins and showing their teeth, the self-righteous preachers camouflage their carnal intentions, and I hear them say, "We're all sinners, Sisters, all sinners." I smell barbecue chicken and pork ribs in churchyards.

The con-artists choose their black beauties carefully, one at a time, saying, "Come, Sister, come on, please, won't you be the mother of my church? My don't you look pretty today."

I watch the self-ordained fight the whiskey anesthetic weighing down their eyelids.

Immigrants weigh good against evil and decide isolationism is protective; it protects my cousin and me. Sicilians don't read Darwin, nor know about the Galapagos Islands, nonetheless, they believe isolationism will ensure their survival. But in one generation America's diversity uncoils their genetic code, and my generation becomes like everyone else.

In the playground I learn about other things besides Negroes. I learn about sex. I learn about it Cuban style.

"*Una mano o dos*," Hernando, an older Cuban, writhes in the dirt with trousers unzipped as we look on. "One hand or two?" he screams.

"Yeah, he's having epilepsy," my cousin says.

"Yeah, yeah," Hernando says, "Love it. It's what happens when you become a man."

"Wonder if it'll happen to us?" I say.

"Well, at least, he didn't swallow his tongue," my cousin says.

It's what teachers do when children seizure, hold on to tongues for dear life. A few of our classmates are afflicted with the embarrassment. I learn Hernando is taking puberty into his own hands, initiating his own affliction in our hideaway, creating his rite of passage, beating himself into manhood.

Oh, I occasionally sneak in and see naked women at the ailing Broadway The-atre. The theatre is trying to stay solvent, so it rolled up its silver screen and imported live burlesque. I'm ashamed of the Broadway's downward moral spiral. It reminds me of the fall of Rome. Bad movies have done it in. Cubans make fun of our club's debacle, knowing burlesque is only a stopgap measure in its inevita-ble decline. But while the good times last, it's fun. I love looking at coming attractions of three-dimensional flesh in lobby posters—sort of like delicacies promised to us under plate glass. Women with names like Blaze, May and Naughty Marie light up the club's neon sign outside.

I don't see Papa standing outside the club. It's where he normally hangs out after dinner. That's where many Italian men gather in the evenings to catch a breeze. The old man who takes tickets allows his cronies to enter without paying, and he's also there to keep young boys out. That's another reason the Italian Club is in the red, too many old cronies tweaking G-strings free.

"Frankie, your Papa is in the back of the theatre. We better get out," a friend says after a successful sneak in.

"Where?"

"Leaning up against the wall."

"Yeah, but wait. He's pretty engrossed. We'll go sit on the other side. If he moves, we'll leave out the side exit."

It's strange watching burlesque with Papa in the place. I feel as if I'm betraying him. I'm sure there are things a man does not wish to share with his son. There is no familiarity in our relationship—none of this "best friend" stuff today's genera-tion prides itself in. He has his job description and I have mine.

I learn about pasties, G-strings and old ladies with sagging breasts. It's a great feeling becoming a man.

My cousin and I integrate before Civil Rights, long before.

"Poor guy, barefooted and soles like leather," I say, seeing James come into the Negro Catholic School playground.

"Yeah," my cousin says.

"Hush."

James is a skinny Negro boy who isn't too swift and talks disjointed Negro talk. He has big, white teeth and dresses in ragged clothes and shines shoes.

"James, you wanna play ball?" I say.

"Okay," he says. "Or you wanna wrestle? I learned a new hold," he says.

"Okay, we'll wrestle," my cousin says.

James is our unacknowledged friend. He tells me about life in colored town. He doesn't attend the Catholic School, goes somewhere else, where Negroes go, but he provides cover, a justification for us to play on black turf, gives the appearance of propriety, as if we've been invited by one who belongs. He gives me insight into a black boy's plight in the South, confirming the outrageousness of segregation, but our parents are correct in their assessment. Negroes in our neighborhood have no culture. When we wrestle, I feel his hair is different than mine. His palms are lighter than the rest of his skin, and his skin feels like sandpaper.

That evening, kinky hairs clings to my clothes like Velcro.

"Papa, I want to shine shoes," I say at the kitchen table.

"What the hell do you think you are, a Negro?" he says.

"No, but it's a way to make money."

"No son of mine is going to shine shoes. You're Italian and Italians don't shine anybody's shoes."

"He's been playing with coloreds again, Filippo. That's where he gets his ideas." Mama leans over and picks kinky hair off my shirt.

"If I find out you're playing with Negroes, I'll break your legs. Understand?"

"*Sì*, Papa."

Most of the houses in the South don't have basements. They're built on elevated foundations of short brick columns. That's how houses aerate in the hot, humid climate of Tampa. They float a few feet off the ground, allowing me to crawl underneath and spend summers in their shade. It's a way to ensure privacy and play with fire, smoke cigarettes and catch itchy ringworm from dog and cat excrement.

James says he screws his younger sister under the house, and since we're good friends, he keeps asking if we'd like to poke her, too.

"Maybe we should," I say to my cousin when we're alone.

"I don't think so."

"But it's for free," I say.

"If my papa finds out, he'll break my legs."

"Yeah, might break more than your legs."

"Right."

We are just starting to pry open puberty's door, but James is inside enjoying dessert. There are many Negro girls victimized by older brothers, cousins, uncles and men who frequent their mothers and grandmothers. Childhood pregnancy is traditional and worse than segregation. It's seen as young as twelve in colored town.

Papa doesn't use the word *tizzune* like my godfather. He embraces a "live and let live" policy, mixing it with "don't tread on me." Times are better economically, so Papa and I take clothes to a black woman who lives in a shanty near the Italian Club Cemetery. Her name is Anna Mae. She's what is called a washwoman, washes and irons clothes in her home. She's huge and molds her big ass in a rocker on her front porch. Fat creases cut her neck like necklaces of black pearls.

We still don't have a washing machine, clothes dryer or hot running water. Papa drops off scraps of lumber from jobs on her front yard. She smiles when he piles it not far from a laundry tub sitting on red bricks. It saves him a city dump fee, and she laughs in a thankful way. I see black men. Many go in and out of Anna Mae's house. Other women live there, too. There are always young women holding black babies with crusty noses. Papa joins Anna Mae's laughter, and the two mix broken English and Negro talk.

One summer evening, Papa takes me along. He parks in front of Anna Mae's house and stuffs a couple of dollars in my shirt pocket. "Take the basket in and pay her."

I knock on a screen door. It's unlocked. I hear nothing, so I walk in. I see Anna Mae in bed with a white man under a white sheet. Both are surrealistic in the dark room. She jumps up and says, "How is you, Frankie? Didn't hear you come in."

Sagging breasts flip out of a full slip, and she slips them back in. The slip is loose, hangs on her frame like her tits do. Swaggering towards me, she smells of bourbon. The white man grunts and turns away on his side—stiffens—makes unintelligible sounds, but I make out—"Shit."

I say, "I came to pick up the clothes."

"Puts the dirties in that corner. The clean ones is in the next room."

I lay the basket down and hand her the money.

"You tells your daddy I needs more wood."

"He's doing floors this week," I say.

"Well, be sure not to forget."

"Oh, I won'ts."

It is easy to fall into Negro talk, sort of picks me up and carries me along, and perhaps, that's why redneck talk is indistinguishable from that of blacks, been in bed with them too long in the Deep South.

"Colored town," circa 1930s. Afro-Americans hand washed clothes for whites. A fire-blackened washtub sits on bricks in foreground.

28

I'm thirteen or fourteen and see a jar stuffed with tobacco leaves. "Ma, what's *capa* doing in the refrigerator?"

"It's good leaf, Franche. Leave it alone."

"Going to make cigars at home?"

"No, no, need it to allow me to meet quota."

"I never see Aunt Felicia put *capa* in her refrigerator."

"That's 'cause she's fast. She doesn't care what she puts out."

"Won't it smell up the refrigerator?"

"It stays pliable in there," she says.

"Like lettuce?"

"Something like that, so don't try to smoke it. They've been giving out terrible *capa* at the factory. It cracks easy because the weather has been so dry," she says in Sicilian.

"How about if they catch you, Ma?"

"They won't."

Capa is the Spanish word for tobacco leaf. I never question the name or its derivation. It is just how things are, but the word means cape or cloak in Spanish. I never think of cigars wearing a cape or a cloak, but I guess they do. Preoccupation with cigar making is all I hear at the dinner table night after night. There are no discussions of world affairs, civic affairs or anything much above the ghetto level. It is part of the isolationism illiteracy puts on the table for ghetto children to eat, and the less Papa knows about something, the more passionate and opinionated he is. My parents don't realize the impact. How can they? They know no different, but I am constantly being told how much better I have it than they did, and I do. I'm not working in a cigar factory and never will.

At age twelve, my mother decided six years of schooling was more than enough for her. She could read and write at grammar school level and that put her above most of her peers. She was one of the lucky ones and didn't know it. Her father wanted her to continue school, never insisted she quit, but she did.

"Too shy to start a new school," she'd said to me, and when she told her father she didn't want to continue he said, "If that's what you want, Maria? I'll get you a job. Your mother can teach you how to roll cigars at home while I search."

It was what Mama expected, and her mother did not object. It was what all the girls of her generation did—work, get married and have children.

She tells me stories about the factories, about how it was when she was a girl.

"Franchito, they hid us in store rooms and in men's restrooms, depending on the sex of the inspector. Truant officers came unannounced. It made me feel I was doing something wrong. Woodrow Wilson did it when he passed child labor laws—made it illegal for poor people to work. Now the government has passed another law to keep cigarmakers out of work."

Mama's concern is minimum wage, a new requirement imposed on factories. America does its best to quash piecework, but factory owners find loopholes. They impose quotas.

"Filippo, I don't think I can make 225 cigars every day," Mama says. "Not with bad leaf."

"Well, make what you can, Mary. We'll get by," Papa says.

"Ma, that's about 4000 cigars a month," I say.

"I had a good year last year, Franche—didn't get laid off much, so I rolled near 50,000," she says.

The numbers boggle my mind. Why do they need automation? Mama is a machine.

"Your aunt Felicia rolls over three hundred a day. She's *larga*, but she puts out lots of terrible stuff. If I could just get a better paying *vitola* it would work out to minimum wage, and I won't get fired."

Papa says, "Talk to the *capotasso*, Mary. You're not that slow, and he's not going to want to lose you. You roll such beautiful cigars."

It's about cigars again. I eat broccoli mixed with fragmented spaghetti and a tad of olive oil and Romano cheese on top—another form of *minestra*. *Minestra* is eaten with every conceivable bean and vegetable. The most common are: lentils, fava beans, red beans, collard greens, string beans and broccoli.

"How's a better paying *vitola* going to help?"

"Well, Franche, figure it this way. Minimum wage is based on an eight-hour day, so divide how much money I make by piecework by eight. If it comes out to minimum wage or more, I'm okay."

"Hell, Ma, you're still getting paid piecework."

"It's worse, because I have the pressure of meeting a quota to make it appear they're paying me minimum wage. If piecework comes out to less than minimum wage—I'm fired."

Slowness is not Mama's only problem. Mama's been laid off more than a couple of weeks and returns to work.

It's midday, a summer vacation day, and I'm sitting on the duplex's front porch. I see Mama moving fast on the sidewalk. She starts to run up the cement steps.

"Franchito, open the door. I'm about to vomit." Ashen, her face hangs on to a barf. She darts a straight shot to the bathroom.

"I'll make *tilo*," Anna yells from the kitchen.

I hear Mama vomiting, and my grandmother makes a Spanish tea Latinos call *tilo*. It's a cure-all made from *tilia* flowers. I run into the bathroom and lift Mama's head and aim it into the toilet bowl as best I can. Her eyes bulge at the explosive force of relief. Her face is crimson and drenched in sweat. I hang on to it, stabilizing it—keep it on target. I rip toilet paper off the roll and hand it to her. She grabs more paper and heaves again and again. Repulsed, I watch yellow liquid gush out of her nose. Angry gastric juices reek acrid in the tiny room, and the strong smell of tobacco vaporizes from her hair. A fine spray of barf hits my bare feet.

"Is there anything I can get you, Ma?"

"No, need to lie down."

She leans on me, and I help her to her bed. She burps, passes gas all at once, and says, "*Perdona.*"

I pardon her. What else can I do? Her eyes glaze, and I yell for my grandmother. Nonna holds ammonia salts under her nose. Mama's head yanks away from the ammonia. Her eyes open. She sees I'm perturbed. She smiles, doesn't eat lunch, lies in the bed a while and returns to the factory. After two to three days the symptoms abate, and all is back to normal. Mama is reacclimated to nicotine.

Cigarmakers seldom talk about acute nicotine poisoning. None of the women smoke, and it's accepted as a mere inconvenience.

At the kitchen table Mama says, "Filippo, I can't eat."

Papa looks up from his bowl of *minestra*.

"I just can't. My mouth hurts," she says.

"I think they've got to come out, Mary," he says in Sicilian.

Nubbins have replaced her front teeth, protruding just above her gum line.

"Mama, do other cigarmakers chew *capa*, too?" I say.

"I never did," Papa interjects.

"It's a bad habit I picked up trying to make heads perfect."

"Mary, you got to stop doing it."

"Easy to say, but it's tough to make heads without working them with your mouth."

"Mary, you got to use the *chaveta*. It's sharper than your teeth."

"When tourists come to watch us work, the *capotasso* warns us not to put cigars in our mouths. I can't roll a good one until they leave."

Mama chews on one side of her mouth. "Factory owners don't want tourists to see we get saliva on cigars. Rich people are strange that way, Franche."

"But I thought you use spit to stick wrappers?" I say.

"No, no, we use a special gum. The Health Department is threatening to inspect cigar factories. Say there's too much TB among cigarmakers."

"That's crazy, Mary. It's not a restaurant. Maybe you'll have to get a chest x-ray like restaurant workers?" Papa laughs, but Mama doesn't see his humor.

"They're thinking about it," she says.

It's pain that drags cigarmakers and their families to dentists, severe pain, and it's usually for extractions. Mama's front uppers and lowers are replaced with prosthetics. She continues to tear at leaves with her new teeth. She never looks like Mama again, but I say to her, "*Sonno naturale*, so natural, Mama, so natural."

I'm sure I commit a venial sin, but in this case, it would be a mortal sin not to lie.

From my porch, I watch cigarmakers trek to factories and back. Lunch and evenings they saunter by. Fast bunch-makers and rollers lead the parade. Slow ones roll out of factories last. Women shade themselves with parasols, and men wear straw hats with stiff, serrated brims, *pagliettas*. Women and men seldom mix. Women walk side by side and men with men, and solitary workers fix their eyes on sidewalks.

All are creatures of habit, people with monogrammed walks. They appear and disappear predictably each day, sequenced, as if released from a starting gate. When I enter puberty some women change.

My cousin and I sit on the porch. I'm flipping a baseball.

"Frank, here she comes," he says.

"La Señorita?"

"Yeah, man, ain't she something?"

"Yeah," I say.

"Look at that low cut. Hot stuff, man, hot stuff."

"Quick, let's go play catch on the sidewalk," I say.

"Yeah, look at those hips, man." He watches them swing back and forth like a pendulum.

We notice adult women, real women, see them in a different light of day, different shades, different from immature school girls. We never find out La

Señorita's name, but she's a Spanish woman, all right, perhaps Cuban, and she walks to and from the factory like clockwork. We christen her La Señorita because of her Spanish style. She sets a new standard. An ardent reference point of sensual attraction brings out feelings we didn't know existed. Perhaps, it is then we learn the difference between pretty and attractive. Attraction turns out to be a woman's worth, what counts. Her hips wave at my hormones from across the street. She's in her thirties, and that's old to pubertal boys, real old, but she arouses my cousin and me in ways only she can.

She carries a brightly colored parasol and shifts it from shoulder to shoulder, contrasting jet-black hair. She shifts it casually, unintentionally provocative, inadvertently spinning it, cradling it on a bare succulent shoulder. An embroidered, white blouse hangs low, filled to the brim, and sometimes, it sits cockeyed, exposing one voluptuous shoulder more than the other. She's typical of our conceptual image of a Spanish *señorita*. All she needs is a rose in her hair, so I imagine one there. She walks on the opposite side of the street. I throw the ball at her feet. It bounces off the sidewalk into the street gutter, and I run up, bend over and reach for it, looking up gawking, gaze into her eyes, and she into mine.

"*Ola, señora.*" She's surprised at my presumptuous Spanish hello.

"Excuse me, *perdona señora, pero,* I pick up *la pelota, perdona.* My cousin threw the ball wild."

"*Es o* right, Nino. *Es nada.*" She interrupts motorized hips and smiles, says it's okay, and I smile.

She's more beautiful up close than I imagined. She's blessed with full lips, dark Spanish eyes and a subdued smile. She never walks on my side of the street letting me know she's not interested in pubertal boys, yet she continues swinging hips as our eyes follow her out of sight.

"How does she look up close?" my cousin says.

"Great."

"What did you say?"

"I said she was a most attractive *señora.*"

"Wow. You said that?"

"Yep."

"What did she say?"

"Nothing."

"Nothing? Naw, she said something. I saw her lips move."

"Oh, that."

"Yeah. Come on, don't hog it all to yourself. Tell me."

"She just said I was a handsome young man."

"No shit."

"Honest."

Women grow old in front of my eyes. Most keep walking long after husbands die, and there is no infusion of new blood into the industry. No one takes up cigar making anymore, no one, so back and forth cigarmakers roll in front of my eyes, walking past my front porch. Some wave and watch me grow up. Widows dress in doleful black down to their shoes, contrasting pale, cosmetics-free faces, but those with husbands brandish lipstick-smeared smiles. I just know they're still making it with husbands in dingy bedrooms. In the nearness of *tabaquero* huts, occasionally, I hear one moan, and I smile.

Women of the *barrio* reflect their heritage. Latin women let loose early; soon after a pregnancy or two, they balloon. They wrap their big hips and breasts in print dresses, but in ensuing years, I see matronly forms abandon the garishness of youth, abandon bright floral prints that once draped young buttocks. In time, breasts sag, too, and the back and forth rhythm creates the repetitive beat of a death march. Sturdy and stout, they float by day after day like vintage battleships of the Spanish Armada. And I, well, I wave at them and smell gardenia perfume. Men age, too, but they smell the scent and follow it, and like fireflies, they switch on. Perfume acts like the aphrodisiac Spanish fly. Tired hormones rejuvenate Italian men, too, as they walk in the wake of sashaying hips. Covertly they interject a skip in their shuffle, a Sicilian shuffle, I'm told. It is one Cubans can't initiate or imitate. In time, husbands die, and black dresses dominate the scene, and colors fade, fade more under sweaty armpits.

29

He stands in front of the refrigerator gulping cold water, drinking it from a Florida Dairy milk bottle on a hot July day. He's done what Mama said for me never to do, drink out of the water bottle she keeps in the refrigerator. But he's drenched in sweat. A tee shirt sticks to his skin, and his khakis are soaked through at the crotch as if he just pissed himself. A layer of dirt clings to his sparse hair, and his arms and chest are dusted with yellow sawdust as if it were pulverized dew.

Papa says, "Better make something of yourself, Franche."

Make myself into what? There are no blueprints out of the ghetto.

"Better finish high school," he says, thinking I don't get his drift.

Parents of my generation are not tactful. Tongues are the hammers that pound in the nails.

He keeps repeating the mantra, but that's as far as it goes.

There is vagueness in his words telling me he can't tell me more. His responsibility ends with, "Better yourself and don't be a damn fool."

I know a white dress shirt and a necktie or an office job or selling Craftsman tools at Sears and Roebuck will quench his thirst.

"As long as you don't have to break your back like me," he says.

Frustrated, he berates himself. "*Somma ama bitcha, somma ama bitcha.*" It happens because he can't read, or when he can't add numbers and shortchanges himself calculating small jobs.

Tampa teenage years are tough years. Termites plague Ybor City homes. Papa's an expert on termites, and he demonstrates the extent of diseased floors to customers with a straw broom. He elicits a hollow sound when he sweeps the floors.

Papa says, "It's hopeless. Need to replace all of it."

The customer bows his head and Papa shakes his.

"How much?" the customer says.

"Well, I'll give you a contract price and a price by the hour. It's a higher by contract because I can't tell what I'll find."

Papa is like a surgeon, holding off prognosis until he tears up the floor.

He thinks all a man has to do to prove himself trustworthy is produce on the job. Producing is the quintessential of being a man.

"Do a good job, Franche," he says. "Do it right, and they'll call you back."

But he doesn't understand the finer aspects of carpentry. He's what is referred to as a rough carpenter, roughing-in and framing-in houses. That's what he does when he works for contractors, but he lays the most beautiful floors in the *barrio*. He doesn't understand architectural design and esthetics. If it's good enough for him, it should be good enough for everyone. He's a man dedicated to function and builds things stout in a postwar building boom.

"They're pasting slivers of wood and fooling the public. It's no longer wood. They call it plywood," he says. "Cheap shit."

My days off from school start out in Papa's slow boat to China, Papa's pistachio green, one-quarter ton, 1949 Studebaker truck. I sit in the cab as he drives to the job, never exceeding 25 mph.

He replaces a pine floor, and I see the sweat drip on his smile like dew rolls off petals of a black-eyed Susan. His face is dark, baked in the sun and grimy. It blossoms out of a yellow tee shirt, but it isn't dew covering my father's face. He finds strength among termites, legions of *somma ama bitcha*s, yet he knows they're his benefactors.

"Franche, go to the truck and unload the two by sixes. Be careful coming through the house. Don't scratch the walls. Don't just dump them. Lay them down easy."

Unloading new lumber is a snap. It's clean and without nails to gouge my hands.

"Stand back. I'm going to be swinging hard. Don't need to worry about you."

"Yeah, Pa, I'll stand in this corner."

I watch like all the times before and hear lumber screech as he rips it out of the clutches of tenacious nails. Steel pounding steel gives off sparks in a dim room as hammer meets crowbar time after time. Groaning, he leverages and lifts planks, rips them out of steel roots. Each grunt synchronizes a swing, and the pounding of steel on steel is as close I get to *Il Trovatore*'s anvil chorus.

He shouts, "*Sonna ama bitcha*." He shouts it again.

He revels in the decapitation of floors, relishes a swinging crowbar that comes from the right, then left, shaking all things loose. I cover my ears. The noise jolts my daydreams out of existence as I balance on exposed beams. I survey the view of under the house. There, Florida sand had been protected from the air currents of time. Undisturbed and preserved for nearly a century, I imagine mounds of sand are Egyptian pyramids. I dream of uncovering treasures, perhaps a strong box, a murder weapon, an Ybor City relic from its exalted past, but all I find are aggressive fleas and yellowed *Tampa Tribune* newspapers blown there by the wind.

Papa marks a pine board with his pencil. He bends over it and picks up his circular saw. He plugs it into an orange extension cord and squeezes the trigger. With his left hand, he pulls up his heavy, wet pants. I see exposed buttocks when he bends over to make more cuts. I find bittersweet humor in the pale skin. I'd forgotten how he'd started out milky white. I gaze at his buttock's perpendicular smile. I never utter a word. Mama is right. He has no ass at all.

"Franche, don't get creosote on you. It burns."

"*Sì*, Pa," I say, "I know."

Brown fumes overwhelm the room, but he doesn't relent. He soaks wood beams, drowning hunkered-down termites. I stay clear of the creosote, ducking flying nails and splintering wood and on occasion, a slipped hammer, too. I hang loose and never get nailed. Loose is the word, loose as a goose, on exposed beams.

He says, "Let's take a break."

We drink water unless the homeowner offers a Coke. After making sure we can't be seen by the woman of the house, we stand back to back. He's my Commander-in-Chief, my General Custer, and he watches my back, creating our last stand among the termites. He can't see my smile, and I can't see his. Like a man I unzip, take aim and piss on the sand. It's another day in becoming a man.

"Franche go back to the truck and bring in the rest of the lumber. Don't scratch the door coming in. The wife is particular, notices everything. We don't have all day," General Custer commands in Sicilian.

So, how do I get there from here? I don't know where there is, or if I can achieve whatever it is I'm suppose to achieve. It's a time of cutting up in school, playing baseball and thinking about girls. I'm told I'm leaving childhood behind, or maybe its left me.

"It's time to meditate like a man," he says, but I don't know how, don't know what or which way to go. I bury my thoughts in Florida sand, and I accept I'm a beneficiary of time—stuck in Tampa—mired in mounds of sand under the house.

On a cold night Mama says, "Franche, take a Cuban bath."

"But I ain't dirty," I say.

"Go wash up. Hear me?"

"But, Ma, it's cold."

I take what she calls Cuban baths, lots of them. It's pretty cold in winter in the middle of the state with only a two-burner space heater, particularly when it sits way out front in the parlor, the other end of the house. Besides it's barely ever lit, and when it is, heat never makes it to the back of the house.

"A Cuban bath," I'm told is how Cubans take baths, and I believe it, yet I don't have the guts to ask my friends if that is what they do. Mama thinks herself better than Cubans, all Sicilians do, and all Spaniards do, too. I never have an image problem, never. Columbus discovered America, so what could be better? Papa says all the great art is in Italy, and I know Mama and Papa will never see it, but it's nice to know that's where it is—like money in the bank.

A Cuban bath in winter is sensible in a house without hot running water or heat. A Cuban bath consists of scrubbing with a washcloth, octagon soap and a small pan of tepid water in front of the bathtub or kitchen sink. The kitchen is next to the bathroom, the coldest place in the house, the north face. It's my preference to stand in the kitchen naked where it's a bit warmer when no one is around.

Papa gets up early in winter and spills wooden matches from a Diamond matchbox on the stove. Scratching on the box, he lights one and sticks it into the oven, gagging it into an explosive start. I react and feel the kitchen shake itself loose from the gripping overnight cold. The oven door gapes open like a stiff lower lip, spewing heat on my skinny ass, for it is there, standing, I dress for school on cold mornings. Clothes in winter are as cold to the touch as is the room, so I hang them on the oven door and shiver, wait and hope they don't burn. The heat is soothing, and the smell of gas numbing like airplane glue. It dulls my senses and relaxes my muscles, so I succumb to the warmth commandeering the room.

Cuban baths are stopgap measures until opportunity to bathe with a bucket in the bathtub cycles again. There are tons of stopgaps in cigarmakers' lives, lots of stops and lots of gaps, but everyone manages—no one complains. Lots of things happen between cold snaps, and feelings are put off until a warming trend. It's the Italian way.

When temperature rises, Mama says, "The water's boiling, Franche, go take a real bath; wash your feet, get that ground-in dirt off those ankles. What a *mala figura* if you have an accident and end up at *l'ospedale*, and doctors and nurses see those nasty feet."

"Yeah, yeah, Ma, I'll try not to embarrass you."

"Joke around, but I told your father he should have never bought you that damn bike. Hanging on to trucks like an idiot. The neighbor saw you."

I'm older, emancipated and carry my own hot water bucket from the kitchen stove to the tub. It's a real bath, nothing Cuban about a "bucket bath." I wrap a washcloth around the bucket handle, lessening its sting. I treasure the galvanized bucket like a hot water faucet. I set it inside the tub below the faucet, and with a beat-up pan, designated for taking baths, I repeatedly pick up hot water from the bucket and mix it with cold. Bursts of lukewarm showers cover my head. Linoleum covers the floor, and pieces of it drape the tub's rim on three sides, nailed to walls like perhaps a bed duster hangs on a bed, guiding water inside the tub. There is no shower curtain to keep the water or warmth in, and the wood siding in the room isn't nailed tight, letting in the cold.

In summers showers are hardship free and economically brief.

Papa says, standing outside the bathroom door, "What are you doing?"

"Taking a shower," I say.

"Use too much water, Franche."

He's learned to speak great broken English at the shipyard and is proud of how he sounds. He's the bold one now. He doesn't mind making mistakes. I watch Mama cringe.

He tells me to shut off the water, so I shut him off, shut off water, in that order.

Electricity is another coveted commodity.

"Why you no turn off the light?" he says. "We going to get a high electric bill."

Papa thinks if he speaks English he's more effective, so as I stand pondering at the refrigerator, he says, "What you look for so long? You know what is inside. No let out the cold."

It's my directive to be decisive, be quick, grab a leftover, and move on. Shut, shut, and shut off is his theme song, making himself impeccably clear in English.

Summers are raunchy cockroach months for cigarmakers.

"Franche, be sure you turn on lights before you walk into the kitchen," Mama warns in Sicilian. We pronounce the endemic creatures *cacarouges*, and no matter how often Papa sprays the kitchen, roaches resurrect themselves. It seems someone rolls away the stone while I sleep, releasing them from crevices in furniture, appliances and walls. Roaches hatch and leave behind dried out cocoons stuck to bottoms of tables and chairs. I scrape off the crispy shells with my fingernails.

On the drain board and stove top, Mama creates moats, like those of miniature castles, keeping bread and Graham crackers cockroach and ant free. She fills a large, deep dish with water, and in the center, a bowl supports another plate containing leftovers. Roaches are poor swimmers, but ants can't swim at all.

"Mama, they're mixed," I say turning on the kitchen lights, finding a dual population of roaches scurrying for cover on the floor. "Are the little ones babies?"

"No, Germans, different breed. They sneak in inside grocery bags, can't see them, you know, sneak in as eggs, but they're not really Germans. Cubans breed them all. All damn Cubans," she says. I wait for the floor to clear.

"If Cubans would keep their homes clean we wouldn't have so many roaches. Franche, they come across the yard and crawl inside. I've seen them."

Our roaches are the Best of Breed. I never walk barefooted into the kitchen on summer nights, but by turning on lights, they evaporate. I have an aversion to washing roach juice off the soles of my feet.

They're all Cubans, all right, for like Cuban outfielders they're agile and fast on hairy legs. They catch flakes of crispy Cuban bread crust on the fly, on antenna tips; against baseboards, all on the run; they're all versatile and sinisterly dark.

My young teenage years are a time of segregated schools, colored restrooms with white toilets, and colored drinking fountains spewing colorless water. It is a time I live unabashed without newspapers, magazines or books to complicate life.

I spell words phonetically, phonetically distort them, for the bilingual first generation survives on oral tradition. Most of my relatives are illiterate in English and Italian, so phonetic mistakes go undetected in Italian and English, recycling themselves with each new generation.

Sicilian is dialect without a written text. I speak incorrectly, fade in and out of one language and another, fade in and out of double negatives, and punctuate sentences with "you know," illiterate America's one two punch, "you know," the sine qua non of—I can't say what I wanna say, so won't you please understand me and say it for me, so I say, "You know" or "don't you know?"

Mine is a mindset of an ideology embracing "ain't." Ain't got this and ain't got that, but what I ain't got don't matter, for nobody in the neighborhood ain't got nothing neither.

There are no Kmarts or Wal-Marts broadening my horizons with English-speaking loud speakers, and there are no golden arches. McDonald still lives on a farm. I believe public libraries are for sissies, and restaurants are segregated not just for blacks, but for me, too. Immigrant families are segregated by frugality, defacto segregation of poor whites. But nothing is as rude as "Colored" and "White" signs. There is a difference, a life-size difference, for I don't see a black face in the mirror each morning. I don't go to a Negro school, don't sit in the back of the bus, and I can walk into a restaurant even though I never do.

Growing up is comical, a tragic comedy Latin style. I feel like a thesaurus in a bookless home, or a dictionary replete with misspelled words, but that's not accurate either, because I don't know the word "thesaurus"—don't know such a book exists.

30

Public schools I attend are all west of where I live, so education takes me constantly west, a straight shot west on Columbus Drive. After Ybor Grammar School, I hit Washington Junior High. By now, I've developed a little more torque and lift to my smile, but in seventh grade I begin to shun schoolteachers and every other word I say is fuck. I never look back though, as I move away from the tower of El Reloj, away from my cultural theme park.

It is a small Catholic high school I transfer to in my junior year, thirty-three in the graduating class. Thirteen boys sitting on wood benches in the large public Jefferson High School are converted to Catholicism to play ball. The Catholic school's modus operandi is clear; recruit one or two boys to play sports, and the rest will follow. The good news spreads fast, like gospels to the deprived wannabes warming up benches, and some of us not even that in what Catholics call a heathen school. I see the light for the first time. It's not the enlightenment religion classes teach, but the lights of stadiums and highlights in *The Tampa Tribune*'s sport section that brighten my life.

I'm no different than any boy who wants to be a sports hero. All of us who leave the public school to play for the Catholic school are Latinos and we're short without the physiques and prowess of Anglos, but we have heart—what the Spanish-speaking bunch calls *cojones*. Although I love baseball, it is football, the wave of the future, propelling me into the winner's circle in after-game parties, cheerleaders and horny girls. I put on a football jersey and wear a white sweater with a stripe on its sleeve and a big letter O on its side for Our Lady of Perpetual Help. I make the transfer to structured religion. All I had to do was sell my soul, and I do.

It's an exhilarating experience after being raised pragmatically. But I can see the power of the spirit—see it in cheerleaders with short skirts, stadium lights, cigarette smoke, small crowds and a ten-piece band that spurs me on with the Notre Dame fight song as if I were a twelfth-century crusader chasing infidels across a football field for the Pope. The irony is I never played football before. It's not a sport popular among Latins. My father doesn't know the game, nor does he care. Cigarmakers from Cuba are interested in the Cuban sport of baseball, and my father is no different. The seminal sport event of the year in the cigar factories and Ybor City is the World Series on radio.

I make a name for myself in scrimmage colliding with a two-ton fullback, Raul. He isn't tall, but he's wide, and his legs have the girth of a Clydesdale. That's where I throw my tackle. It is a form of suicide—throwing myself in front of an oncoming train. A lightweight Sicilian is no match for steel legs of a black-bean-eating Cuban-American. I bring down Goliath with a clean tackle in broad daylight, labeling me "Kamikaze Frank" the rest of the year. All I have going for me is *cojones* and my pride, believing I'm better than any Cuban.

I dust myself off, and Coach Bittner says, "Good tackle, Frank."

"Yes sir," I say.

My head swells, and my chest follows. Raul lies at my feet. I feel like Donnatello's *David* lopping off Goliath's head with the giant's own sword. I, too, relish victory.

Raul limps to the sidelines saying, "*Conyo*, good tackle you son of a bitch."

I grin. "I hope you're okay."

"That's all right. Get you next time, Italiano."

At the school I meet my first Irish priest, my first Irish anything. I become an apostle of Father Mallen who is a disciple of the Roman Catholic Church, and like any born-again, I embrace faith with fervor. Father Mallen lives in a different world than mine, a world that is mystical and strange to me. None in my family ever say turn the other cheek. Papa says *somma ama bitcha* and is ready to swing, and both my Uncle Tonys want to swing harder.

Scrimmages inside the confessional are tougher than those in the sandlot where the team practices across from the school. The rectory is full of holy smells and sounds that I begin to associate with three squares, clean sheets, pool table, television, wine, cooked meals and all the cigarettes priests can smoke, and when a priest gets old, there's a retirement home waiting for him somewhere. It isn't a bad setup for just believing in Jesus. It's a life unfamiliar to those of us raised in the *barrio*. No, not much has changed from the days of Sicily—priests still lead the good life while the proletariat works in cigar factories.

When Father Mallen says, "My son..." says it as though he means it, says it as if he understands emptiness. I respond to the singularly possessive phrase, and he is not even Italian. I don't know he's Irish, don't know Irish names like O'Connor, O'Dwyer and O'Meara, other priests in the school—don't know there is something called corned beef or shamrocks—don't know of their affinity for drinking or where Ireland is, and certainly I've never heard about Saint Patrick.

Father Mallen belongs to the order of Redemptorist Fathers. He's in his forties, and mornings he stands at the altar all in white. He raises a silver chalice above his head. It is what Catholics call consecrating the Eucharist, and I have no idea why we sit, kneel and stand in pews, but I do it, taking my cue from class leaders, goody-goody boys and pious girls. Father Mallen is thin on top, but his smile is broad and wide, and I believe it fills God's shoes. Hung up in Latin, he tarries, filling the church with his ethereal voice. Father's incantations seem to soften the harsh wrinkles of abstinence creasing foreheads of old nuns, and young ones with bright smiling faces line up, too, line up at the altar, kneeling in rows like a squadron of Cinderellas—all at his feet. I see their faces light up as they smell incense mixed with Father's aftershave. Like vestal virgins they close their eyes when he struts by. Shafts of stained light come through tall windows and form celestial rainbows inside the church. It all adds to the aura when the nuns open their mouths and satisfy the Host.

Students are grouped by grades. Pews are filled in progression from those nearer my God to thee in front rows, to seedlings being whipped into shape for first communion. Each year the children distance themselves from the altar of God. First, second and third graders are committed to absolute obedience to nuns, but in the rear of the church, the student body effaces into high school. And it is there girls harbor coveted thoughts and rebel against obstinate nuns.

Dressed in yellow and green uniforms, the young girls smell of cheap perfume, and their shy eyes hide behind faint mascara shadows. In unison adolescent girls kneel like primordial Madonnas, and *macho* wallets, in hip pockets of high school boys, brandish the imprints of rolled rubbers. Virgins sitting behind the boys admire the potential size of the ring.

Students kneel and stand and kneel and stand again and again, and some do it piously, and others haughtily. Some do it with debonair shrugs, but stand they do, for they all must. Standing, some cross legs at the ankles as if loitering on street corners. Others seek refuge in fidgety hands, gripping backs of pews. Back and forth they sway, participating in phony push-pull play. It is how boys accentuate triceps, show them off to girls, extending their arms while they extend themselves. Trojans in hip pockets wait for the miracle in the back seat, but soon, Trojans lose their seal as burnished benches rub them thin. Buttocks slide on and off seats, simulating pious fornication, escaping the discomfort of sore knees from unpadded kneelers. Many give in, and sit half and half, buttocks on bench edges, and knees, not bearing weight, never touching kneelers. With hands clasped they lean forward onto the backs of pews. And so kneelers discipline the student body, and little children, well, like rows of corn, they are picked over by Notre Dame nuns.

Father Mallen belongs to the family of God who doesn't question vows, vows opposing instinctual desires and biological needs. Vows, vows, and more vows define commitment to faith by the clergy and nuns of the era. But it all boils down to celibacy, and they expect me to stay celibate, too.

"Bless me Father for I have sinned." I see his silhouette on the other side of the black screen, sitting in judgment, leaning toward the cloth that separates me from the shadow of God.

"Good morning," he says.

"Hello, Father," I say.

He knows who I am and and I know it's him, but we pretend we're strangers. That is what seasoned students tell me I must do.

"Bless me, Father, for I have sinned," I give him the opening line.

"How long since your last confession, my son?"

It's all formatted to gain my confidence—make me a practicing Catholic. Father refers to me and the other recent converts from the public school as his sons. It's strange to call someone other than one's father, Father, but it's a name that hits home at a time when many of us feel our fathers don't care about us. They're preoccupied with survival, putting food on the table, and perform parental duties in a detached, perfunctory way, don't follow academic progress or high school baseball scores. There isn't involvement in school at any level or allotted time for chitchat about adolescent conflicts. Going to school is a job to be fulfilled militarily, expected to pay dividends at graduation in the form of a job. My father is happy if I don't play sports, belong to school clubs, attend school dances, for he views extracurricular activities as frivolous, if not folly.

"It's been a week since my last confession, Father," I say.

"All right. Go on."

"Well, there's not much to tell."

"Well, you're here for a reason, right?"

"Saw my girlfriend a few times."

"And?"

"Same old stuff, Father. We didn't do anything really bad. She's a good Catholic."

"Good," he says.

"I just had some bad thoughts about her."

"Well, did you try to influence her?"

"Guess I did."

"Like how?"

"Well, I don't remember, Father, but nothing real bad."

"You're sure?"

"Oh, yeah, real sure."

"Anything else?"

"I guess I took the Lord's name in vain a few times."

"And how did that make you feel?"

"Not so hot."

"Is your girlfriend a student here?"

"Yes."

"Do you know if she had bad thoughts, too?"

"Don't know."

"And all you had were bad thoughts?"

"Yeah, bad thoughts."

"That's all?"

"I guess it was more than just bad thoughts."

"You want to talk about it?"

"Well, there ain't much to tell."

"You sure?"

"Yeah, real sure."

I undergo a spiritual change as well as a carnal one for I fall in love with my first nun. Sister Mary Coaina flattens me like the weighty cross of Calvary the moment she walks into the classroom dressed in black, except for a white rim framing her face. I am seduced, and I wish there is something I can do to relieve the prickly heat she complains of in the days before air-conditioning. I dream of rubbing her down with cornstarch like my grandmother did me when a child, for at one time or another during summer months, all of us are plagued with the devil's rash. And it is indeed as if the devil's pitchfork stabs, for the sensation is one of stinging and pricking.

"Sister, do sisters really cut off all their hair?" I say.

"Can't get the headdress on otherwise."

Silence.

"Frank, who do you want to take to the senior prom?" She smiles, for she knows.

"You know, Sister," I say.

"Would you like me to see if I can convince her uncle to let her go with you?"

"Yes, Sister, but I don't think it'll happen."

"I know she likes you," she whispers.

"I know, Sister, but her uncle is strict, real strict," I say.

"I'll see what I can do." She walks away.

She possesses a most gentle voice, and if anyone is the Virgin Mary, it is Sister. Her complexion is unblemished and her movements ethereal, floating in and out of classrooms in a black habit rustling an inch off the floor. I think Father Mallen favors her, too, and it has been rumored a classmate saw them holding hands. I don't want to think of such a devastating possibility. I am no competition for the Satan slayer. I'm still squeezing pimples and covering them with Clearasil before class. I feel solace knowing Sister is safely married to God. I know she can't sin with a spirit, not the way I view sin. After all, she wears Jesus' wedding band on her hand. Other nuns are kind, and some tough, but Sister is an angel, a seductive angel, and I know I'll never forget her.

The Nun's Story confirms the unimaginable as I watch Audrey Hepburn's hair chopped off. Though she is a movie star, she runs a distant second to Sister's beauty and grace. I imagine Sister a redhead, a strawberry blond, an ordinary blond and even a mousy brunette. Sister glows, so color never matters. She is forbidden fruit like the apple she talks about in religion class. I accept she is the apple I'll never taste. She is magnificent, exemplifying simplicity but ravished by the insatiability of convent life. There is nothing I can do, nothing, but say an extra amen when she enters the room.

I chase a girl who turns out to be as difficult to court as a nun. She's the most virginal thing I've ever laid eyes on, and she can't speak English and is a year older than me. She has emigrated from Italy and is placed a couple of years behind me in the tenth grade. She's a slight girl with dark hair and hazel eyes, a beauty mark on her right check. She's not buxomly, but my Papa says not to pick fully packed ones, for they're the ones who will explode into Mama Mias after a first pregnancy.

"Skinny ones do best in the long run," Papa says.

Adina is the Annunciation of love, my Italian from Italy no less. I don't have to settle for a watered down Italian-American. Adina is something I know Papa will approve of, and I want his approval, want it badly.

Conversing with her is difficult because she speaks a different dialect, but it doesn't keep me from falling in love. I'm a bit shy, but there's no stopping the tumble.

We meet clandestinely near her uncle's home. Her uncle is the guardian, guardian-in-chief and grand inquisitor. She is his ward all right, imprisoned like Rapunzel but with dark hair instead of gold.

I don't have a phone, so I walk to the western border of Ybor City and talk to her from a pay phone, and there, her words turn on my smile. The grand inquisitor intercepts calls as if he can tell from the ring it's me.

A *vendétta* simmers inside. Sitting in my Uncle Vincenzo's Model A Ford with Vince, I see the old man's big, black Buick heading our way. Cars in my neighborhood are old, so it's not unusual for teenagers to learn to drive in relics. Soon we'll be flashing by each other at top speeds of forty miles an hour for a split second.

I notice an old slipper with a wooden heel laying in the back seat. I pick it up and stand on the running board, waiting for the moment the old man's car comes alongside, and at that moment, I let fly, and the wooden heel of the slipper shatters the rear window behind the old man. Vince pushes on the accelerator.

Days later, Papa comes home from the Italian Club waving the slipper in my face. "Franche, *che fachisti*? What do you know about this?"

"What, Pa?"

He slams the slipper on the kitchen table. "Tell me what is this all about. It almost cost me twenty-five dollars, a fancy, damn Buick. Couldn't you've picked a Ford or a Chevrolet?"

I say nothing.

"Miste Manna was kind. Said he just wanted me to know what you did. He thought the slipper was mine, so he returned it," my father says.

"I'm sorry, Papa."

"He had to replace the window, you know."

"I'm sorry, Papa."

"You *somma ama bitcha*?"

"I had to do it," I say in defiance.

He slips into English. "But, why, Franche, why, he a nice man? What's wrong with you?"

"I wanted to take his niece to the prom, Papa, that's all. She wanted to go, but he wouldn't let her."

"Well, that his right. Maybe, he no know you a nice boy. Maybe, he no want you take advantage of the girl. He got big responsibility you know," Papa says.

He doesn't know I respect Adina. She is my first love after Sister Coaina. I would never try anything without her consent. I'm the victim of the Madonna-whore syndrome like most Italian men, but I have no idea what the syndrome is, or that it even exists. Courtly love is expressing itself in the streets of Ybor City. The unattainable is attainable, but I don't know it.

Papa composes himself and slides back into Sicilian. "It is your fault the old man doesn't trust you. What kind of behavior is that? Almost killed the man with a slipper."

I have only kissed her behind bushes near the old man's house and talked to her on the phone—no more than that, but reality is making itself clear.

I say, "I don't know why, Papa."

"I'm lucky he didn't make me pay for it, but I offered. He owns a business, sells building material, you know, so I have to face him when I need material for jobs."

"I won't do it again," I say.

Sister Coaina has made it clear to Adina's family I'm a good kid, and maybe it is also clear I come from a poor family, not from people who'll make it big in America. And big to little fish need not be much. Papa is a *tabaquero* turned carpenter, not a building contractor, not a developer. No, Papa is hired cheaply, does repair work, grunt work, replacing termite riddled floors, and we live in Ybor City, and Adina's uncle has done well by immigrant standards. The old man has distanced himself from my people, moved closer to professionals like schoolteachers and businessmen.

I just know my family and I aren't good enough. In Catholic school the son of a carpenter is not folly but scripture. Adina should convince her uncle, but she doesn't, so I go on without her, and like Father Mallen says Christians should do, I turn the other cheek and let someone else kiss me.

Isabel is a beautiful girl with olive skin, green eyes and thin. My cousin calls her *flaca*. It means skinny, not a word girls take to kindly, for they know boys are interested in big breasts, big bottoms, big everything, a big something you can feel through clothes as if one is right in there shaking hands with love. It is the Latin way, but I always remember Papa's admonition—it is not the shapely ones that do best in the long run, and if any one is going to do well, it's skinny Isabel.

I've been visiting her home for months, but we don't go on dates. I tell her Papa is stingy when it comes to giving me money for dates. He doesn't think I should be spending money on strangers. My newspaper route pays a pittance, and no one where I live gets an allowance. I don't think the word allowance or the concept exists. Isabel's parents are Spanish and strict. Nonetheless, Isabel and I plan a date, not in Ybor City but downtown.

Her mother warns, "Frankie, be sure you bring Isabellita home by midnight. I want her home before her father comes home from the restaurant, *comprende?*"

"*Sí, sí,*" I say.

"He doesn't go for dating, you know. If it weren't for me Isabellita wouldn't be going anywhere with you or anybody else," she continues in Spanish.

"*Comprendo, señora, comprendo.*" I stand erect and nod to amplify my earnestness.

Her father tolerates me on his front porch and parlor and occasionally nods but never smiles. The whole time I visit, he and I never exchange a word. I never penetrate beyond the parlor or anything else for that matter. There's no question of whose side he's on, but fortunately he's usually at work, a phantom father. Ours is an adversarial position from the start. It's an inherited stance, inherited because the man is her father, and he is like all Latin fathers. She's his only child, and that's why her parents call her Isabellita, the diminutive, precious commodity. I know she connotes regal territory, for the old Isabella was a hell of a queen and gave Columbus three ships, but this Isabella gives me no chance. To her I'm a landlocked Sicilian, and her virginity is worth more than the Niña, the Pinta and the Santa Maria.

A formal date is a milestone in the career of a Latino father, a milestone to be avoided. It is said in the neighborhood it is the American path to hell. It is one no father wants to experience. He's a proud Spaniard, a restaurant waiter, dressing like his thoughts in black and white. He waits on tables at the famed Columbia Restaurant. All Latinos know it's the cat's ass—"the gem of Spanish restaurants." Isabel tells me he doesn't like Italians.

Her mother is understanding of young people, and she's one of the sexiest women I've seen in the *barrio*. She swings her big hips unconsciously, bending over tidying up when I arrive. Someday I know my Isabella will flesh out and no longer be a *flaca* and make a hell of a bed partner, but that's a long way off.

Evenings I wait for her mother to turn in, so Isabel and I can kiss, French kissing is in, and sometimes we kiss to her father's snoring. The sound penetrates the parlor from the bedroom—typical setup in a shotgun home. I know I wouldn't be sleeping if I was in bed with Isabel's mother, but all I have to work with is innocent Isabellita. I'm a virgin, too, but the nuns at school tell us that's what a marriage made in heaven is about, all about virginity.

My parents don't like me going out with non-Italians, but they tolerate Isabellita. She's sweet, underdeveloped, and they believe she poses no threat.

On this date night, Isabel and I bid her mother goodnight and catch a bus several blocks from her home to go downtown. We watch the feature movie and share popcorn, and I feel self-conscious. There's only one movie, no double feature downtown, letting me know it's uptown, upscale, for that's how everything is outside the *barrio*, pay more, get less. Isabel gets up once during cartoons to powder her nose.

"Frank, do you want to go to the bathroom or anything?" Isabel says, standing in the theatre lobby as we're about to walk out to Franklin Street.

"No, let's go. Got to get you home on time, Isabel."

I need to go, but I'm *macho*. I can hold it, I know. It's not a long bus ride, and the truth is, I'm embarrassed to go in her presence, to have her wait in the lobby and think about what I'm doing. Once I drop her off, it's just a couple of short city blocks to my home. Sure, I'm a little uncomfortable, but it's a real date, it's expected, and the formality of it all seems to manufacture more urine. I certainly don't want her to know I piss and go to the bathroom. It's all so unromantic, and I do want her to hold my hand.

The bus sputters, stalls a few blocks from the movie theatre.

The driver hits the starter again and again. "Ladies and Gentlemen, I just can't get her going."

The driver flags down a bus crossing the intersection, runs over, talks to the other driver and returns.

"The company will be sending another bus," he tells the passengers. There are audible sighs all around us.

We wait, and my bladder nudges me into the purposeless movements of a paramecium or an amoeba. Isabel makes small talk, gossips about cheerleaders, but I'm uncomfortable and hold on to the armrest and flex my toes. I look out the window and see a filling station across the street. It's closed. It's over an hour and we're still stalled.

"Okay people, it's here." The driver stands and opens the bus door. "All right, let's file out."

We roar off in the new bus. I'm not talkative.

"You sure got sweaty hands, Frank," she says.

I see our stop and pull on the cord hard. We get off.

"Why are we walking so fast?" she says, "It's a beautiful moon."

"Yeah, but we're late."

"I know, but my high heels aren't made for running."

"Okay, okay."

"Frank, this is really our first date, you know. Our first night out for all the world to see." She squeezes my hand. "I wonder who saw us at the movie. Maybe Aleida or Maggie Diaz? They got big mouths you know."

"Yeah, that's 'cause they're sisters. How about Father Mallen or Father O'Connor? Priests go see lots of picture shows, you know. Probably go 'cause they're horny."

"Don't say that."

"Okay."

"You're built like Kirk Douglas, Frank. Do you know that?"

"Not Victor Mature?"

"Well, him, too, but you're more like Ulysses, so debonair."

"Not Sparticus?"

"Well, him, too, but Ulysses was a Greek, and you're Sicilian, kind of close."

"A Greek. No thanks," I said. "I hear they were queers."

"Well, that's not what I meant. Wouldn't be with you, if I thought that."

We walk down dark streets, but waves surge. I just can't hold it. It's two blocks to her house, and I still can't hold it. I'm pressured by urine into confession.

"Isabel, I got to take a leak real bad," I say.

She stops and looks at me under a street lamp. "You can go in my house if you really gotta go."

"Naw, I'll just step into this alley. You wait here. I'll just be a minute. Just a quickie, okay?"

"Okay, if you gotta." She sighs, but it sounds like a snort.

I can't worry about what she thinks at a time like this. I walk a short distance into the alley. I can hardly breathe, about to pop. The urine pours and clangs on something, so I point it in another direction, on the weeds that grow between tire paths.

"Are you okay in there?" she says.

"Yeah," I yell back. "Hang on."

I clamp down in midstream and move deeper into the alley, making sure she can't hear me. Someone has made a backyard fence out of tin roofing, a common form of recycling in the neighborhood. Nothing is wasted where I live.

I flow freely. I hear a growl, and fiery eyes meet mine. The growl barks, and other barks on the other side of the alley chime in.

"*Quién esta?*" yells a man.

Back porch lights flick on, and still pissing, I move around to avoid the light. I see an old man in underwear cradling a double barrel shotgun. More lights flip on, closer to me.

"*Tiene que es un* Negro."

"*Sí, un moreno,*" a woman says.

They think I'm a Negro up to no good.

"*Sí, es un* Negro, *el perro sabe.*"

She says her dog knows Negroes, and he barks like that when Negroes come through the alley on garbage day. I tuck it in, don't shake, and get urine on my trousers. I've lost the urge.

I run out of the alley. Isabellita is waiting with arms crossed across her flat chest.

"You could have gone at the theatre," she says. "It's almost one o'clock in the morning. If any of those Spanish people see me, I'm going to get a bad reputation."

"Yeah, I guess your father's home by now, right?"

I put my hands in my pockets trying to fan my trousers from within, but it's just three blocks to her house. They'll never dry. What's the old man going to say when he sees a wet crotch? Isabel doesn't see it in the dark, but inside the house, with light, to experienced eyes it will be a lynching epiphany.

"Isabel, something is moving on the porch," I say as we approach.

"Oh, oh," she says.

"The whole house is dark," I say.

"Yeah, I know, it's really late."

I'm sure it's her father, but if I don't have to go inside, if he doesn't turn on the porch lights, it won't be as incriminating as it could be.

"Well, it's about time." The rocking chair brakes, and a dark silhouette stands.

"It's your mama. Thank God," I say.

"*Buenos, al fin,*" she says.

It's a blistering one liner, at last!

"Mama, don't be mad. It's not Frank's fault. The bus broke down and we had to wait for another one."

"Isabella, go inside and don't wake up your father. He went to bed a half hour ago."

"Sorry, Mrs. Fernandez. It's true," I say.

"Better go home, Francisco."

"*Buenas noche*, Mrs. Fernandez," I say. "*Buenas noche,señora.*"

I walk around the corner high-tailing it home, home-stretching it without a good night kiss and a wet crotch. The wall of the Fernandez house abuts the sidewalk, hugs the corner, so as I round it, I hear Mr. Fernandez snoring. His snore has never failed me. Whether it's when I'm kissing his daughter or now, it's reassuring. I don't go out on a date on a bus again. I realize I'm like all Latin men. I don't want to give up control, and you do give it up riding a bus.

31

School was never a priority. It's something I did while waiting to grow up, but now there is no thirteenth grade to be shoved into.

"Gonna register?" a friend, Jack Mangione, says. "Not a bad deal."

"What's this registering all about?" I say.

"Well, signing up for classes. That's what it's called."

"Oh?"

"Yeah, think about it. In four years, you can teach school, be a coach or get a job with a necktie."

"What do you think, Frank?" Vince says to me after Jack leaves.

"Don't know."

"It'd be nice to be a coach."

I have a blue-collar outlook on life—get a job, marry and make love on the couch after *pasta* on Sunday afternoons listening to the *Italian Hour* on WFLA. That's what many of my buddies do after high school.

"Frank, let's check it out," he says.

"Okay."

"You gonna tell your father?"

"Nothing to tell."

"But don't you think…"

"Naw, it can wait. Hell, we don't know shit from Shinola."

Vince picks me up the next morning, and he drives west on Columbus Drive in his father's Model A Ford, always west for enlightenment. I've never been to a university, never received any kind of brochures, never bothered to look at catalogs or seen photos of one.

The Tampa Bay Hotel was converted into a university in the '30s. It naps on the west bank of the Hillsborough River, across from a sleepy downtown. It's beautiful in its own way, wood and red brick, lots of wood. It has nothing to indicate that it's a university except a brick sign facing Grand Central Ave. reading—University of Tampa. All of my friends refer to it as Tampa U, as if the word university doesn't apply, doesn't fit inside their mouths. Most of us from the ghetto slur over words we can't spell or pronounce, so we chop, chop and keep only the "U" alive.

As a child, its campus, Plant Park, a public park named after Henry B. Plant, a railroad tycoon who built the architecturally Moorish hotel in 1887, was my zoo. It housed a lazy alligator fenced in a pond and a black bear caged under Florida live oaks drenched with Spanish moss.

The Civic Auditorium to the west and the Hillsborough River to the east flank the converted hotel. The building's six minarets and numerous cupolas, capped with moon crescents, spiral into the sky. The Islamic Moorish design looks like something from *The Arabian Nights*.

I remember rare Sundays Papa drove Mama and me there to while away an afternoon. It was touted a major outing. Papa wore a suit and tie with a Sons of Italy tie pin, and Mama put on her Sunday dress with puffed up shoulders—all to see a sleepy gator and black bear.

The structure, distinctively Victorian, is filled with students who work part-time or fulltime, and Latinos hail from Ybor City and West Tampa. It's a work-ingman's college, all right, but I'm not comfortable, for it's a university, a place I was told by high school counselors to never attempt. Registration is held in the old lobby where bronze sculptures, dressed in eighteenth-century clothes, are poised to dance Mozart's Minuet. I listen to professors who sit around shaky card tables like U.S. Marine Drill Sergeants at recruiting stations. I fill out cards, hand them back, and I'm told I'm a fulltime student. No one makes a fuss over curriculums, schedules, GPAs, and there are no SATs to inhibit ambition.

"Vince, let's look around," I say.

"This place is kind of spooky, don't you think?"

"Well, yeah. Maybe it's just because it's old."

The veranda outside is huge; everything outside Ybor City is. The porch encircles much of the building and displays elaborate woodcarvings, gaudy Victorian gingerbread. We walk up a wide staircase to the second floor overlooking the lobby and look down. I savor cleavage and conclude the biggest breasts belong to Latin girls, but a few blond bombers in low cuts are targeted, too. The hall leads straight back to the department of Biological Sciences, squeezed in between stacks of specimen jars where formaldehyde reeks.

"Let's peek in here," he says.

"It's tiny. Part of a bathroom."

"A hotel room, all right," he says.

"What the hell did you expect?"

Converted classrooms line an endless hall. Air conditioning units hang out of windows. Acorns ping on them, bounce off and bounce again, and then are silent until they hit the ground below. Honeymoon suites boast brick fireplaces.

"Cool," he says. "Real cool."

"Yeah, it's okay."

"It is, Frank, it is."

We know beggars can't be choosy, and our glances and shrugs communicate it's our destiny. We move along the corridor, peering in wherever we can, sizing up coeds.

"The main thing is a lot of our friends are here."

"Yeah, Vince, can you imagine what it'd cost to go away to a real college?"

"I bet the girls ain't any better."

"Shit. I'm taking fifteen hours. Makes me a fulltime student, and I don't have to be here no forty hours, right?" I say.

"Yeah, something like that, but I ain't clear on them kind of hours either. It's not like work."

I'm not clear on a lot of things, but school is cheap, and living at home makes it cheaper. Of course, it isn't college to fancy dudes who go away to the University of Florida at Gainesville or Florida State at Tallahassee, but, now and then, I see rejects return and check in at the old hotel.

"Hey, Manny, thought you were at Gainesville?" I say.

"Oh, just thought I'd take a semester home. Personal reasons."

Personal reasons, my ass, yeah, no brains.

Next semester, I see him with the same grin trying to survive General Chemistry.

"Thought you were here for just one semester, Manny?"

"Well, its not a bad place, kinda got used to it."

Yeah, flunked out of the big time—did your father a favor.

I'm a Spartan—a Tampa Spartan. That's what the school's football team is called. *The Tampa Tribune* publishes articles with captions—*Spartan fullback ran into a stonewall* and *Spartan quarterback fumbled at goal.* I don't know there was a Sparta or a Troy or someone called Homer. I never make connection with Achaeans and Trojans. I never know about the ten-year war or the wife of the Greek king Menelaus, Helen. I've never heard of the woman that launched a thousand ships. I don't know about Achilles, and I don't care.

The university gives me a chance for a mediocre education, or maybe it's a poor one, but I hope it will get me into a necktie. I have a problem though. Bluntly put, I'm pathetically dumb and ill prepared, couldn't get accepted to a state school if Papa were Rockefeller. The ghetto created an attitude in me that tells me what I don't know isn't worth knowing, but I don't cancel reservations.

I'm comfortable in my Motel 6—fits my laid back style, and all I do is sleep in English, French and History classes. There is no checkout time at the hotel.

Things are in disarray at home. Mama says, "Doctor Torretta says Nonna Sara has TB."

"What?"

"Don't eat there anymore, Franche, please, no more."

I feel as if I disown my grandparents, but my health is at stake.

Days later Mama comes to me. "Franche, Doctor Torretta says we need to get chest X-rays. We've all been exposed."

Papa drives us downtown to a mobile X-Ray truck parked in front of a white building on Tampa Street, the Hillsborough County Health Department. The technician that takes our chest X-rays tells us we'll be notified if any abnormalities are found. Two weeks later I receive a card.

"Ma, look, it says I need to see my doctor for another chest X-ray."

"*Mama mia*, better call Torretta." There's consternation on her face, for no one else received one. I know I have the dreaded disease.

"Franche, make an appointment right away."

Right away means it's serious.

Diesel fumes inflate my lungs sitting in a bus heading downtown. Tall buildings shade Franklin Street. I see storefront windows housing white manikins—no blacks, yellows or browns. Some I recognize, met them briefly when I was a child standing outside Maas Brothers and O'Falks Department Stores on cold nights.

It was the Christmas season when I begged Mama to take me inside. Mama said the stores were not for us, too expensive. There was a sled and a snowman with a scarf wrapped around his neck, and I wondered what it would feel like to own one. Red maple leaves lay strewn on make-believe snow. It was so picturesque. I'd always dreamed of snow, but I knew there wasn't a chance in hell of my ever seeing the real stuff.

Across the street Doctor Torretta's office building is a pyramid built on the American dream—nothing like the Italian Club medical clinic on top of Lodato's Pharmacy. No, this is first-class, big, big-time, and it is there he sits like a pigeon in a hole near the top. That is where successful Italian-American doctors roost once they've left Ybor City. I stand in front of shiny elevator doors in the lobby and watch a brass sundial above them, waiting for a slow-moving arrow to point to *G*. The door slides open, and passengers move out.

"Going up. Going up," a gray-uniformed Negress says. "Watch yo' step."

The elevator operator, in white gloves, seals my fate with the steel door. I ascend and watch her do her machinations, steering the elevator into flight. Back and forth she slides the Harlequin grate, unfolding it, refolding it and sliding the shiny door open and shut. Stopping and picking up passengers as we move up in a stop-and-go fashion. I'm not used to elevators. There are none in the ghetto, nothing above two or three stories exists. The elevator elicits a dropping sensation inside me, as if I'm leaving my guts behind. Adjusting and readjusting to floors, I reposition my feet, broaden my stance, stabilize my legs and forget about tuberculosis, forget I'm the sacrifice ascending a Mayan pyramid, and the scalpel of Doctor Torretta waits for me at the top.

The elevator door opens. "Ninth floor."

I get off and see a black charwoman on all fours scrubbing a white marble hall floor. I think back to a story Mama told me when I was a child.

"Franchito, her mother was a Negro who scrubbed floors, but her daughter looked white."

"White?" I say.

"Oh, yes, white. Everyone thought the little girl was a white girl, even went to a white school."

"Nobody knew?"

"No."

"A white school?"

"That's right. The mother worked as a maid for a white family, so the little girl went to school in a white neighborhood."

I say nothing, never heard of a Negro in a white school.

"In time the little girl began to believe she was white."

"She looked that white?" I say.

"Oh yes, as white as you. She didn't want to be seen with her mother, and when she was, she said the Negro lady was her family's maid."

I look up quizzically, don't know much about maids, but I've seen Negro women dressed in white, standing on street corners, waiting for trolleys in white neighborhoods.

"It was very, very sad."

"I don't like sad things, Mama," I say.

"The Negro woman understood though."

"But why, Mama? Why was the daughter so mean?"

"Because sometimes people around us make us feel inferior if we are not like them or have nice things. The girl was ashamed, didn't want to be different."

"I would never be ashamed of you, Mama."

"I know, but we all grow up, Franchito." She smiles a lazy smile. "It was a good movie. It made me cry."

I see Mama's tears.

"How does the movie end?" I say.

"The mother dies, and the daughter drapes herself on the casket and screams, Mama, Mama in front of all her white friends. She was grown by then, so she understood how much her mother had loved her. The movie was called *The Imitation of Life*."

I don't know what to say, don't know the word *imitation*.

"It was too late, Franchito, too late," Mama says, looking me in the eyes.

Joseph Torretta, M.D., Physician and Surgeon, is stenciled on the upper half of a frosted glass door. Physician and surgeon is a fancy way of saying he's a general practitioner.

A bleached blond in her thirties greets me at the reception desk.

"I'm here to see the doctor about an X-ray," I say.

"Sit down. Doctor will see you soon."

I sit in the waiting room and pick up a magazine from a coffee table in the center of the room where magazines are strewn. Most have the doctor's Davis Island home address on them. The room is full of Italians comparing miseries, blood pressures, blood sugars, and occasionally a woman lowers her skirt minimally to show off a scar.

"Buy Buitoni," a fat widow in black says to another fat woman.

"You mean brown pasta?" another says, questioning the advisability of brown.

"*Sì, sì,* Buitoni, it's made from wheat. Is good for you if you have diabetes."

"You think is better than *semolina*?"

Torretta opens a door. "Frankie, come in. We'll get X-rays in a minute."

I stand.

"I remember you as a baby," he says.

"Doctor, I don't know what this is about. I feel fine. It's the X-ray from the Health Department. The card said I should see a doctor." I hand him the card.

"Relax, we'll listen to your chest. Your grandmother has cavities, you know," he says. "I'm treating her with streptomycin, so it's possible you got it from her."

After he percusses and listens to my chest, he has me stand in front of a black X-ray machine. He flips a switch and the machine hums and lights go out in the room.

"It's that damn fuse, Frankie. Be back in a minute."

He repositions me, placing my hands on my hips, pressing my chest against the machine's coal-black steel, cranking it up to chest level. He pushes my elbows forward making my chest concave, and my elbows protrude like hollow wings.

"Don't breath, don't move." Running out of the room, he adds, "Hold it. Hold it."

I hear a series of clicks.

"Okay, relax," he says.

I wait in the examining room.

He comes in waving a chest film. "A P view. Want to see your X-ray?"

He points to shadows in the upper part of my lungs. He calls them apices, but all I see are white ribs.

"Well, it's a good thing you came to see me. Got spots on the right and left, Frankie." He looks at the floor and says, "Bessie, draw up a gram of streptomycin."

"I got tuberculosis?" I say.

"We can lick it, Frankie. In about a year, you'll be as good as new."

"But, I feel fine, honest I do."

"Maybe you think you do, but if I don't treat it you're going to die." He points to my trousers. "Drop them."

"Will I have to go to the TB Sanatorium?" I say.

It's my greatest fear.

"Look, we'll keep it quiet, between us Italians, okay? You can stay home. I won't report it to the Health Department."

"*Grazie*, Doctor. I'll do whatever you say, anything. Just let me stay home. Should I quit my job?"

"Good idea, Frankie. Take it easy, eat well, something more substantial than *pasta*, and keep it in your pants." He smiles when he says keep it in your pants. He pushes bubbles out of the syringe and plunges the needle into my buttock. "Also a good idea to keep plates and utensils separate. Don't eat with *la famiglia*. Eat in your room or after the family. No kissing. Tell your mother to boil your things separately."

"She washes dishes with leftover, hot *pasta* water, Doctor. We don't have hot running water. Is that good enough?"

"No, no, need to boil it."

"Okay."

"You got a girlfriend?" he says.

I nod.

"Better break it off. There will be a whole new school of fish when you're cured," he says. "Okay, see you each week for your streptomycin shot. Bessie can give them to you. It's the first time we've got something to fight TB. You're lucky."

"Yes, sir, real lucky."

I wait for the elevator.

"Going down," the elevator operator says.

It's the same black woman, and this time she smiles kind of shyly. I manage to flip back a smile.

Riding the city transit bus home I think of tuberculosis, the Red Death, think of Doc Holiday, Wyatt Earp's drinking buddy in Tombstone, coughing up leathery lungs at the O K Corral. Red Death is the name given tuberculosis by old timers. Profuse hemorrhage from lungs warrants the colorful name.

A sanatorium sits far west on Columbus Drive, and a new one is being completed to accommodate a surge of new cases. Some of Mama's coworkers from the factory live there. It's more than a disease among Latins; it's a social stigma like mental illness.

Cigar factories are breeding grounds because workers are squeezed side-by-side without adequate ventilation. It's hot and humid, ideal for incubating the tubercle bacillus. If the word gets out I have TB no self-respecting Italian girl will marry me. Cigarmakers warn their children. I hear a patient is never cured, only arrested, and Papa and Mama know people who relapse, so it's more than a scare. It's a curse—my curse.

I live a solitary existence, quit my job, eat alone, have no dates and barely mingle with students at Tampa U. I visit Torretta's office weekly and bare my ass for streptomycin shots. I get a sense of what doctoring is about. People treat Torretta with respect, and he writes prescriptions with an awesome Schaefer fountain pen. He writes Latin words I can't read with style and flair in ink that flows through a gold tip. He wears dress shirts and a necktie, and his Italian patients thank him profusely as if he were a saint.

When I drop my pants, Bessie rubs me down with an alcohol sponge and says, "Don't tighten up, Frankie, relax."

After the injection she pats my ass. Her soft touch and the cold alcohol sponge, before and after the injection, are pleasurable.

I read what I can at the university's library about TB and find I have no signs or symptoms of the disease. I'm confused, so I make an appointment with a bona-fide internist on Davis Island, near Tampa General Hospital, not far from the University of Tampa.

Doctor Nathan Marcus takes X-rays and says to me, "I don't see any signs of TB."

I'm ecstatic, for he's touted as one of the best in Tampa.

He says, "Let's put a skin test on, a PPD."

"What's that?" I say.

"It will tell me if you've ever been exposed to tuberculosis." A tiny needle puts a welt or blister on the inner skin of my forearm. "Needs to be read at twenty-four and forty-eight hour intervals."

He requests that my family brings in my grandmother. A radiologist interprets her X-rays as emphysematous blebs from chronic asthma.

"You don't have TB, never have. Doctor Torretta doesn't know what the hell he's talking about," he says on my last visit.

I'm impressed. I've seen a lot of bad medicine in the *barrio*. Now I've felt the sting first hand, and I wasn't even sick. I'd love to become a physician and make things better for the people in my *barrio*, but I don't dream of becoming one—can't. A ghetto mentality won't let me.

University of Tampa The original building has not materially changed.
The school made higher education possible for me and other Latinos. It
was my "Harvard of the South" before I knew Harvard existed.

32

"It all happened such a long time ago," I say.

He doesn't say a word.

"How in the hell did we ever make it out of this place?"

"Had enough of the old neighborhood?" he asks.

"It's turned to shit, Vince, but it's hard to get it out of the system."

"Me, too," he says.

"Still, in some ways it feels as if I never left."

"But you did, Frank, you did."

It was a blue-collar neighborhood from its inception, but I never saw the blue. Cigarmakers didn't wear dungarees or coveralls. They dressed decently and inexpensively—men and women. It was a village, to use the vernacular, of tin-roofed huts built to house short stature people—people I took for granted and never quite understood. I never thought of myself as different because I was the son of cigarmakers, never did. Certainly didn't think it would be anything I'd ever want to write about. It was a unique place even by today's standards—Democrats who would have never tolerated a liberated woman, and it was cockroaches that staggered in the streets, not winos, and Cubans sang the ditty "La Cucaracha No Puede Caminar"—Cockroaches can't walk because they need to smoke marijuana.

I remember the lyrics and sing. I pound a Latin beat on the steering wheel with my fist as I press on the accelerator.

"La cucaracha,
la cucaracha, no puede caminar
porque le falter, porque le falter
marijuana para fumar."

"You gone crazy?" Vince says. "Look at 'em all looking at you, and you're singing about cockroaches."

"It's different—a whole different place, Vince."

"That's what I mean. We should get out of here, not attract attention."

I grin. "Yeah, yeah, but I've gone *loco*, real *loco*, so I can say anything I want. Don't have to worry about political correctness in a black ghetto, right?"

I burn rubber and focus on the duplex in my rearview mirror. The black columns loom. The duplex is no longer home, hasn't been for a long time. It's wasted and Vince's home, though still standing, is condemned, hollowed out like a bomb shelter that suffered a direct hit. Like cemetery tombstones, ghostly houses are flanked in rows next to alleys where we caught butterflies, dragonflies, bees and grasshoppers, and moved aside to let garbage trucks go by.

The slumped cement steps of my duplex make no effort to rise and greet me. They seem unable to seesaw against the weightlessness of time.

Vince says, "Want to go to the cemetery?"

"Why not? I don't know these one-way streets though," I say.

I can't see the red bricks under the asphalt, can't hear or feel their vibration under my tires, but inside my head, it's all still there. Cement slabs of sidewalks have cracked in the wake of time, and weeds have grown rampant. Discarded washing machines and junk cars litter front yards, and torn up upholstered chairs act as lawn furniture on front porches.

"It's gone, Frank. It just never got a funeral."

"A damn shame—a meltdown," I say, pressing on the accelerator harder, pressing the images in the pages of my mind. The people—the homes—the culture—all gone.

Vince looks out the passenger window as we drive by Tony Labruzzo's Fish Market a couple of blocks east of the duplex. It's abandoned, condemned and boarded up—no more chicken feet there. Winos and crack cocaine and methamphetamine addicts sleep off homelessness under cover of the building's second-story overhang.

"They're a different kind of dead fish," I say.

He says nothing.

"Vince, we're what people call emeritus. Did you know that?"

"Usually that implies one is connected to an institution or something academic."

"Well?"

"Well what?"

"Don't you think we're still connected?"

He nods rather than let his voice crack.

"It may have not been academic, but it taught us all we know," I say.

"Long time ago," he says.

Sure, we can now count without fingers, read to ourselves like Miss Hood preached in third grade, but now, V.M. Ybor School stands boarded with a few window panes spared, just a few leftovers for the next generation of unruly blacks to toss bricks at our past.

"Damn, I'm not sure if this street will take us there," I say.

"Take a right. It's just a few blocks. Didn't think you'd ever forget, did you?"

"Never did."

Omnipotent time has done its job. In the '50s cigarmakers carried home their tools—*chavetas* and *machinettas*. They brought them home for the last time in brown paper bags, tucked under sweaty armpits. That was when Ybor City fell apart. Automation in cigar factories hit its stride, developed enough technology to replace the hearts and fingers of passionate people. It was about the bottom line. Factory owners knocked the straight-back chairs the cigarmakers had sat on for a lifetime out from under them. They were old, infirmed, gasping their last breath. Some started shops in storefronts, garages and homes, so-called *chinchales* or "Buckeye shops." *Chinchal*, the Spanish word for bedbugs, implying it was where bedbugs gathered—not legit, but still the possibility of making a few dollars and change. It was the dance of the dead cockroach they were doing on their backs and treading air with all fours. In the late fifties, Fidel Castro took over Cuba, and in the early sixties, President Kennedy placed an embargo on Havana tobacco. That was as far as Ybor City would roll. It was the end of the world as I knew it.

Vince wears bifocals. He doesn't have to tell me it happened. The time elapsed can't be covered up with his smile or tossed out the window like my Honduran cigar.

"Sure this street will get us there?" I say.

"That used to be Blanco's Bar over there. It's just a couple of blocks from here—keep going."

"I delivered newspapers there. It's boarded up."

"But it's still standing."

The arch at the entrance dwarfs us as we drive under it. L'Unione Italiana Cemetery reads the wrought iron that's been worked into an intricate sign. Three Italian words mixed with one lonely English. I never realized the incongruity in the name, but that's how it reads, always has. Upper case letters arch like colors of a rainbow nailing down my dead, resurrecting all those Sunday mornings I visited with Papa. Some of the paint-starved shanties that rimmed the cemetery have been razed. Others are fixed up and freshly painted—pink, purple, green, orange and lavender—letting the white man know colored town has survived civil rights.

"Neglected wood siding," Papa called it when we visited, but it wasn't only wood that was neglected. Although not always visible, I knew colored children lived inside the shacks. I could see the barren sand they trampled free of weeds in their yards. Tampa was one large sandbox without skyscrapers, condominiums and sailboats littering Tampa Bay. I tried to imagine how pitiful black lives were. It seemed there were so many living in material squalor. Children my age and younger housed with destitute mothers and grandmothers. I knew colored men were recycled hard, heard old immigrants say it was the way of the blacks—one man in the front door and another out the back. Italians likened them to dead whiskey bottles, affirming Pearl Bailey's theme song—"Bill Bailey Won't You Please Come Home."

Vince looks around. "It's pretty desolate."

"I think we'll be okay." I pull the Bronco over to the grass, careful not to hit a tombstone.

"Scarcely anyone visits," he says.

"Don't worry, I still have the magnum."

"I don't see a soul."

"It's broad daylight, Vince. Don't have to worry."

His nostrils flare. "Better leave it in the car."

"Still got film in that camera?"

"Lock up your side." He steps out.

"Okay. Let's roll," I say.

He comes around my side and tries the door.

The cemetery hasn't changed since Papa, Nonna Anna and I made rounds according to the proximity of blood. The same clusters of Italian cypress trees are grouped next to mausoleums, breaking up bleak monoliths with moving shadows. The Italian imports were mere bushes then, but like me, they've grown, but unlike me, they never roamed. In springtime, around Easter, I remember junipers drenched with tiny gray berries, spherical and smooth. Their bitter taste told me it was the flavor of death.

No, I wasn't comfortable in the cemetery. Never was, but after awhile I couldn't help but believe there was one cemetery meant for me. It was where I expected to be buried, and although children didn't consider death a reality, those who frequented cemeteries couldn't help but think of death as a living role model. Sure, perhaps it was an immigrant way of thinking, but I was a son of an immigrant.

Names were kept straight. Remarried widows and widowers were reunited with original spouses after death. Their children saw to that. There were no children of second marriages—no his, hers, and theirs. Immigrants remarried late in life—middle age and beyond—marriages of conveniences—"For companionship," the old people said.

Divorce was almost nonexistent among immigrants. Italian women never divorced spouses that played around or had mistresses, and the women were never unfaithful. Divorce came with the first American born generation. Horns were the physical metaphor for adultery—index and little fingers shoved in the air. Divorce was the honorable way out of a cuckold relationship, and the greatest dishonor was the man who didn't shed his.

I'd read in *The Tampa Tribune* the cemetery was 114 years old, filled with five acres of Ybor City Italians. It was home to over 3500 of them. It also boasted graves of the first black Episcopal priest in Tampa, buried in 1889, and the first black woman supervisor of Hillsborough County Black Schools, Blanche Armwood Washington, buried in 1939. A few more were buried later, but as a boy in a segregated South, I didn't realize the cemetery housed blacks, never saw them planted near its east gate, but it was their land before it was Italian.

The cemetery was a place immigrants visited, made peace with Mother Earth long before she embraced them. The cemetery was eternity's address despite what beguiling priests preached at rosaries and funerals. A plot was finite, not abstract like a lofty P.O. Box in the sky. It was as definite as anything they ever relied on.

I see the cemetery's "Bates Motel" near where we parked. As a boy I knew about the gore inside the Licata Mausoleum. I can still hear Mama those Sundays she and I walked the cemetery aisles. I was about five, and there was comfort in holding her hand, especially in the cemetery.

"Franchito, a whole family is in there. All died on the same day." She squeezes my hand, and I look up.

"Mama, tell it to me again."

All conversations prior to my starting school are in Sicilian.

"Walking into the factory one morning I saw *tabaqueros* peering out of windows. I went and looked out, too, and saw bodies being carted away on stretchers from a house across the street. There were five in all."

And there are five each time I count. I can count up to about twenty, so I count crypts as if expecting numbers to change. It is about the time I count cars in funeral processions. Mama scolds me, but it's the way my cousin and I learn to count. There is no end to funeral processions. Italian funerals are lavish—outdo the Cubans and Spaniards. And Sicilian families brag about the number of mourners that attend.

"Franchito, how many times do I have to tell you it's bad luck to count funeral cars, *mala sorte*, understand?" she'd said to me on an afternoon she caught me counting them from my front porch.

"We don't need bad luck, *capisci*?" she'd said.

"Like the kind of bad luck you get if you throw away hair or finger nails?"

"No, that's different."

"But isn't all bad luck, bad luck?"

"No, there are two kinds. One is plain bad luck, and the other is witchcraft. Witchcraft is the reason I don't throw out body parts like hair and nail clippings. You never know who might go through the garbage. All they need is a piece of you to put on the curse."

"The curse?"

"Yes, that's different from ordinary bad luck."

"Different?"

"There are gypsies from the Caribbean called *brujas* that worship the devil. You know Cuba is in the Caribbean, and there are lots of Cubans around here. Those women make rag dolls. The doll becomes a miniature person when they put human hair or fingernails on it. Even a piece of clothing works. *Brujas* stick the doll with needles and make you sick enough to die, Franchito. It's best to play it safe. I never sweep out hair or nail clippings. Burn them or flush them down the toilet."

Mama starts to walk away from the mausoleum, pulling me along.

"Mama, I want to look at the pictures close-up," I say, letting go of her hand.

"Hurry." She stands a few feet away while I walk up to the mausoleum and peer through its glass doors.

I see the photos of the Licata family: a child, father, mother and other siblings—some smile.

"He used an axe on all of them, Franchito," she says. "I heard there was blood everywhere in that house."

I stare at the photographs as if each one is a detached head.

"A crazed son butchered his family while they slept. The police found him sitting on the toilet smoking marijuana the next morning."

It's a time the marijuana is not called weed or pot, and I don't know about Lizzie Borden and her forty whacks.

"Franchito, promise you'll never smoke marijuana. It made that boy go insane." She looks at the mausoleum as if she's interceding for the dead.

"That's what you always say, Mama. Don't smoke marijuana, don't smoke marijuana."

"I'll tell you as many times as I want."

"Are you afraid I'll kill our family?"

Her index finger transforms itself into a metronome in front of my face. "It's not funny, so don't make a joke of it. Just promise me, Franchito, that you'll never, never smoke marijuana."

"I promise, Mama, I promise."

That was how the war on drugs was fought, and children buried in the cemetery, particularly infants, didn't have photographs on headstones. Their graves were adorned with sculptured lambs and angels. Most were old graves, for infant mortality had been high during previous generations. I didn't realize lambs represented Jesus, the sacrifice. I just assumed they were placed there because children love to play with animals. That's how it was being unaware of certain truths or untruths. It was all in the point of view.

Oh, I visited the cemetery once with my children years ago when they still went on vacations with me, when I still impressed them, and they asked questions, but they were too young to understand. I didn't know it then, but I sentenced them to American diversity, which espouses homogeneity of thought. Somehow I felt I had dropped the baton in the cultural race, one of many dropped along the way, and it was too late to run back and start over.

Vince and I succumbed to freedom, ignored the teachings of our parents. He and I married outside tradition, outside our culture and customs. For years I swallowed my native tongue and feasted on the American dream and found it eventually digesting my pride. I wanted my children to be a part of my heritage, but it's mothers who raise children, always have. Ironically, I wanted it to be for them as it had been for me but without poverty, provincialism and most of all a muzzled mind.

I hope when my photograph is embedded in stone, they'll roam the cemetery in search of themselves. I know it will never be their cemetery. To them it'll be just a place Daddy raved about, an archaic place they might mention in passing to their children. A place they might refer to as, "You know, that cemetery in Ybor City, the Italian one, the one grandpa was so crazy about. They'll say it at a get together with about as much flavor as the store-bought barbecue sauce they'll pour on spareribs on a Fourth of July or a Memorial Day in a gated suburban backyard.

"Vince, look, buried in 1918." I point.

"October, November, a slew of them."

"A grouping. That's when my great grandfather died, 1918, during the great flu epidemic," I say.

"I've never heard you talk of him." Vince folds his arms on his chest and scans stones.

"He's the one who founded Castellano & Pizzo Italian Imports, you know, but Castellano and Pizzo aren't blood. Castellano and Pizzo married into the family. His only son, Jimmy, died young of TB."

"Is this it, Piz—zo—la—to?" he says, breaking up the name into syllables.

"That's him—PIZZOLATO, PIETRO—*nato Otb. 20, 1855—morto Set. 13, 1918.*"

Old tombstones are chiseled in Italian, and it's more than a sluggish camera lens holding down their smiles. I look at his face as if we'd just met in the trick cycle of time. First he was here, and I was nowhere. Now, he's there, and I'm here, and soon I'll be there, back to nowhere. I accept the shuffle, as we all must, recalling an inscription on a gravestone in Tombstone's Boot Hill—*Once I was one of you, soon, you'll be one of me.*

I realize I'd never given thought of who he was, yet he had walked the same streets I did, loved some of the same people, but all I can do now is brag tritely to Vince, "He's my great grandfather."

His photograph is embedded in marble, old marble, and the curlicues of the inscription are tastefully done in Italian, but who was he? What had he stood for?

"The flu epidemic?" Vince wrinkles his face quizzically.

I clean off the photograph with the palm of my hand. "It killed like forty million worldwide."

"Wow."

"The good old days weren't so good when it came to medicine, Vince."

"Do you know much about him?"

"Worked in gold mines in Socorro, New Mexico before settling in Tampa. He belonged to a group of Sicilians known as Gheg ghegs, from La Contessa Entellina in central Sicily."

Originally I'd thought the language might be Greek, but I learned it was Albanian. Albanians came to Sicily centuries ago fleeing Ottoman Turks.

I experience nostalgia and a sense of solace knowing his bones are at my feet; a physical representation of what he was. Sure, a skeleton by now, some eighty years later, but bones have to make do, and strangely enough they do. But what did he look like? If I were to shake his hand, say, *como se,* Nonno Pietro, would he smile, hug me, and if so, how would he smile?

"Vince, do you see a resemblance?"

"Well, he's got a mustache." He shrugs his shoulders. "Maybe but it's hard to tell."

I wonder if the tables were turned, him above ground and me below, would he be as thrilled to find my grave? Italians say family members are cut from the same timber. The grain and knots run constant, but it is the cut that determines what shows—whether it's the beauty of the grain or the weakness in the knots. It's all combination and permutations of genes, and somewhere, surely, I have a few of his.

"My mother's grandfather, Vince. Can you believe it?"

He glances at me in a strange way.

"Mama told me she remembered him on his deathbed during the epidemic when she was seven. It was a time musical bands accompanied corpses. Corpses were paraded through the streets with a retinue of mourners, some in carriages but most walked. The crowd joined the funeral at the Italian Club and terminated the procession at Fifteenth Avenue and Twentieth Street. That was the corner where Mama lived. From there family and close friends went to L'Unione Italiana Cemetery. So, right here on this spot mourners stood that September in 1918, Vince, right here."

He says nothing.

"I bet you don't know he was the last corpse the band played for."

He chuckles. "A little before my time."

"But you must admit it must have been neat."

"I guess," he says.

"There were daily funerals, so out of empathy for those stricken, the band disbanded. That I heard from Mama. The requiem music depressed them."

"I'll take some close-ups, Frank, I know you'll want several."

"Make sure you're not shooting into the sun and don't shake the camera."

"No sweat."

The photograph is pristine. There weren't many pictures handed down, for between inaccessibility to cameras and frugality, there were few taken. That included photographs of me as a child.

I can date the cemetery time-line by the presence or absence of smiles. Older photographs have horizontal lips, unaffected by vanity, most impressionable to a boy. Those were the ones whose eyes followed me when, as a boy, I dumped stagnant water and rotten flowers out of vases. Their eyes have not changed—still search the horizon.

I don't remember latitudes or longitudes walking the cemetery, but I remember landmarks. I see a path lined with sandspurs. Paths are just as sandy as they were four decades ago. I see a headstone—see Anna's picture in her nineties with a smile, and Ciccio, younger, with a stern look. It feels as if I'm visiting a neighborhood my grandfather founded, and the rest of my family followed. Paths have not been rearranged, widened, nor one-ways created. The cemetery is still as bucolic as I remember it.

"They sure were a no frill bunch," I say.

"Yeah, no one smiled in those days."

"You can make out the timeline by the presence or absence of smiles."

"It's hard to remember it all, Vince, damn hard."

"You don't have to, Frank."

He pulls a few weeds encroaching on my grandparents' slabs. We admire our grandmother's photograph taken a few years before she died in 1959, and I remember Anna before I left the *barrio* to chase the American dream.

Anna tells me if she can make it one more winter, she'll be around another year and says winter is the enemy of the old, culls them. I realize her truthfulness because it's what I saw in movies as a boy—American Indians—the old and sick—dragged by horses, on outriggers made of aspen poles. The young braves dropped them off in the snow. It happened to Indians, but she's no Indian.

She fears baths in winter, for baths usher in pneumonia, she says. Says that's what happened to her friends. I wait for spring and secretly pray for a mild winter, pray she'll make it one more time, and she does. Life is uncomplicated, and one day merges into the next, and I merge with them, and she's part of each day.

There is serenity in her thoughts. All are attainable, so, when we talk about death, she says her wish is to die a natural death—no hospital, no operations, no intervention, and she trusts God will oblige her.

She's my Buddha sitting under an olive tree instead of a bo tree, and enlightenment, well, it's like all things—it's taught Sicilian style.

"Franchito, why don't you shut off the radio?"

"Okay, Nonna."

She doesn't understand American voices spewing out of radios and lives in America longer than Sicily, yet never becomes an American citizen. There are no railroad tickets, bus fares or airfares in her life, and seldom does she ride in a car. She sees all of man's achievements: city water and sewers, paved streets, cement sidewalks, electricity, radio, telephone, automobiles, airplanes and finally television, but she's unaffected. The entire time she lives in Tampa, she never travels outside the city, never goes downtown. Not much chance of a violent death, yet she prays for a natural one and dreams more and more of death.

She keeps asking, "Why is God keeping me here?"

"Because he likes you," I say.

She doesn't know the curse of Methuselah, yet she knows it well, knows it first hand. She's learned the power and tenacity of *why,* and why not to ask why. Nonetheless, she keeps asking, but I have no answer except to say, "Tell me another story, Nonna, a story of the old days."

Twenty years she's cloistered in black. Sicilians call it *il lutto,* a mourning custom dating back centuries. The custom is symbolic of spousal fidelity, and like fidelity, subsequent generations find the meaning trite. Her daughters try to convince her to bring it to an end, shed the black, bring on the white into what's left of her life—a little, just a little, it won't hurt. Put an end to this preoccupation with black.

I no longer sleep in her room. I haven't for five or six years, moved out at fourteen when Papa added a room to the duplex.

"Franchito, there are Negroes in our parlor," she says.

She's not excited, just concerned. "Who let them into the house?"

"Nonna, it's just black people singing on TV." I know she's lost it, but she's ancient. It's expected. I've seen the behavior in old relatives before, heard their children complain, heard it from those who are now dead. There's nothing to worry about. If she comes into the parlor, I'll shut off the tube.

"It's okay, Nonna. They're going home soon. You go to bed. Don't worry."

"Franchito, tell them not to stay late. They should sleep in their own homes."

"Yes, Nonna."

Her white hair is never colored, never curled, combed straight back into a bun anchored by long, wavy hairpins. Her hair is the only thing that's not black, even her rosary is black, and her olive skin has the patina of age. She takes to bed and sleeps hard, doesn't wake when the doctor pinches her chest. She takes all her body parts with her, bequeathing only rotten teeth to this earth.

Her daughters have their way. All in white, Anna sleeps, sleeps without a bun. Her hair has been permed and styled. Fingers are frozen on white rosary beads, and a white-carnation wreath covers her. Death has plucked her clean of all life's black.

At ninety-four the black bird of paradise will sing the Ave Maria no more. I will no longer hear stories from a gilded cage. The dark lady flies away without a goodbye, without a kiss, without one toothless smile. I am not there. I read about her death in a newspaper a fellow student brings to my attention. I still don't subscribe to newspapers, and my parents didn't call me. I'm twenty-three, trying to make good, trying to make my immigrants proud. I cry and call home. It's too late, I know, but I call.

"She was buried today," Papa says.

"Did she die in the hospital?"

"No, in bed."

I am told it was inevitable. She was lucky—did not suffer.

"A natural death," Papa says.

I hold back tears.

"Don't lose sight of your goal, Franche, don't let it affect you, study hard, for all old people must die."

I step back on America's fast track without missing a beat, and it whirls me away. I try hard not to think about our room at the top of the duplex.

Standing in the old cemetery with Vince brings it all back—the soft sand, the sandspurs and all those familiar headstones. I reflect on the funerals I attended as a boy, recalling eulogies that stretched into dinnertime. Mellifluous words mesmerized the crowd as I stood in the shadows of those dressed in black.

"*Compare e comare* in *la vita tutti siemo poveri, pero in morto tutti siemo ricci, e csosi e questo uomo qui se va a la terra,*" the eulogist said. "In life we are poor, but the dead in paradise are rich, and so shall it be with this man."

His voice reined in the crowd, and children glanced at each other and flipped whites of their eyes, and I, too, wondered when the eulogy would end. Funerals were held in late afternoon when the sun was ebbing. Cigarmakers had cut out a half hour early from factories to get to the funeral home. One thing was certain—immigrants kept score. "You no come to mine, I no go yours." And so, at home, at night, after a funeral, trying to sleep, I rubbed my eyes and erased the image of a face morticians went heavy with rouge.

The eulogist used the words *pui* and *lui* and *questo* and *quella* long before I heard the aria *Questa o Quella* in Verdi's *Rigoletto*. He made his sounds full like a tenor, distinct with precise diction, formal and erudite—so full of Italy. But Sicilians in Ybor City never said *questa* or *quella* (this or that). My people spoke slipshod Sicilian.

Lord & Fernandez funerals were not cheap, but they were affordable lay-away plans. Men were buried in stilted suits, and women, in passé dresses, sported *bon voyage* corsages. Folding chairs, inside green tents, propped up overweight Sicilians who parsed ponderous thoughts waiting for the perishable crate to be unloaded.

The Cadillac arrived first, always did. Its up-sweep tail fins established that it was a first-class hearse and funeral. After the crowd gathered, the hearse's back door opened, and hand signals from morticians guided self-conscious pallbearers to the hole. Humanism mattered, for at that moment, the person in the box was the measure of all things.

At eighteen I watched Nonno Domenico's casket touch down—watched it plumb itself over a deep hole rimmed by green outdoor carpet. Not unlike a space mission, he waited the descent from a steel rack. The squeal of a ratchet told me my grandfather was being erased.

Along with five others I carried my grandfather to his grave, and although he no longer held my hand, nor I his, I was close to the man, knew his thoughts, smelled his cigars, and I looked the other way when he broke wind. Despite his wisdom, I thought him singularly alone that day; without an umbrella for the first rain; alone without an overcoat for the first frost; alone without his cigar in smoky eternity; alone without my grandmother for a while; alone, asleep in the Italian Club Cemetery with the rest of dead cigarmakers.

33

"Got a light?"

I never hear the man walk up. He's disheveled and middle age.

"Sure," I say.

"I don't smoke," Vince says with a disapproving tone in his voice.

"I take care of this place," the man says.

I hand him a book of matches.

He lights up. "Feel a hell of a lot better." The drag floats his eyes.

"What's your name?" He spreads his legs and pulls up his baggy trousers.

"Urso," Vince says. "Vince and Frank, cousins."

"I'm Victor Testasicca. Nice to meet you all." He puts out his hand.

Vince and I smile, for we know Testasicca translates into dried head in Italian. We shake his hand. He's unshaven—a yardman in the land of the dead. He looks older than us, but he tells us he's our age. I detect the odor of stale alcohol, as if perhaps he went to bed cuddling a cold six-pack the night before.

"Small world, ain't it?" Victor says. "I know lots of Ursos, know where most are buried."

"No shit," I say.

His accent is distinctive like all Italians raised in Tampa. It's a mixture of a southern drawl, Sicilian and Spanish.

He scratches his crotch. "But what you going to do?" he says. "Got to make a living anyway you can, right? Nobody is going to give you a damn dollar when you get old and decrepit."

He's decrepit, but he doesn't know it. It hasn't slugged him some of our classmates are already seeding his lawn.

"It's happening," Vince had said months earlier when he read obituaries to me over the phone. I was content not living in Tampa, not waking up to "happenings" in *The Tampa Tribune*. Vince kept score and attended funerals and memorial services. It was a down home feeling I was glad I did not experience.

"Riiight," Vince says to Victor, "riiight," he says again with the same drawn-out inflection young people say right on, saying a prolonged yesss as if experiencing a sexual climax—Yesss, Yesss, Yesss—bragging to the world they're making it.

Scratching first with one hand and then the other, Victor widens his stance and digs into his crotch. He doesn't know he's doing it. I know how it is. It's second nature. I remember the syndrome, considered it a harmless mannerism. Besides it was one I couldn't do anything about. It was like breathing, for one is never conscience of breathing unless it goes awry.

It'd been awhile since I scratched, and a good scratch was one of the simple pleasures I left behind. So I scratch where I hadn't in a long time. Why not? I'm among friends who hear nothing, see nothing and say nothing. The men around me taught my generation to scratch and how to scratch; taught it to me on front porches, the Italian club, cafés, funerals, weddings and wakes while they could still scratch.

My mother said never to scratch there, but there were more important things to refrain from, and scratching wasn't a sin, no, not nice—but never, never a sin. It was what boys did. It wasn't until I left home and married, it bothered anyone. Of course, I worked at abstaining, trying to get nice, be accepted by etiquette. That's what my wife called it, and, if I didn't stop, she curtly followed with a caustic, "Quit playing with yourself."

"So, you work here full-time, Victor?" I say.

He wipes his brow and flips sweat aside. "*La vita e brutta. Eh, tu che fa?*" He speaks Sicilian, saying—life is brutal and asks what I do for a living.

"Retired," I say.

"No, shit, made your bread, eh?"

If he didn't have to work, he'd rather not. I understand the mentality.

"What did you all do before you retired?"

"Oh, I haven't," Vince says. "I'm a high school principal, and Frank was a doctor."

"*Mischa*, you guys did damn good—a *maestro* and a *dottóre*."

Vince smiles.

"*Famiglia* had money enough to send you to medical school, Doc?"

"Our families were cigarmakers," I say.

He's raring to show off his stuff, now, show his competency to professional men. He shifts into high gear and goes into one aisle and then another. He points at tombstones like a tour guide, releasing bits of Ybor City history, and now and then, scratches his ass, digging in hard with the hand I just shook.

"Trafficante is in the big mausoleum," he says. "Want to go see?"

"That's all right. He's not representative of my people," I say.

"You know he was the big *capo-boss* from Tampa, right?"

"I know. Nice family but he didn't roll cigars."

"Did you guys play football for Jefferson?" Victor gets into the *barrio*'s sub-text—nitty gritty of gridiron.

"No, you're thinking of our cousin Ernest. A big guy for a Sicilian."

"That's who I was thinking of—Ernest. Yeah, he played guard, right?"

"No, tackle," Vince says.

"All City?"

"All State, too," Vince lays it on thick. "His brother, Tony, played for the University of Tampa."

"So, you guys didn't play ball?"

"We were wimps, Vic," I say with a deadpan face.

"Sure we did. We played for the O.L.P.H. Bears," Vince says.

Victor scratches his head digging for enlightenment.

"Our Lady of Perpetual Help, the Catholic school, you know," Vince says.

"Oh, yeah, yeah, right, O.L.P.H., right, the fucking Catholic school."

"It's no longer around," I say. "It's been razed. Even the Pope couldn't keep it afloat.

Vic gives me a quizzical look.

"It's been torn down, Vic," I say.

"Oh, yeah," he says. "Every damn thing is being torn down."

Victor has all the information he needs to judge us, for some things in a *barrio* never change. His questions and comments stir buried feelings, deeper than those buried around me. In the old days, most of my friends focused on sports, confined intellectual prowess to: sports heroes, scores, batting averages, and runs batted in. Most Ybor City kids who went to college went to the University of Tampa and worked part-time or fulltime. Most became schoolteachers, but many got left behind, didn't go to college. A few went to state universities, and very few became doctors, lawyers, engineers and dentists.

Aspirations and expectations weren't high, and *A Mid-Summer Night's Dream* was making out at Courtney Campbell Causeway with a girl in a back seat, but for a few of us, education changed all that. The caretaker keeps dialing long distance, wanting to talk about the old days, but I'm not about to answer.

"So, tell me, why did you quit doctoring, Doc? Don't look old enough to give up all that bread."

"Maybe I just wanted time to myself before you start weeding my pad."

He says, "Hell, Doc, you didn't have to bust your ass, wore a tie, sat around in an air-conditioned office, right? Screwed all those young nurses I bet."

"Right, Vic, I wore a tie."

"Think you could spare a few bucks for cigarettes? Forgot my damn wallet at home," he says, looking at his feet like I'd seen immigrants do when asking for the price of an item they couldn't afford.

Vince and I glance at each other and speak the silent dialect of eyes. The caretaker's expression upgrades into a quarter smile when he sees me pull out my wallet.

"That's all I got." I hand him three dollars.

He reaches. "Well, it's my lunch break, fellas. Thanks for the cigarette money. Drop in anytime."

Victor walks into a shed and closes the door.

"Drop in anytime. Vince, did you hear that? A hell of a note," I say.

"Not anytime soon. I hope."

"What does one do to be buried here?" I say, not revealing there is no better place when one is divorced, no better place when your children are grown, no better place when they didn't inherit Italian traditions, no better place than to be with your own people. I lived the American dream, but the one I left behind was sweeter.

"I don't know. Maybe you can't anymore." Vince looks at me as if I'm being trivial.

"What's so funny?" I say.

"I've heard all the plots are spoken for, Frank. Only place left might be in the big mausoleum. I hear they're expensive, but you'd be with Santo Trafficante." He lets out a short laugh. "You wouldn't have to worry with a godfather like him around."

"Funny, funny," I say. "So what if it's expensive? Are you going to let your wife decide where you're going to spend eternity?"

He wrinkles his brow.

"This is all there is, you know," I say.

"You believe that?"

"Isn't that what most cigarmakers believed?"

"Don't be so cynical," he says.

"You know, Shakespeare left his wife, Ann, the second best bed when he died—didn't give a shit," I say.

"What are you talking about?"

"Never mind, Vince. You're too damn politically correct."

"I got a responsible job at the high school."

As a boy, fresh heaped up mounds of Florida sand alerted me to recent check-ins or check-outs depending on point of view, but during my sabbatical, gravediggers tunneled like gophers, ravaging consecrated soil. It is now priceless real estate in colored town and a historical marker sign is posted at the front gate of the cemetery.

"Frank, the *barrio* did funny things to people, don't you think?"

"The *barrio*? Shit, Vince, nothing wrong with where we lived."

"But it's in the middle of colored town. Makes it tough on children if they want to visit."

"That'll give them an excuse. Have you ever brought your kids here?"

He doesn't answer. None of us fought Americanization.

"Our bellies are fat, and we've lost our identity. We paid the price, Vince."

"Getting hungry?" he says, shaking his head as if he's shaking off the futility of our conversation.

"Hell, Vince, colored town was always part of us."

It's mid-afternoon. The biological needs of the living outstrip the dead's.

"Vince, just a sec, I gotta take a leak."

"Can't you wait?"

"Why?"

"Well, someone might see you."

"It's desolate. It's only a piss."

I step behind a headstone and point away from anyone's face and look down at thick-bladed Saint Augustine grass. I'm tempted to whistle, look up at the sky, and make myself invisible like I did when I was a child.

I had one more thing to do before returning home the next day. I never attended the funeral, for schools didn't do funerals when I was a boy. I didn't know where Augustine Fraga spent the last half of the century until Vince mentioned him during our sojourn through the Italian Club Cemetery. Augustine was buried at Wood Lawn Cemetery on the other side of Ybor City where a mixture of Spanish, Cubans, Italians and Anglos are buried. The next morning I drive to Woodlawn and locate a familiar face whose scar I once pitied. He's exactly where Vince said he'd be, in an aisle near Vince's maternal grandparents.

"I'm sorry, Augustine," I whisper.

The cemetery is deserted, so I think it's the wind I hear, but the accent is unmistakable. "I understand, Frankie, a matter of honor, right?"

I look around—see nothing.

"You didn't become a Mafia boss after all. Would have made a good one."

I shake my head like a drunk shakes off cobwebs. I stand among sandspurs and marble and recall the day I abandoned my duplex, left my people behind and never looked back. Hell no, I never did. I believed the ends justified the means, always did, still do. Papa bragged to his cronies at the Italian Club he had a son in medical school, and that alone made my leaving worthwhile. But it was more than that. I'd made something of myself and lived a life far away from the ghetto. I knew I'd done the right thing, for I was the last runner in an immigrant relay race, and I had to catch up. Besides, Ybor City was a sinking ship. Even the rats were scrambling to get out when the blacks moved in.

In the marble reflection of Augustine's headstone I see my parents, my god-parents and both my widowed grandmothers. All of them are standing and waving to me from the front porch of the duplex on East Columbus Drive. It's a Sunday that's tattooed in my brain; the Sunday morning I left for the University of Miami School of Medicine. I see a beat-up Studebaker emerge from the narrow alley behind my home. The car turns onto Nineteenth Street and comes across Columbus Drive. My arm is sticking out waving, waving goodbyes, interrupted only by a sinking sensation inside me. The emptiness is fear, and it's hard to describe, but I force myself to drive south, driving by rows and rows of cigar-maker huts to pick up Adamo Drive and pick up a highway to a dream.

Spanish moss hangs heavy in the humid air surrounding the centuries-old oak trees. It hovers over me like indelible memories hang. Woodlawn Cemetery is old, over a century old. Everything is old. Old is home.

Augustine's ceramic face lines up next to his sister's and his father's—all facing the morning sun. Fraga, Fraga, Fraga—the names read. His father has since died, too. All three lie in a short-coupled row near the cemetery's entrance.

I think back to V.M. Ybor School and days in fourth grade and a barren playground. I think about hide-and-seek, tic-tac-toe and mother may I. I whisper, "Mother, may I?"

"Only one giant step, Italiano, *uno nada mas.*" The wind fills my ears.

I take a measured step, just one, and my shadow embraces a mildewed stone. I wipe an unwrinkled brow in a photograph smooth and pristine. I adjust my glasses and see in the picture the reflection of an old man bending over a child.

978-0-595-33537-4
0-595-33537-3

LaVergne, TN USA
04 March 2010
174912LV00001B/92/A